THE IMPORTANCE OF
SHINZO ABE

Celebrating
30 Years of Publishing
in India

Also edited by Sanjaya Baru (with Rahul Sharma)

*A New Cold War: Henry Kissinger and
the Rise of China*

THE IMPORTANCE OF SHINZO ABE

INDIA, JAPAN

AND THE

INDO-PACIFIC

EDITED BY

SANJAYA BARU

HarperCollins *Publishers* India

First published in India by HarperCollins *Publishers* 2023
4th Floor, Tower A, Building No. 10, DLF Cyber City,
DLF Phase II, Gurugram, Haryana – 122002
www.harpercollins.co.in

2 4 6 8 10 9 7 5 3 1

Anthology and introduction copyright © Sanjaya Baru 2023

P-ISBN: 978-93-5699-360-0
E-ISBN: 978-93-5699-359-4

The views and opinions expressed in this book are the authors' own
and the facts are as reported by them, and the publishers are not in
any way liable for the same.

Copyright for the individual essays vests with the contributors.

Sanjaya Baru asserts the moral right
to be identified as the editor of this work.

All rights reserved. No part of this publication may be reproduced,
stored in a retrieval system, or transmitted, in any form or by any
means, electronic, mechanical, photocopying, recording or otherwise,
without the prior permission of the publishers.

Typeset in 11.5/15.2 Bembo Std at
Manipal Technologies Limited, Manipal

Printed and bound at
Replika Press Pvt. Ltd.

This book is produced from independently certified FSC® paper to ensure
responsible forest management.

CONTENTS

ABE AND JAPAN–INDIA RELATIONS

ABE AND THE INDO-PACIFIC

FOREWORD

A PERSONAL TRIBUTE

S. Jaishankar

IF THERE IS A single individual who can be associated with the emergence of the Indo-Pacific as a strategic reality and the Quad as a cooperative platform, that is unquestionably Prime Minister Shinzo Abe of Japan. It is not often in contemporary times that Japanese leaders are credited with fresh thinking in international relations. Shinzo Abe was an exception because of his political boldness, his perceptive grasp of global changes, and not least, the political longevity to translate ideas into reality. And that is why his tragic assassination is a loss that is felt so deeply across the world.

In analysing the impact of such leadership, we are guided on most occasions by contemporaneous accounts and the impressions of others. In this particular case, I was greatly privileged to be a witness for over two decades to the strategic developments in question and the evolution of Abe's thinking on the subject. As it often happens, someone of this consequence would be viewed from differing perspectives. There would be those who understandably would place him in the context of the constitutional debate in Japan and the assumption of greater military responsibility. Others may see him more driven by the immediacy of his neighbourhood and overcoming many legacy issues. Much of what he advocated and practiced was grounded in the established security relationship with the United States.

My experience was, however, directly connected to the growth and development of the India–Japan partnership. The many conversations with Abe over an extended period affirm that he envisaged India as a natural partner if Japan were to undertake greater global responsibilities. In this regard, he was an unusual mix of political calculation and personal proclivity. The latter may have begun with his attachment to his grandfather Prime Minister Nobusuke Kishi, who first reached out to India after the war. But it deepened as his own experiences and relationships grew with Indians and India. There is a very good reason why India, perhaps more than most, feels his loss so keenly.

My first interaction with Shinzo Abe happened sometime after I arrived in our Embassy in Tokyo in January 1996. To be honest, it is hard after so many years to put a time and place to it. The recollection is much sharper of him in the run up to Prime Minister Yoshiro Mori's visit to India in 2000. Abe was then the deputy chief cabinet secretary and very much part of a political effort to get the relationship past the difficulties in which it found itself after India's 1998 nuclear test. I have a strong memory as well of his contribution to the deft finessing of the impasse that then led to the lifting of the Japanese sanctions. Our acquaintance through mutual friends grew sufficiently that I kept in touch even when I continued to visit Japan thereafter from my posting as ambassador in Prague.

When I returned to the Ministry of External Affairs in 2004, Shinzo Abe and his wife, Akie, happened to be in India on a private visit. By now, he was the acting secretary general of the ruling Liberal Democratic Party. We met at a social occasion, and I was surprised to learn that he had no contacts planned with anybody in the government. Some of that may have been Japanese self-effacement, some perhaps a feeling that he was a party representative; but there was also the fact that few in Delhi understood his importance. I felt that the then Prime Minister Dr Manmohan Singh—who had a long association with Japan—should meet him and approached his media advisor, Dr Sanjaya

Baru, and suggested to him that he may consider arranging a courtesy call for Abe. Dr Singh readily agreed to the suggestion and met him the next day. What was planned as a courtesy call became a substantive meeting.

The feedback from Dr Singh was that he found Shinzo Abe a very untypical Japanese in many ways. Given the Prime Minister's vast experience with Japan, there was clearly a good basis for that judgement. Even then, Abe spoke out on what many in his country considered to be sensitive matters. And in doing so, he was clearly trying to break out of the mould. In due course, he became chief cabinet secretary, and then Prime Minister in 2006. I saw him intermittently, obviously in an unofficial capacity given his higher office and greater responsibilities.

It was during this period that Abe sought to synchronize the progress in India–Japan relations with his promotion of a trilateral between India, Japan and the US. The latter initially took the form of a Track-2 dialogue, whose seriousness was nevertheless evident due to the involvement of American policymakers close to Abe. When I look back from the comfortable situation in which we find ourselves today, those early initiatives certainly look somewhat awkward, if not actually forced. The joke at that time was about the challenge of how to get the Japanese to start talking and even more difficult, how to get the Indians to stop doing so. Only American intermediation could deal with this!

This period witnessed Abe move decisively on his strategic vision, perhaps to a point where he got well ahead of the ability of the systems involved to support it. At the end of 2006, Abe floated the idea of a Quad comprising of Japan, India, the US and Australia. He also gave his famous 'Confluence of the Two Seas' speech to the Indian Parliament in August 2007. The first meeting at an official level of the Quad had just taken place. But it seemed in the coming months that Abe's enthusiasm did not evoke sufficient commitment from the others. Abe himself had relinquished the Prime Ministership very soon after his defining speech, which slowed the momentum at take-off. The Australians were the first to back out publicly and to many, this seemed a quixotic venture. For those of us who continued to converse with him from time to time, there were nevertheless indications that he had not abandoned this quest.

From 2007, I was high commissioner to Singapore and after 2009, ambassador to China. Our meetings were obviously occasional but I could always sense his keen interest in the status of our ties with both the US and China. He understood the larger significance of the India–US nuclear deal and was anxious that the ensuing negotiations should be brought to a successful conclusion. I was naturally hesitant to even approach him once he became Prime Minister again in 2012. It was typical of Abe that on one occasion, he learnt of my presence in Tokyo on a personal visit from one of his close advisors and insisted I see him at the Kantei. Dodging the watchful Japanese press on my way out was not without its challenges. In the years thereafter, the opportunities to interact with him naturally increased.

As foreign secretary from 2015 to 2018, I had direct jurisdiction over the development of our ties with Japan. And I often accompanied Prime Minister Modi to various international summits, especially the G20 and East Asia Summit, where a bilateral meeting with his Japanese counterpart was pretty much the norm. Since we had a practice of annual summits, there were regular occasions to see Abe and hear first-hand his views on the international situation. His relationship with India remained an abiding one and the last occasion to meet him in person was in May 2022 when, having just taken over the chair of the Japan–India Association, he and his predecessor came together to meet Prime Minister Modi, who was in Tokyo for the Quad summit. It said so much for his commitment to India that Abe had chosen to accept this post even in his days as an elder statesman.

The personal chemistry between Prime Ministers Narendra Modi and Shinzo Abe was a particularly visible one. To anyone who worked with them, this was hardly surprising. Both were deeply nationalistic with a strong sense of their own culture and history. But personal traits aside, they were also united in their desire to establish the right place for their country in the international order. I remember Abe once mentioning to me that he found India's thinking to be a value because of its intrinsic independence. Modi, on his part, has always held out Japan as a pioneering example of traversing the road to modernity without compromising on culture and values.

Since I was still ambassador to the US in 2014, I was not present at Modi's first visit to Japan as Prime Minister that year. But thereafter, I could note their growing comfort with each passing year. Increasingly, their conversations became strategic and freewheeling, often interspersed with particular thoughts or insights that one wanted to share with the other. Sometimes, this would even be done with reference to what they had read or heard which they thought to be of relevance to their worldview. Both leaders made it a point to underline their special feelings by inviting each other to their respective homes. The rapturous welcome accorded to the Abes in Ahmedabad—with them riding in an open jeep with Prime Minister Modi—is undoubtedly the most enthusiastic public reception accorded to a foreign leader in recent times. On his part, Abe too was very understanding of the value of respecting cultural traditions and his participation at the Ganga Arti in Varanasi in 2017 clearly struck a deep chord with his host.

It is natural to ask what set Abe apart from other Japanese Prime Ministers—and indeed from world leaders of his era—where India was concerned. To begin with, he was engaged in a task for his country that his Indian counterparts—especially Prime Minister Modi—were doing for theirs. It was evident that there was a deep churning underway in the international system. But rather than let events take their course, Abe was obviously among those of his generation who was prepared to shape developments actively. The related aspect—and again one to which Indians would identify with intuitively—was how to position Japan best in the transformation underway.

Quite obviously, Japan's relationship with the world would undergo a profound change. But its extent, pace and intensity were all subjects of debate. More than other powers in the second rung, Japan was also encumbered by history. Perhaps, part of the energy of the partnership with India was derived not just from a broadly shared objective but also from the knowledge that this could be realized with a forward-looking perspective. Usually, leaders of change do not set out their worldviews with explicit clarity or great detail at one go. Reading from multiple interactions and deducing from policy decisions, it would be fair to conclude that Abe perceived India as just the right partner in travelling with Japan to the next level of its global engagement.

This probably explains as well how much he was willing to go out on a limb for India. One of the most complex negotiations that took place during his stewardship was on our nuclear cooperation agreement. Even when the US–India agreement was under negotiation, Abe understood its larger significance. He, therefore, readily concurred with the thought that something similar should be undertaken with Japan as well. This also had a direct industry relevance since Japanese companies are very much a part of the global supply chain. At the same time, there were understandable sensitivities on the Japanese side that derived from their own nuclear experiences. Abe's leadership enabled the two sides to walk this difficult path with the dexterity required to finally reach our destination.

Less contentious but equally significant was the domain of defence cooperation where Abe steadily encouraged the conclusion of enabling agreements and the implementation of complex military exercises. Even when it came to the bullet train project, he readily appreciated that its true significance lay in the larger technology upgrade that it would trigger. On many of the discussions that accompanied its implementation, his consistent approach was to look beyond the benefits of the first project. This same bent of mind he brought to bear as well when it came to encouraging Japanese investments in India. He truly envisaged them as making a strategic contribution in helping to create a more multi-polar global economy.

That Abe took a geostrategic view of world politics was quite evident. His conversations and even questions were often historical in nature. The long view that came through was, of course, always balanced by the compulsions of the day. It is therefore eminently appropriate that Abe should be remembered for the profound contributions that he made to the strategic debates of our era. There are three inter-related ideas that he sought to realize in his time: the Indo-Pacific as opposed to separate

Indian and Pacific oceans, the Quad diplomatic platform, and the Free and Open Indo-Pacific. It is a reflection on the strength of his beliefs that lack of success the first time did not deter him from pursuing his dream for another decade, until he achieved success. Sometimes, the nature of political polemics tends to dumb down complex initiatives.

What Abe was seeking, in fact, was the actualization of new cooperative arrangements that transcended the orthodoxies of the earlier era. And, as events have demonstrated, it is only through doing it that the viability of such plurilateralism could be credibly established. Abe was also among those who went beyond traditional Westphalian beliefs in an era of globalized agnosticism. His emphasis on values resonates today in an age where the importance of trust and transparency has become more apparent. But when he first tabled it, like on so many other issues, Abe was a prophet before his time.

It is by now widely accepted that Abe's mission was to get Japan ready for an uncertain, volatile and different world. He left before he could accomplish these goals in substantial measure. It is for his successors to take that forward. But for partners like India and the rest of the international community that shared a vision of new ways of cooperation, Abe remains a powerful inspiration. His mix of optimism and realism, openness to global ideas, confidence in his own heritage and respect for that of others are traits that those of us who had the good fortune to interact with him will always cherish.

I am delighted that Sanjaya Baru has taken this initiative to publish a book of essays by eminent Japanese and Indian writers familiar with Shinzo Abe's important contribution to Japan's resurgence, to Japan–India relations, to the Indo-Pacific region and, indeed, to global affairs. As we commemorate the first anniversary of his tragic death, it is only fitting that we pay tribute to Shinzo Abe's leadership and vision.

INTRODUCTION

Sanjaya Baru

SHINZO ABE, AN INTERNATIONALLY respected statesman and highly regarded Asian leader, was not only the longest-serving Prime Minister in Japan's history but was also the most consequential leader of post-WWII Japan. He re-energized a nation that had begun to stagnate through the 1990s, shaped the geopolitics of the Indo-Pacific region and laid the foundation for the emergence of a 'New Japan' in the twenty-first century. Mr Abe's shocking assassination in July 2022 has been widely mourned in Japan, in India and around the world. This collection of essays is the first of its kind and pays tribute to the memory of a great leader of Japan and Asia, a great friend of India and a global statesman.

It would be no exaggeration to suggest that Shinzo Abe was the only head of government who could claim to have had a good personal equation with both Prime Ministers Manmohan Singh and Narendra Modi. Tomohiko Taniguchi—a former special aide to Prime Minister Abe and one of the authors in this volume—says that Mr Abe regarded Dr Singh as his 'mentor' and Mr Modi as a 'close friend and partner'. Mr Abe played a vital role in constructing the new edifice of Japan–India relations from 2006 to 2022, building on the foundation laid by his two immediate predecessors, Yoshiro Mori and Junichiro Koizumi.

Presently, Japan is the only country with which India has a virtually problem-free and productive bilateral relationship. Mr Abe is to be credited for this. He was not only the architect of a new Japan–India relationship but also the principal visionary behind two major geopolitical ideas of our time in Asia: the 'Indo-Pacific' and the Quadrilateral Security Dialogue (Quad). India's external affairs minister, Subrahmanyam Jaishankar—who knew Mr Abe well—notes in his preface to this volume that, 'If there is a single individual who can be associated with the emergence of the Indo-Pacific as a strategic reality and the Quad as a cooperative platform, that is unquestionably Prime Minister Shinzo Abe of Japan.'

Jaishankar sums up the essence of Abe's historic role in world affairs, Asian security and Japan–India relations when he writes,

> What Abe was seeking, in fact, was the actualization of new cooperative arrangements that transcended the orthodoxies of the earlier era. And, as events have demonstrated, it is only through doing it that the viability of such plurilateralism could be credibly established. Abe was also among those who went beyond traditional Westphalian beliefs in an era of globalized agnosticism. Abe was a prophet before his time.

Taniguchi—who also served as Mr Abe's speechwriter—tells us that when Mr Abe returned to office in 2012 after a period of illness that had caused him to demit office in 2007, he may well have viewed his return to represent Japan's return to the global stage. Post-WWII Japan had fought shy of its regional and global role, given the legacy of Japanese imperialism in Asia and its defeat in the war. Japan's citizens became avowedly pacifist after the experience of being the only nation to have suffered a nuclear attack.

There was a brief period in contemporary Japanese history when the Japanese elite sought to reassert their presence and personality. It was at this time that Shintaro Ishihara and Akio Morita co-authored the famous polemical tract, *The Japan That Can Say No* (1989), in response to Western bullying in the 1980s. The United States had imposed restrictions on Japanese imports and the European Union cited competition from Japan as the reason for creating a 'Single Market'.

However, Japan's economic stagnation in the 1990s and the new lovefest between the West and China forced Japanese elites to once again adopt a low profile.

During this period, Japanese foreign policy became increasingly driven by its search for markets and investment opportunities and its requirement of imported energy. Japan sought to revive relationships with countries in what was termed the 'Asia-Pacific' region—which excluded India. At the turn of the century, when Brazil, Germany, India, Japan and South Africa laid claim to membership of the United Nations Security Council, many in the West saw little prospect for Germany and Japan achieving this goal when compared to the other contenders.

A second feature of Japanese foreign policy during the 1990s was the enthusiastic outreach to China. China emerged very quickly as the single largest recipient of Japanese aid and investment and the two became key trade partners. It was a decade during which India sought to attract Japan's attention but was repeatedly rebuffed, with Japan even imposing economic sanctions on India in response to the latter's nuclear tests of May 1998 that established it as a nuclear weapons power.

It was only at the start of the twenty-first century that India and Japan entered a new phase in their bilateral relations. The initial thaw occurred during the brief but productive tenure of Prime Minister Yoshiro Mori. It was, however, the summit meeting between Prime Ministers Manmohan Singh and Junichiro Koizumi at New Delhi in April 2005 that became the turning point in the relationship. The two leaders signed a joint statement titled 'Japan–India Partnership in the New Asian Era: Strategic Orientation of Japan–India Global Partnership' and issued an action plan titled 'Eightfold Initiative for Strengthening Japan–India Global Partnership'. At the time, Mr Abe was the chief cabinet secretary to Prime Minister Koizumi.

As Jaishankar and Ravi Velloor note in their essays, Mr Abe had made a non-official visit to India in 2004, when he was the acting secretary-general and chairman of the Reform Promotion Headquarters of the ruling Liberal Democratic Party (LDP). It was during this visit that he was given an opportunity to call on Prime Minister Singh, and in this meeting the two discovered a shared personal interest in bilateral relations. Mr Abe was the grandson of Nobusuke Kishi, who in 1957 became the first post-WWII Japanese Prime Minister to visit India. After that trip, Mr Abe had his first introduction to India from his grandfather's lap.

Dr Singh too had an important Japan connection. Prime Minister Indira Gandhi had named him co-chair of the India–Japan Study Committee when he was deputy chairman of the Planning Commission in the 1980s. When serving as Union finance minister in subsequent years, Dr Singh took a keen interest in the bilateral relationship between the countries. Thus, both future Prime Ministers were adequately primed to recognize the importance of this bilateral relationship in the geopolitics of the post–Cold War era defined by the rise of China.

In August 2007, Mr Abe's historic address to the Indian Parliament demonstrated his desire to truly establish a global, strategic partnership with India. India heartily responded. The 'Confluence of the Two Seas' speech was magnificent and it set the tone for Japan's subsequent engagement with the world.

In December 2022, Prime Minister Fumio Kishida unveiled three national security policy statements that reflect Mr Abe's 'grand strategy'. The documents are Japan's National Security Strategy (NSS), National Defence Strategy and a Defence Build-up Programme. The NSS revised the 2013 strategy paper of the Abe government, which commits Japan to a more robust defence and deterrence posture in the light of new challenges to security, both domestically as well as in Asia and the rest of the world. The Japanese government proposes to increase defence expenditure to 2 per cent of GDP. The political and ideological groundwork for this historic shift in Japan's defence planning and strategic capability was done by Mr Abe and reflects his vision and strategy.

The first section of this book examines the domestic politics of Mr Abe. The author of the first essay is Tomohiko Taniguchi, who was a senior journalist with Japan's premier media outfit, Nikkei, before his close alliance with Mr Abe. There is perhaps no one better placed to offer us a ringside view of Mr Abe's thinking than Taniguchi. His essay draws attention to four aspects of Mr Abe's premiership. Firstly, he believes that Mr Abe may have felt 'destined' to play a role in Japan's rise, and not just because he was the grandson of a former Prime Minister. Because Mr Abe's first stint ended all too briefly due to health problems and his return to office was not assured, Taniguchi thinks he was a 'born-again' political leader. On returning to office in 2012, Mr Abe had declared, 'Japan is back.'

The second aspect to Mr Abe's premiership was his focus on Japan's economic revival through what has come to be dubbed 'Abenomics', and the third was the role he played in convincing the United States to take the rise of China more seriously. In pursuing this thought, Mr Abe became the architect of the notion of a 'free and open Indo-Pacific' and the Quad. Finally, Mr Abe devoted considerable attention to closer ties with other Asian countries—including India.

An economist by the name of Heizo Takenaka was invited to join Prime Minister Koizumi's ministry as minister for economic and fiscal policy, financial services and postal privatization. When Mr Abe became Prime Minister, he invited Takenaka to join a small group of economic policy advisors that guided and steered his economic reforms programme. Takenaka believes that while Mr Abe is known around the world for his foreign policy initiatives, the success of these depended critically on the success of his domestic economic reforms programme aimed at reviving Japan's sagging economy.

The quiver of Abenomics comprised three arrows—monetary policy easing, a flexible fiscal policy and a growth strategy based on easing supply-side constraints including the shortage of manpower. Takenaka lays emphasis on the continuation of the 'legacy of Prime Minister Abe', which he sums up as providing political leadership to policy management, managing the media to influence public opinion in favour of reform and strengthening national security.

Nobukatsu Kanehara, presently a professor at Doshisha University, Kyoto, was assistant chief cabinet secretary and deputy director general of the National Security Secretariat in Prime Minister Abe's office. In his comprehensive review of Mr Abe's vision and leadership, Kanehara views him as Japan's 'man of the moment', given that he reminded a new generation of Japanese of the challenges their country faced. The millennials had grown up in the post-Cold War era and had become unaware of the challenges posed by great power rivalries. Mr Abe managed to get his country to focus on China's rise and deal with it within the parameters of Japan's pacifist constitution.

Kanehara believes Mr Abe showed an 'image of a new Japan' as a leader of the liberal international order. He managed to override left-wing and conservative objections to Japan ensuring its own national security. Kanehara writes that Mr Abe 'gave the young Japanese purpose, hope and confidence'. He emphasizes Mr Abe's commitment to free trade at a time when the US had become increasingly inward-looking on trade.

Interestingly, Kanehara views Mr Abe's outreach to India as being based not just on amoral power politics but on his admiration for Indian democracy, 'birthed by Gandhi and nurtured by Nehru' and, therefore, based on a commitment to liberal democratic values. Kanehara attaches importance to Japan's relationship with India both because of India's liberal democratic credentials and its role as a voice of the 'Global South'.

Robert Ward and Titli Basu offer valuable introductions to the maze of domestic politics in Japan. They write that after a frustrating history of short-term Prime Ministers and revolving-door governments, Mr Abe emerged as a new ray of hope for a beleaguered Japan. Both Ward and Basu believe that Mr Abe's top-down approach to governance in his second term and his centralization of power within the Prime Minister's office enabled him to undertake difficult policy reforms both on the economic and national security fronts.

Ward suggests that Mr Abe's most important domestic political legacy is perhaps his 'embedding of foreign and security policy issues in Japan's domestic political debate'. He drew lessons from his first term as

Prime Minister to make his leadership in his second term more effective. The three things that Mr Abe prioritized in his second stint were: paying greater attention to voters' concerns; securing better control over the 'levers of power'; and prioritizing stability of administration. Getting a hold over LDP's factional politics and empowering the Prime Minister's office enabled Mr Abe to push for significant changes in Japan's domestic and external policies.

Basu's essay deconstructs the influences, ideas, values and vision that shaped what many view as the 'Abe phenomenon'. She examines the roots of Abe's political aspirations and his ambition for Japan. The influence of his family and his mentor, Koizumi, were merged with many intellectual influences on 'an elite political dynasty', which were reflected in his political philosophy, writings and historic speeches delivered over two decades. These demonstrate that Mr Abe was 'a leader on a definitive mission: rewiring Japan's prestige and standing in the international system as a respected, trusted and a strong power ready to step up as a foremost "promoter of rules and guardian of the global commons"'.

Both Ward and Basu draw attention to the intimate link between Mr Abe's domestic political powerplay and his success in projecting a new image of Japan globally. Nowhere is this link between domestic politics and external security better seen than in Japan's nuclear policy. As the only victim of a nuclear attack, Japan has self-consciously remained pacifist and anti-nuclear. Yet, Japan is acutely conscious of its increasingly nuclearized neighbourhood, writes Manpreet Sethi in her review of the nuclear issue during Abe's tenure.

Despite rising hostility from China and North Korea, Japan's ability to enhance its nuclear deterrence posture has remained constrained by a staunchly anti-nuclear public sentiment. Faced with this dilemma, writes Sethi, Mr Abe followed a 'two-pronged' approach of ensuring the US maintained its nuclear posture in the region while at the same time attempting to 'push the envelope of thinking' on the issue at home even in the aftermath of the Fukushima tragedy.

Sethi sees this as Mr Abe's 'hedging strategy that grappled with Japan's deteriorating regional security environment' and a possible fraying of the 'American nuclear umbrella'. Whatever the policies of future governments, concludes Sethi, there is little doubt that Mr Abe has made Japan think 'practically about nuclear matters in the context of the real-world challenges' that it faces.

≈

The second section of this book is devoted to an examination of Mr Abe's impact on India–Japan relations. I compare the bilateral relationship in the post-WWII and post-Independence period across three phases. The highlight of the first phase—of 'engagement'—was Prime Minister Kishi's visit to India and the Nehru–Kishi partnership. However, this phase soon evaporated without delivering much during the Cold War era, a period that saw little of substance happening between the two democracies. Japan was allied with the US and India remained non-aligned while moving closer to the Soviet Union.

The second phase—of 'partnership'—in the 1980s saw growing Japanese economic and business interest in India, but that declined rapidly in the 1990s when Japan began eagerly exploiting the China opportunity. The third phase—of 'courtship'—began with the meeting between Prime Ministers Mori and Atal Bihari Vajpayee. After sinking roots during Koizumi's tenure, the relationship took off under the leadership of Prime Ministers Abe and Singh and only grew during the Abe–Modi partnership. There was a sharp increase in bilateral engagement during this last period. It is Prime Ministers Abe, Singh and Modi who have come to define the India–Japan relationship in the twenty-first century.

Among Japan's most senior scholars with an intimate knowledge of India is Takenori Horimoto, who sees the rise of China as defining the Japan–India relationship in the post-Cold War period. It was left to Mr Abe to steer the relationship against the background of Chinese assertiveness in the Indo-Pacific region and the changing US assessment of China's rise. Along with his Indian counterpart, Prime Minister Abe was able to give a new direction to the bilateral relationship. However, Horimoto emphasizes the urgency for Japan to find the resources to defend itself in the context of reduced US investment in Asian security. Horimoto's cryptic last sentence is a question for Mr Abe's successors as much as it is to Indian political leadership. In these uncertain times, Horimoto worries whether 'Japan and India are heading into unknown waters with no nautical chart'.

Deepa Gopalan-Wadhwa was India's ambassador to Japan during Mr Abe's consequential second tenure and had a ringside view of the emerging India–Japan relationship. Recalling the very emotional response in India to Mr Abe's death—with Prime Minister Modi penning a very personal tribute to 'my friend, Abe-San'—Gopalan-Wadhwa attributes it in part to the fact that 'India loomed larger in Shinzo Abe's worldview' when compared to any Japanese leader of the past several decades. This was reflected not just in Mr Abe's statements and writings but also in his actions—such as sharply raising development assistance to India, supporting the Delhi–Mumbai Industrial Corridor project, signing up to an India–Japan Investment Promotion Partnership, funding the 'Japan–India Make in India Special Finance Facility', among others.

Gopalan-Wadhwa draws attention to what she refers to as the 'two prongs' of Mr Abe's outreach to India. The first is co-opting India into his framework for a restructured regional order defined by the concept of the Indo-Pacific and the creation of Quad; the second is establishing a defence partnership with an aim to safeguard sea lanes of connectivity in the Indo-Pacific region, which is critical for Japan's economic security. The 'two-plus-two' dialogue that brought together ministers for both external affairs and defence from each side signalled this new security partnership.

What made Mr Abe enhance Japan's engagement with India? Was it merely emerging geopolitical challenges and economic opportunity or was there something deeper in his psyche and memory that created a special bond with India? Suhasini Haidar explores this fascinating question, delving into political influences on a young Abe whose grandfather instilled in him a special regard for India.

Haidar admits that Kishi could not have imagined the geopolitical architecture of the world in which his grandson would lead the nation. However, she writes, 'It is clear that so many of Mr Abe's ideas and his worldview came from what he had learnt from his grandfather.' Haidar shows that many of Mr Abe's policy ideas, including his recipe for Japan's economic revival, have their origin in Prime Minister Kishi's attempts to revive post-WWII Japan.

Mr Abe's assassination came at a time when he was preparing to visit India's northeastern region. Japan had begun to invest in the region and had emerged as a major benefactor for infrastructural development there. In 2019, Mr Abe's visit had to be cancelled due to political disturbances in Assam triggered by proposed changes to the Citizenship Act. The visit could never be rescheduled.

Sanjoy Hazarika's essay points to the rising Japanese commitment to the development of the Northeast—especially Nagaland and Manipur—and the region's connectivity to Southeast Asia. Japanese agencies have taken a keen interest in the region's development, funding the 'India–Japan Sustainable Development Initiative for the Northeastern Region of India' that was established in 2017. The memory of Japan's historic association with the region provided the context for India's 'Act East Policy'.

≈

The third section of this book examines in detail Mr Abe's conceptualization of the Indo-Pacific and Quad. It is widely regarded that he was the principal architect of both these key geopolitical constructs of the early twenty-first century. In his essay, Purnendra Jain notes that Mr Abe did not just define these concepts but in fact pursued them for securing global recognition of the relevance of both constructs. Jain reminds us that Mr Abe also introduced a new and important term, 'Broader Asia', which highlighted India's centrality in Japan's vision of Asia.

To show how Mr Abe pursued the Indo-Pacific concept across continents, Jain refers not only to the famous and prescient speech in August 2007 to the Indian Parliament but also to an address in 2011 to the Indian Council of World Affairs, New Delhi and another at the 6th Tokyo International Conference on African Development (TICAD) at Nairobi in 2016. In an essay published posthumously in 2022, Mr Abe had visualized the expansion of Quad, writing: 'While Japan, the US, Australia and India have forged an extremely important framework for countering the threat (China), it is important to deepen our ties with countries that share our values, including European countries.'

Kanti Bajpai challenges the standard narrative on the Indo-Pacific and Quad, viewing both as redefining Japan's post-WWII grand strategy, which had been defined by what is known as the Yoshida Doctrine. Bajpai suggests that the latter emphasized the centrality of a military alliance with the US and the rebuilding of the post-WWII economy, whereas the Koizumi–Abe worldview focused on the rise of China and the relative decline of the US. It emphasized building global alliances as well as Japan's own military capability.

According to Bajpai, the triumvirate of Koizumi, Abe and Taro Aso defined the new 'arc of freedom and prosperity' stretching from Europe to Japan as the rimland that encircled the Eurasian heartland. Bajpai believes Mr Abe saw the Indo-Pacific and Quad as nothing less than a quasi-military alliance aimed not at containing China but deterring it, whatever diplomats in the region might wish to say publicly. Bajpai sees a continuity in Japan's post-WWII worldview that will help maintain Japanese support for the Indo-Pacific approach, which is yet another construct aimed at ensuring Japan's role in shaping the Asian regional order in years to come.

Inquiring into the roots of Mr Abe's Indo-Pacific vision, Ravi Velloor concludes that it was shaped by Japan's new grand strategy, which sought a role for Japan in a world with a shifting balance of power between the East and the West. Mr Abe understood the importance of Japan building its own defence capability even as it strengthened its alliance with the US and reached out to Australia, India and Europe.

Velloor writes that Mr Abe was neither a 'reflexive China sceptic, as some in Beijing, and a few in Southeast Asia, have sought to see him', nor a 'sentimentalist, as thought by some in New Delhi'. He was open to cooperating with China but at the same time sought to build new alliances to keep Beijing in check. Velloor concludes that Mr Abe 'was a man acutely attuned to the shifting sands of global geopolitics, the relative strengths of nations and what it could mean for his nation'. He sees future Japanese leaders continuing with the approach that Mr Abe systematically thought through and defined for his nation.

In step with the views of Bajpai and Velloor on Mr Abe's grand strategy, Yuka Koshino also emphasizes the historic significance of his worldview. Mr Abe's tenure as Prime Minister is significant, writes Koshino, because he was among the first to craft a strategy that appreciated and responded to the rise of China. His was a realistic and pragmatic strategy that combined diplomatic, military and geo-economic tools. This, believes Koshino, stood in contrast to many other countries that for far too long viewed China's rise as a largely benign phenomenon. Mr Abe sought a 'stable relationship' with China through diplomacy, economic relations and people-to-people exchanges, even as he ensured that Japan played a 'bridging role' between the West and the Indo-Pacific.

To emphasize the integrity of Mr Abe's worldview, Koshino points to what she terms as his 'de facto political manifesto': *Utsukushii Kuni E (Towards a Beautiful Country)*, published in 2006. He had come to power with a vision of the future of Japan and systematically worked towards realizing that vision in terms of policy at home and overseas, overcoming the hurdles imposed by 'enduring domestic constitutional, fiscal and normative constraints' on Japan's capacity to fulfil its ambitions.

Rohan Mukherjee offers a detailed account of the evolution of Mr Abe's grand strategy and wonders if Japan's new thinking was only on account of Mr Abe or whether any other Japanese leader in his place would have pursued a similar policy. Other leaders who shared his ideological commitments—such as Taro Aso—may well have steered the ship of state into similar waters as Abe did, suggests Mukherjee, but it was Mr Abe 'who led Japan through a tumultuous period, bringing some semblance of stability to domestic politics and greatly enhancing Japan's stature and status on the world stage'. Mukherjee concludes that by imparting a visionary's perspective to a pragmatic and realistic policy, Mr Abe leant weight to his policy initiatives that the world came to appreciate and applaud.

Taken together, these essays underline the global and historical significance of Japan's most consequential and longest-serving Prime Minister. Shinzo Abe was without doubt a leader among his peers and his thinking and initiatives will be viewed as having come to shape the world order in the first quarter of the twenty-first century. These essays in tribute to the memory of Mr Abe will be of interest to readers not only in Japan and India but also all over the world—for Mr Abe was a global statesman who left his imprint on the emerging world order. In India, he will always be remembered for his contribution to enabling the 'confluence of two seas'.

ABE'S LEGACY FOR JAPAN

1

SHINZO ABE'S JAPAN AND A NEW ASIA

Tomohiko Taniguchi

W HEN SHINZO ABE RETURNED as Prime Minister of Japan on 26 December 2012, there were fears that Japan would end up becoming a 'tier-two' country. It was precisely this concern that Richard Armitage, Joseph Nye Jr and others highlighted and reported on in the summer of that year. The domestic economy was not growing at all. During the Democratic Party's tenure, Japan's relationship with the US—its most important ally—had been weakened. In addition, the earthquake and tsunami that struck Japan's northeastern coast on 11 March 2011—and the consequential nuclear catastrophe—robbed the Japanese people of hope for a better tomorrow. Prime Ministers changed every year. Could Japan really remain a 'tier-one' country?

Prime Minister Abe visited Washington, D.C. in February 2013 and answered yes to this question, using both present and future tenses. His straightforward response to Armitage and others was: 'Japan is back'. 'Because I am back,' Abe would have thought, 'Japan, too, must do the same.' Shinzo Abe was a 'born-again' political leader at the time, though not in the Christian sense.

At the age of sixteen, Abe was diagnosed with ulcerative colitis. He became Prime Minister in 2006, but the illness forced him to resign from his position after only a year. Then, at the age of fifty-six, he tried

3

a new medication. The effects were remarkable. After forty years, he was finally able to put his illness into remission.

Only those who have suffered from incurable illnesses can imagine how much courage and energy this gave Abe. No longer afraid of anything, Abe told himself that he should only move forward. Projecting this belief onto his country, Abe felt that Japan too could, and should, only move forward.

Abe wanted to rebuild the economy first. Japan's national budget is larger than the GDP of Saudi Arabia or Turkey. However, 70 per cent of it disappears in just three areas of expenditure: redemption of government bonds and related interest payments; subsidies to local governments; and social security expenditure, mainly on healthcare for the elderly. For long-term growth, more money must be spent on basic science research and education, but as long as the overall pie does not grow—that is to say, as long as economic growth cannot be achieved—money cannot be spent on anything future-oriented, be it education or defence.

Abe's well-known economic policy, termed 'Abenomics', started as a short-term demand stimulus and then began to try a series of measures to help the economy grow. This policy can be termed a success. Before the COVID-19 pandemic hit Japan and the world, Japan could achieve full employment: ninety-eight out of hundred university students could find jobs upon graduation. The same figure applied even for those looking for employment after finishing high school, with 98 per cent of such individuals finding stable work. For the first time since the bursting of the speculative bubble in the early 1990s, young people in Japan were allowed to believe that there would be hope for the future.

In September 2013 at Buenos Aires, Tokyo was awarded the right to host the 2020 Olympic Games. The presentation ended with a speech by Prime Minister Abe, who spoke about the importance of dreams. He described the irreplaceability of dreams for young people while referring to scenes he saw at the 1964 Tokyo Olympics.

I was part of the delegation to Argentina at the time. On the way back to Japan, our government aircraft landed to refuel in Los Angeles, allowing me to check my emails. Among the flood of messages that came in was one from one of my former students. She was then in her mid-twenties.

She wrote in her email:

Congratulations, Professor! I could see your influence in the words of the Prime Minister's final speech. The vision he created was so sparkling. When Tokyo was chosen, I picked up the phone and spoke with my fiancé, who is in East Timor (but was also born and raised in Tokyo). I said to him: 'I am sure we would have had a baby or two in seven years' time. Let's go to the Olympics together. There will be a lot of people, but we can carry our kids on our shoulders. Let's show them the festival for peace.' It was then that I realized that I had until then never ever expected that there would be something shining waiting for us seven years down the road. I always felt that I had grown up in a country of permanent decline, so it was the first time that I felt upbeat thinking about a bright future that I can believe in. It's nice to live in a time of hope. Thank you so much.

This email illustrated the fact that young people took Abe's message to heart. The economy is based on human activity and people change their behaviour depending on whether they are optimistic or pessimistic about the future. Whether in Japan or India, there are only three paths through which an economy can grow: increase in labour input, increase of capital stock or increase of total factor productivity. That much is in every economics textbook. What no textbook touches on is the fact that none of these factors could be increased without people, especially entrepreneurs, having hope for the future. Unless people believe that the future will be better than the present, nothing positive will happen.

However, economies where hope is a rare commodity are so rare that standard economics textbooks dare not mention the importance of hope. Japan was that rare exception: the economy where hope was the rarest of all scarce commodities. It was Abe's eagerness to give young people hope for the future that led him to do all he could to attract first the Olympic Games and later the World Expo—which is to be held in 2025 at Osaka. I would like to state that Abe's achievements in economic policy have given young people hope.

The biggest problems plaguing the country are the dwindling number of children and an ageing population. It is not an easy problem to solve. There are no textbooks to consult to help tackle this issue. Japan's solution may well set the first such precedent in human history. What is certain is that nothing will be resolved unless people have hope for the future. And for the Japanese people to have confidence in their country's future, stability in the external environment is essential. Fewer people would invest in Japan—and fewer children would be born—if they think the country might become dependent on China in the future.

The challenges for Abe therefore were firstly to grow the economy, secondly to use the fruits of that growth to constantly improve defence capabilities and thirdly to expand Japan's strategic space and neutralize Chinese coercive activities by strengthening relations with India and Australia in addition to its long-standing alliance partner, the US. These three challenges create a self-reinforcing causal loop, both positively and negatively. Prime Minister Abe was keenly aware of this dynamic. Foreign investors visiting Tokyo advised the actors in his administration to focus on the economy rather than security. But for Abe, the economy and security were as inseparable as his own vitality and health.

When Abe first met Donald Trump, who had just won the US presidential election, he persuaded him to see that the biggest challenge to the US–Japan alliance was not North Korea, but China. Tokyo's attempts to confront the Chinese threat can only be achieved through overcoming all three of the challenges mentioned in the previous paragraph: it must strengthen its economy, build up its military and make its cooperation with Australia, India and the US as strong as possible. In the process, Abe saved the Trans-Pacific Partnership (TPP) from the brink of oblivion and brought it to fruition. He also succeeded in forging the EU–Japan Economic Partnership Agreement (EPA).

Under Abe, Japan became the standard-bearer for a free, open and rules-based international economic order, which was unparalleled in the 150 years of the country's modern history. He developed the arguments he made in the Indian Parliament in 2007 to create Quad. The US–Japan alliance has grown stronger than ever through the administrations of Barack Obama and Donald Trump, and the Australia–Japan relationship has grown to become a quasi-alliance. Japan's strategic space has expanded markedly.

Japan has a constitution that is unique in the world. Article 9, paragraph 1, states that 'the Japanese people forever renounce war as a sovereign right of the nation and the threat or use of force as means of settling international disputes'. This builds on the trend of outlawing war since World War I and is not a factor unique to the Japanese constitution. What remains unique today is that the subsequent paragraph 2 states: 'In order to accomplish the aim of the preceding paragraph, land, sea and air forces, as well as other war potential, will never be maintained. The right of belligerency of the state will not be recognized.' Because of this section, many Japanese constitutional scholars still regard the Japanese Self-Defence Forces (SDF) as a violation of the constitution. This is also the reason why the SDF is not referred to as an army.

For many years, Japan's actions have been constrained by the limited interpretations of its constitution, which state that the SDF 'may not return fire, whether by missiles or artillery shells, unless it is hit by the first shot' and that 'whatever friendly forces are attacked, it may not join in and return fire unless it is attacked itself'. Under this interpretation, in the hypothetical situation of Taiwan coming under attack by China, the Japanese forces in the immediate vicinity will be unable to do anything about it even if their allies such as the US suffer military damage.

Abe's efforts have led to Japan receiving 147 F-35 fifth-generation fighter jets from the US. But no matter how many superior planes Japan has, they are simply useless as long as the interpretation of its constitution remains unchanged. If over a hundred Japanese fighter jets remain grounded despite Chinese aircraft attacking US forces, the US–Japan alliance will at once lose its significance. Japan's security environment would deteriorate instantly and significantly.

In 2015, Abe succeeded in passing a series of legislative bills, the enactment of which changed this narrow interpretation of the constitution. For instance, in the event of a military attack by China on Taiwan, the SDF facilities on Japan's westernmost island (Yonaguni Island) would not be unharmed. The US military would respond by mobilizing from bases in Japan to defend Taiwan. In such a situation of imminent and existential threat to Japan, the Japanese Self-Defence Forces and the US military would be able to collectively exercise their right to self-defence. Abe spent much of his political capital to pass the bills that made this possible. Now, protection of US military assets are a regular obligation for the SDF, and US military vessels and aircraft operate under ever-present SDF protection.

Throughout his second term, Abe continued to win elections for both houses in the Japanese parliament: the House of Representatives and the House of Councillors. In some cases, the ruling coalition gained a 'super majority' (more than two-thirds of all seats) in both houses. This meant that the necessary requirements for amending the constitution could be met. However, the Constitutional Review Commission—a special committee that screens and proposes amendments in advance—did not function at all due to obstruction by the opposition parties. As a result, no movement towards constitutional reform took place. Although the scope of the SDF's activities has been greatly expanded thanks to Abe, the view that the SDF is unconstitutional has persistently remained. This was much regretted by Abe.

Despite this, with his accomplishments in economic revitalization and strengthening of deterrence as a backdrop, Abe faced Xi Jinping of China. The Chinese Communist Party is an organization that believes in power, and power alone, and Xi is the embodiment of such a party. However, acknowledging that Japan's power had been strengthened, Xi began to pay more heed to Tokyo and Abe. Nowadays, the term 'One Belt, One Road' does not appear in global discourse as much as it used to. When Abe fell to the bullets of fanatics, Xi Jinping sent his condolences. The use of the first person in the condolence message was unusual for a Chinese leader. Even Xi must have felt that he and Abe had a kind of friendship.

Similarly, using his varied diplomatic skills, Abe attempted to conclude a peace treaty with the President of Russia, Vladimir Putin.

He met with Putin twenty-seven times and was prepared to make some compromises to achieve his one objective: to reduce the military threat to the north of Japan by bringing military tensions with Russia under control. This would enable him to concentrate any spare SDF capacity entirely on the southwestern part of Japan to defend against China. It was a realpolitik-oriented diplomacy, but it did not bear any fruit. Ironically, Putin was not a dictator who could change relations with Japan by a single decision. Japan imposed harsh sanctions on Russia following the invasion of Ukraine and now relations between Russia and Japan are even worse than they were before Abe began talks with Putin.

Russia, North Korea and China are vertically aligned across the Sea of Japan and all three share borders with Japanese territory. None of these countries has ever experienced anything akin to open democracy, and all three believe in the power of nuclear weapons: in fact, they are increasing their respective arsenals of warheads. This means that no G7 country is in a more dangerous location than Japan. Never in Japan's modern history has its neighbourhood been more volatile.

Japan needed allies. No matter how strong the economy is and how energized the people are, Japan can be weak in the long term if the external environment is so dangerous. Japan had to be able to state with confidence—both domestically and internationally—that it is not alone, that it has partners and allies. It needed a statement that the whole world could understand—one that respects freedom, human rights, democracy and the rule of law—and to declare it to the world.

Creating a new geographical concept and spreading it around the world is no mean feat. It was Shinzo Abe who pursued this in the Indian Parliament in Delhi, in the Australian Parliament in Canberra and in the US Congress in Washington, D.C. It is also to Abe's credit that he launched Quad and fostered cooperation between Australia, India, Japan and the United States, and these diplomatic efforts have reassured Japan and the Japanese people.

The British Empire used Greenwich as the base point to separate the 'East' from the 'West'. Japan was classified as the 'Far East', meaning the furthest zone from the centre. It was only in the 1980s that Masayoshi

Ohira, then Prime Minister of Japan, created the category 'Asia-Pacific' together with his Australian counterpart. APEC was also Ohira's brainchild. However, when Abe first came to power in 2006, he realized that the Asia-Pacific concept had become outdated. He felt that there was a need for a larger concept that would balance China's intimidation as well as a framework that would encompass and emphasize fast-growing India as one pole, both politically and economically. Thus, what Abe created—and the world accepted—was Free and Open Indo-Pacific (FOIP) and the Quadrilateral Security Dialogue (Quad). Under Abe, for the first time in its modern history Japan succeeded in launching a new concept that has defined the world discourse. Abe's success as a politician is unprecedented in the country's history.

When Abe passed, in a eulogy titled 'My friend, Abe-san', Prime Minister Narendra Modi wrote: 'I first met him in 2007 during my visit to Japan as the chief minister of Gujarat. Right from that first meeting, our friendship went beyond the trappings of office and the shackles of official protocol.' When he first arrived in Japan, Modi had the image of being a 'bad guy', someone the US had refused to allow into their country. Abe, on the other hand, was the Prime Minister of Japan. However, Abe followed his own judgement and was happy to welcome Modi. The friendship that developed between the two men was essential for Japan to make India a reliable partner. Abe was a penetrating strategist. He was a systems manager who understood that economy, diplomacy and security are inseparable. At the same time, he was a warm-hearted man who instantly created a friendship with Modi, who came to visit from afar.

Japan has lost one of its greatest leaders in modern history and has lost its compass to guide its course. At times like these, what is needed is the support of friends. Nothing would be more gratifying for Japan and the Japanese people than the friend Abe has made in India.

In closing this paper, I would like to include the speech transcript that Abe was supposed to read in Manipur. He had been invited by Modi to visit Imphal at the end of 2019. Initially, the visit was postponed due to social unrest in India and later due to the spread of the coronavirus that originated in Wuhan. The trip could not be rescheduled before Abe died.

Manipur has a monument and a museum dedicated to the friendship between Japan and India. The original draft of Abe's calligraphy, titled 'Peace', appears below. This piece is framed and displayed in front of the entrance to the museum.

Standing here in Imphal and reminiscing about a time that is now long gone has been a task that I have been trying to accomplish for many years. As time passed from Showa to Heisei and then to Reiwa, the desire only grew stronger.

Now, with the kind consideration of my friend, Prime Minister Narendra Modi, it has become a reality, and I feel a deep sense of gratitude for the fact that it has become a reality.

The Peace Museum, which we have just seen, quietly tells of what happened here during the war, and shakes the souls of us, the present generations. I would like to pay my deepest respect to the efforts of all those who worked so hard to build it.

Annihilation after annihilation. The battlefield was fierce, also cruel. There was no ammunition, no food, not a grain of medicine, not a piece of bandage. A match, moistened by rainwater, would not have easily started a fire.

Young lives, if they survived the fire line, died of malaria, dengue fever, dysentery and even the plague.

To stand here is to at least try to quieten our hearts and listen to the hushed voices of those soldiers, the nurses who died trying to help them, and countless others.

The area from here to Myanmar and Yunnan Province would otherwise have been a land of peace, but war has unilaterally struck the people of this region, causing untold tragedy.

Even if I were to close my eyes quietly, nothing can bring back the lives and property that were lost in the past.

Even so, I hereby pay a silent prayer on behalf of the Japanese people. I offer my sincere repose and condolences for the countless innocent, nameless people of this region, and of course for all those who fought each other, the Allied Forces, the Indian National Army, the Japanese Army and all those who exchanged arms.

For seventy-five years since then, Japan has respected peace, valued human life, and worked tirelessly, both at home and in distant foreign lands, to nurture the human capacity of each and every individual, to cultivate freedom and democracy, and to ensure them.

Fortunately, our efforts have borne fruit in the form of recognition for Japan. Will the people who have died in this region take this as any consolation at least? I hope so, and I would like to pledge that the progress we have made so far will remain unwavering in the future.

A rusted piece of an iron helmet, a rotting piece of a military sword. What clues are left behind? Too many of the remains of Japanese soldiers are still scattered here and there in the region, waiting for their impossible return home.

I would like to express my sincere gratitude to the people of this region who, from the very beginning of the post-war period, helped us to collect the remains. With the generous understanding of the Government of India, I am pleased that in coming years we will be devoting even more effort to the collection of the remains of the deceased. I am sincerely pleased. I would like to thank all those involved.

Prime Minister Modi has made this journey of repose and remembrance a reality. For that I would like to thank you once again, Mr Prime Minister. Thank you, Prime Minister Modi.

— Shinzo Abe, 2022.

2

THE LEGACY OF ABE AND ABENOMICS

Heizo Takenaka

ON 8 JULY 2022, Japan lost a great political leader. In a country supposedly renowned for its safety, Shinzo Abe, the former Prime Minister who had led the longest-running administration in the history of Japanese politics, was assassinated. The assassination not only shocked the public, politicians and bureaucrats, but also was deemed to have a major impact on global politics and economy. It signifies the greatness of Prime Minister Abe's legacy.

Abe was often thought of as a politician with ultra-conservative views. True, he was a conservative who spent much of his political capital on security policies and endorsed liberalization and privatization in economic policies. However, Abe was also a thorough realist. That's why he managed to sustain his administration over a long period and left behind a great legacy.

I pray that Prime Minister Abe's soul may rest in peace and would like to discuss the legacy of his administration in this tribute.

Shinzo Abe as a Person

From 2001 to 2006, I worked with Shinzo Abe as a fellow member of the administration of Prime Minister Junichiro Koizumi. While I had been suddenly recruited from the academia to serve in cabinet positions (including as minister for economic and fiscal policy, financial services minister and minister for postal privatization), Abe had built his career as an influential member of the Diet (the Japanese Parliament) and was already considered to be a future candidate for the post of Prime Minister.

After having served in key positions in the Koizumi administration—including as deputy chief cabinet secretary, secretary general of the ruling Liberal Democratic Party and chief cabinet secretary—Abe was elected to be the nation's ninetieth Prime Minister in 2006. Even though he stepped down due to health problems after only a year in office, Abe resolved to make a comeback. He returned to the government's helm in 2012 to lead his second administration which, as it turned out, became the longest on record. He led the ruling coalition to victory in all six national elections held under his leadership and went on to drive Japan's politics and economic management, contributing to the international community over a period of seven years and eight months, until he resigned—again for health reasons—in September 2020.

After the Koizumi administration came to an end in 2006, I quit government duties and returned to my career in research at university. But when the second Abe administration began, I was invited to be a member of a policy council chaired by Prime Minister Abe and again began taking part in the government's policy discussion. It was then that I came to know Shinzo Abe as a bright and forward-looking person with a personal charm to constantly attract people around him. People are often said to become reticent when they become top leaders. But Prime Minister Abe was always ready to talk to others and win them over. Whether he was talking about serious policy matters or public relations campaigns, he had the power to always give us a positive outlook on the issues discussed.

It was with such a personal character that Abe pursued his various policy initiatives. In doing so, he appears to have followed a distinct pattern when appointing people to key positions on his team—a pattern that was influenced by his father, Shintaro Abe. In his curtailed political career, Shintaro Abe served as minister for international trade and industry and as foreign minister, but fell short of being elected to the post of Prime Minister. His fellow LDP rivals Noboru Takeshita and Kiichi Miyazawa both became Prime Minister after serving as finance minister, but Shintaro Abe died at the age of sixty-seven without ever being appointed to either post.

Before becoming a lawmaker, Shinzo Abe worked with the Ministry of Economy, Trade and Industry (METI) and the foreign ministry as his father's secretary, but is said to have kept a tense relationship with the finance ministry. As a consequence, Prime Minister Abe tapped METI officials (such as his executive secretary, Takaya Imai, and Eiichi Hasegawa, special advisor to the Prime Minister and cabinet public relations secretary) and foreign ministry officials (such as Ichiro Komatsu, who was appointed chief of the cabinet Legislation Bureau) to key posts in his administration, while keeping the finance ministry at a distance. This approach was also reflected in Abe's economic policies.

Abenomics as Economic Policy

Prime Minister Abe's biggest achievements in policy were in the diplomacy and national security areas, as symbolized by the enactment of the Peace and Security Legislation. However, he was fully aware that the foundation of diplomacy lies in a robust base of domestic governance. Due to the complexities of Japanese politics, the administrations of post-WWII Prime Ministers each lasted a mere one year and seven months on average. Abe recognized that the nation's foreign policy had been affected by this fragility in the domestic power base of Japanese political leaders. Therefore, he laid a particular emphasis on economic policies, and the policy package that he put on the forefront of his administration was termed 'Abenomics'. Prime Minister Abe is still remembered for the 'Buy my Abenomics' remark he made during his speech at the New York Stock Exchange in September 2013.

Abenomics had three components, which Prime Minister Abe termed as the 'three arrows' after the maxim by the sixteenth-century feudal lord Mouri Motonari. In concrete terms, the 'first arrow' was a bold monetary-easing policy aimed at overcoming deflation. As the tenure of the Bank of Japan (BOJ) governor expired shortly after he took office, Abe appointed Haruhiko Kuroda as the new BOJ chief after obtaining the Diet's approval, which was needed for appointing a BOJ governor.

Under Kuroda's leadership, the BOJ introduced a set of unconventional, 'new dimension' monetary-easing steps, setting an initial target of doubling the monetary base in two years. This resulted in share prices increasing threefold, with the fall of the yen and the rise of the stock market leading to a surge in exports and capital investments. Criticism against the BOJ's unprecedented monetary easing emerged from some quarters in recent years as the policy was maintained over an extended period. However, the first arrow of Abenomics can be deemed to have had major effects to boost domestic as well as external demand.

The 'second arrow' was a flexible fiscal policy, in which the administration—even as it recognized fiscal rehabilitation as the government's long-term goal—declared its readiness to expand fiscal spending flexibly for achieving an economic recovery. The administration thus distanced itself from the finance ministry, which had put the top priority as rebuilding the nation's fiscal health. Under the second Abe administration—from fiscal 2014 to 2019, just before the nation was hit by the coronavirus pandemic—the government's general account budget expanded by 5.7 per cent despite the persistent fiscal deficits.

It was likely with reluctance that the Prime Minister had to raise the consumption tax in April 2014, just as the economy was beginning to improve steadily. The tax hike had been dictated by a tripartite agreement in June 2012—when the LDP was still in the opposition—with the then-ruling Democratic Party of Japan as well as the Komeito, under which the consumption tax rate was scheduled to rise from 5 per cent to 10 per cent in three years. Prime Minister Abe was personally opposed to such a tax hike, but was obliged to raise the tax from 5 to 8 per cent under pressure from the finance ministry and the business circles. The tensions between Prime Minister Abe—who kept his distance from the finance ministry—and the fiscal authorities continued throughout his administration.

The 'third arrow' was the growth strategy: the most difficult and most important challenge. Normally, what's important for economic growth are tax cuts, deregulation and changes to immigration policy to increase the population. To draw concrete measures for such policies, Prime Minister Abe launched the Growth Strategy Council (later renamed as the Council on Investments for the Future) and served as its chair himself.

As a government council to discuss policy issues, the Council on Economic and Fiscal Policy had already been established. However, that council, for which the cabinet Office served as the secretariat, had increasingly been under the strong influence of the finance ministry. Therefore, Prime Minister Abe separately launched the Growth Strategy Council, and put its management primarily in the hands of METI officials.

The achievements of the administration in terms of the third arrow of growth strategy were widely judged to be insufficient when compared with those of the first and second arrows. It must be noted, however, that whereas monetary and fiscal policy decisions can be made quickly and their effects felt promptly, it involves political difficulties to build a consensus on most components of growth strategy because they necessitate structural reforms. It also takes longer for the effects of such reforms to materialize.

Given such constraints, the Abe administration's growth strategy can be deemed to have had considerable effects on Japan's economy. Even as Japan's population continued to decline, the number of people with jobs increased by more than five million between late 2012 and the end of 2019.

The Struggle with the Media

There were parts of the administration's growth strategy that were considered successes. First among these was the reduction in corporate tax rate. In order to revitalize corporate activities—the primary factors of growth—the nation's effective corporate tax rate, which was the highest in the world at that time, needed to be brought down. Tax cuts amid the huge fiscal deficits were extremely difficult, but the Abe administration put corporate tax cuts on the agenda of its growth strategy, paving the way for a gradual reduction in the effective tax rate. The effective corporate tax rate, which was close to 40 per cent before the Abe administration, has finally been reduced to 30 per cent in recent years.

Other noteworthy endeavours were reforms of the labour market and the corporate governance system that expedited the renewal of businesses and industries. While the administration's major achievements in terms of corporate governance include the introduction of the Corporate Governance Code as the stock exchange guideline, a number of challenges remain unresolved concerning labour market reforms. For deregulation, the administration created the national strategic special zones system as a mechanism to move ahead with regulatory reforms in designated areas. It is indeed politically tough to fight against vested interests, and this mechanism to enforce deregulation in special designated zones ahead of other areas has been partially successful.

For example, deregulation concerning urban development in Tokyo and Osaka significantly streamlined the process at city planning councils. As a consequence, more than twenty-five large-scale urban redevelopment projects are under way in the central parts of Tokyo. Here again, however, challenges remain, such as in decontrol of farming-related regulations.

One of the key features of the Abe administration's economic policies was that it set various policy agendas in ways that anticipated popular interest. The regional revitalization initiative to reinvigorate the declining rural economies and the measures taken to promote women's empowerment drew strong public interest. In terms of the social advancement of women, Japan continues to suffer from a significant gender gap—as illustrated by its rank of 116 out of 146 countries in the World Economic Forum's gender gap index. But women's labour participation substantially increased under the Abe administration.

As for regional revitalization, it is not an easy task to revitalize the rural economies amid a continuing decline in the nation's population—especially as the emphasis today is placed on urban-model, knowledge-intensive industries. Still, Prime Minister Abe created a cabinet position in charge of regional revitalization for the first time. He set aside a budget of 100 billion yen for the task, thereby identifying to the public a policy direction that the nation should be taking.

The reforms introduced at the Prime Minister's initiative brought hope for Japan's economy. But looking back on the management of Abe's administration over the seven years and eight months of his second stint in office, I must point to one change from the first half of that period to the second half. The political scandals that surfaced from 2016 to 2017 put the administrative on the defensive, making it subsequently difficult for the Prime Minister to come to the forefront of efforts to pursue the reforms. That apparently reflected not the intention of the Prime Minister himself but that of the bureaucrats aiding him, who began to balk at reforms driven by Prime Minister Abe in order to shield him from criticism.

In both scandals, it was alleged that the Prime Minister gave political favours to certain groups of people. The allegations against him did not go much beyond the realm of speculation, but the public opinion was heavily influenced by the reports on the issue by parts of the media. The popular sentiment also turned against Abe and there was a growing sense of antipathy to an administration that appeared to be on its way toward an extended rule based on a robust power base.

A key lesson learned from the Abe administration was the importance of the Prime Minister taking the lead for reforms and guiding the economy in a favourable direction. This was demonstrated by Prime Minister Abe, at least in the first half of his administration. Another lesson is that the media tends to feel an antipathy to an administration that has become too powerful, and the popular sentiment heavily influenced by such media reports puts the administration in trouble. Clearly, the management of an administration entails a struggle with the media and public opinion fanned by the media. Such an experience served as a major lesson for the subsequent management of the administration.

The Great Contributions in Terms of National Security

The Abe administration had a number of great achievements, but if its biggest contribution is to be singled out, it would be its success in substantially strengthening Japan's national security framework. Prime Minister Abe was of the same belief. Under its so-called 'pacifist' post-war constitution, Japan had for long neglected to deepen practical discussions on its security. Today, however, the security environment surrounding Japan has radically changed—as illustrated by the US–China confrontation, nuclear weapons tests by North Korea and Russia's invasion of Ukraine. Japan is confronted with a growing risk.

Against this background, the policies pursued by Prime Minister Abe will be considered successful in two respects. Firstly, he engaged in a comprehensive overhaul of the nation's legal basis concerning security. Previously, the government had taken relevant steps in terms of national security to respond to changing circumstances—such as the enactment of a special legislation to enable Japan's support for the war on terrorism and the law for responding to military emergencies. However, these were mostly ad-hoc responses, instead of efforts to build a comprehensive national security system. That is why Prime Minister Abe aimed to build a 'seamless security system'.

In 2013, shortly after assuming office for the second time, Abe announced the National Security Strategy, the first-ever comprehensive security vision presented by the government. The following year, he set up the National Security Secretariat in the cabinet Secretariat under his direct command. Based on the power of the cabinet Secretariat, the National Security Secretariat is to engage in the planning and coordination of the basic direction and other important matters of the diplomatic and defence policies relating to national security. And finally in 2015, he enacted the Peace and Security Legislation, which represented a major progress in the development of Japan's security system as it lifted the self-imposed ban on the nation engaging in collective self-defence.

Abe's second policy success was in defining the 'free and open Indo-Pacific' initiative as a clear concept. It was presumably the first time that Japan advocated such an initiative for creating a broad regional order—and that the concept was widely endorsed by major Western powers. The idea—which calls for establishing the rule of law, pursuit of economic prosperity and securing peace and stability in the region—will play an important role in the post-Abe international community.

Prime Minister Abe indeed played a key role to lead not only Japan but the world, as illustrated by his accomplishments as chair of the G7 and the G20 forums. In his endeavour to develop the national security system, Prime Minister Abe came under severe criticism from the opposition parties as well as the liberal forces in his country. However, he followed through with his beliefs and fulfilled his accountability to the public, and eventually succeeded in having the security legislation enacted.

Japan after Abe

Without a doubt, Shinzo Abe was a politician who left his mark on Japan's history. The sudden loss of such a leader at the relatively young age of sixty-seven has sent shockwaves through Japanese society, making it difficult for us to have a clear prospect of our future. In the world of politics, the death of Abe—a symbolic figure among conservative members of the ruling LDP—will likely alter the balance of power between the party's conservative and liberal forces (of which the current Prime Minister, Fumio Kishida, is deemed a leading figure). This may not immediately result in a major shift in Japan's foreign policy, but it could trigger subtle changes in the nation's relations with the United States and China.

In more concrete terms, the question of who takes over the leadership of the LDP faction formerly led by Abe—which happens to be the biggest party faction—will affect the future course of power struggles within the party. The LDP still tends to distribute key positions among its lawmakers according to the factional balance of power. So far, no clear candidate has emerged to succeed Abe as the leader of his faction. The possibility cannot be ruled out that the faction will eventually break up, setting off fierce struggles among its members.

There will also be changes to economic policies. Whereas Prime Minister Abe put the priority on economic growth through revitalization of public-sector activities with his Abenomics, Kishida has emphasized the importance of distribution policies over economic growth (although more recently he has used nuanced expressions such as 'the virtuous cycle of growth and distribution'). And while Abe kept the finance ministry at a distance, Kishida has edged closer to the ministry, as illustrated by his suggestion to increase the capital gains tax. Such a shift in the focus of economic policies could lead to a more short-sighted management of the Japanese economy.

It is likely that the loss of Shinzo Abe—who led Japan's politics and economic management both in terms of ideals and power—will cause several sets of challenges for managing our society. We need to take to heart the lessons left behind by Abe about the crucial role of leadership in policy management, the struggle with the media that fuels public opinion and the importance of strengthening our national security.

At Abe's state funeral, held in September 2022, Yoshihide Suga—the former Prime Minister who spoke on behalf of friends of the deceased—wrapped up his eulogy by quoting a poem. It was written by Yamagata Aritomo—the Meiji Era political leader who served as the third Prime Minister of Japan—to lament the death of Ito Hirobumi, who was the first Prime Minister. The lines are quoted below:

My friend who served the country with everything he had
Has died before me
What should be done about Japan
Now that he is gone?

3

SHINZO ABE: PRIME MINISTER OF A NEW JAPAN

Nobukatsu Kanehara

PRIME MINSTER SHINZO ABE represented a new generation of Japan. He was born in 1954 and brought up in a post–WWII liberal democracy during an age of spectacular economic development in Japan. He belonged to that age of optimism and liberalism and went on to become one of the nation's first leaders from that generation.

On 8 July 2020, Mr Abe was slain by a cowardly assassin in Nara at the Yamato–Saidaji railway station as he was talking to his supporters about the coming general elections. The light has gone with his death, like in a sudden total solar eclipse. Many Japanese, particularly the young, mourned his untimely death. In his private funeral at Zojoji temple, waves of people rushed to say goodbye to the former Prime Minister. At the assassination site, offerings of flowers piled high. When the state farewell ceremony was held at Budokan in Tokyo on 25 September, a long line of people holding flowers surrounded the building.

While Shinzo Abe had invited the anger of the senior leftist generation, for young Japanese he had represented the 'dawn of a new Japan'. He successfully gave a new identity to Japan as a democratic country of innovation and freedom. Now it is up to the youth to pick up the burning torch that Mr Abe left unextinguished and pass it down to future generations.

Mr Abe tried to put an end to the futile and dividing domestic ideological debate on the strategic direction for Japan during the Cold War period. The division of national opinion still haunts Japanese politics even thirty years after the fall of the Soviet Union in 1991. In the strategic vacuum created by the collapse of the German and Japanese empires in 1945 followed by strong divisive pressure from Washington and Moscow, many divided nations were born: East and West Germany, North and South Korea, North and South Vietnam as well as the 'second China', Taiwan. Japan survived as a single nation, but was divided bitterly inside. As Dr Henry Kissinger correctly wrote in his book *World Order*, 'Japan placed itself legally in the camp of the developed democracies' but 'declined to join the ideological struggle of the age'.

Prime Minister Shigeru Yoshida brought Japan into an alliance with the US in 1952. The informal military arrangement would see US occupying forces remain in Japan for security against the Soviet Red Army in the Far East. The arrangement would also guarantee economic development of a Japan devastated by the Pacific War and avoid the resurrection of the political influence of the Imperial Army and Navy.

But the Cold War confrontation tore Japan into two halves. In 1955, the Japanese Socialist Party grew in strength. To counter it, the Liberal Democratic Party was created by uniting various conservative parties. Unlike the UK's Labour Party, the Socialists of France, Germany's Social Democrats and the Democrats of the US—all of whom represented the interests of labour unions and were in firm support of the ideology of the West—the Japanese Socialist Party swore allegiance to Moscow. The government of Japan and the LDP stood firmly with the West, but the Parliament was completely and ideologically divided. The media and academia were largely sympathetic with the Socialist Party. Marxism and Leninism as well as the idea of class struggle had strong influences until Japan's spectacular economic development of the 1960s and 1970s.

Amid this ideological battle, Prime Minister Nobusuke Kishi—the grandfather of Shinzo Abe—upgraded the Japan–US alliance. Mr Kishi was a staunch patriot who wanted to transform Prime Minister Yoshida's informal arrangement into a formal alliance, which he achieved in 1960.

This upset the Russians, who had wanted to make Japan a neutral country like Austria. Domestically, the socialists and the communists and a large part of the media were opposed to Mr Kishi's actions. Thousands of labourers and student activists surrounded the Parliament and the Prime Minister's office. Prime Minister Kishi refused to resign, but was eventually forced to do so. Shinzo Abe witnessed that political turmoil first-hand as a child.

The Cold War that divided Japan ended thirty years ago. Today's Japanese youth are not concerned with the Cold War and the former Soviet Union. They are instead concerned by the rise of a belligerent China and the decline of the Japanese economy. They needed a leader of a new age. Prime Minister Abe was that leader. He showed them an image of a new Japan that was a leader of the liberal international order emerging on a global scale. He gave the young Japanese purpose, hope and confidence.

The core idea of the liberal international order is that its legitimacy is based upon the consent of free people. Regardless of skin colour, gender, ethnicity, religion or political creed, each person has dignity and inviolable human rights. Conscience is absolutely free and freedom is self-realization led by one's own conscience. For survival and a better life, people can make an inclusive society. The government is bound by law and a mere instrument for the peoples' will. Law is nothing but rules made by agreements among free people.

Prime Minister Abe wanted Japan to be one of the main pillars of this world order. He used to say, 'Japan should bloom proudly at the centre of the world.' In 2013, during his second stint as Prime Minister, he visited Washington, D.C. to give a speech at the Centre for Strategic and International Studies. The speech was titled 'Japan is back'. Mr Abe had returned to the centre stage of world politics with an image of a new Japan and a new belief among Japanese people.

A New Identity for Japan

Mr Abe's conviction in freedom, democracy and rule of law was consolidated after his inner struggle to establish a new identity for Japan and its citizens. He had to come to terms with the past of Imperial Japan. This historical issue was also a bitterly divisive issue in Japan, and Mr Abe had to resolve this issue to achieve his aim of creating a new Japan for future generations. His thoughts on the issue are reflected in his statement on the occasion of the seventieth anniversary of the end of the Pacific War on 15 August 2015.[1]

Mr Abe denounced wars, colonization and discrimination and he concluded that the liberal international order is based upon the tremendous bloodshed and sacrifices of innocent people worldwide in the last century and that it is Japan's and other like-minded nations' responsibility to sustain this liberal international order. He said that Japan should look back at the past one hundred years of world history and learn lessons from it. The world was slowly but steadily changing for the better, but Japan had hastily become a challenger to that world order.

After Japan's defeat, war was prohibited, colonial empires had collapsed, Asian and African nations proudly took back their independence and sovereignty and institutional racial discrimination like apartheid in South Africa was finally pulled down. 'And here we stand,' Mr Abe thought. 'This is Japan's vantage point.' He wrote in his statement:

> More than one hundred years ago, vast colonies possessed mainly by the Western powers stretched out across the world. With their overwhelming supremacy in technology, waves of colonial rule surged toward Asia in the nineteenth century.
>
> At the beginning, Japan, too, kept steps with other nations. However, with the Great Depression setting in and the Western countries launching economic blocs by involving colonial economies, Japan's economy suffered a major blow. In such circumstances, Japan's sense of isolation deepened and it attempted to overcome its diplomatic and economic deadlock through the use of force.

Mr Abe continued:

> We will engrave in our hearts the past, when Japan attempted to break its deadlock with force. We will engrave in our hearts the past, when the dignity and honour of many women were severely injured during wars in the twentieth century. We will engrave in our hearts the past, when Japan ended up becoming a challenger to the international order.
>
> Upon this reflection, Japan will firmly uphold basic values such as freedom, democracy and human rights as unyielding values and, by working hand in hand with countries that share such values, hoist the flag of 'Proactive Contribution to Peace' and contribute to the peace and prosperity of the world more than ever before.

Mr Abe made this statement not only for himself but also for the future citizens of Japan. He concluded,

> In Japan, the post-war generations now exceed 80 per cent of its population. We must not let our children, grandchildren and even further generations to come, who have nothing to do with that war, be predestined to apologize. Still, even so, we Japanese, across generations, must squarely face the history of the past. We have the responsibility to inherit the past, in all humbleness, and pass it on to the future.[2]

The Strategic Vision of FOIP

The greatest contribution of Mr Abe to world politics is his vision of the 'Free and Open Indo-Pacific' (FOIP). He launched his vision on 27 August 2016 at the sixth session of the Tokyo International Conference for African Development held in Nairobi, Kenya. It was a conference that brought together heads of states of almost all African countries.

Mr Abe stated,

> When you cross the seas of Asia and the Indian Ocean and come to Nairobi, you then understand very well that what connects Asia and Africa is the sea lanes. What will give stability and prosperity to the world is none other than the enormous liveliness brought forth through the union of two free and open oceans and two continents. Japan bears the responsibility of fostering the confluence of the Pacific and Indian Oceans and of Asia and Africa into a place that values freedom, the rule of law and the market economy, free from force or coercion, and making it prosperous. Japan wants to work together with you in Africa in order to make the seas that connect the two continents into peaceful seas that are governed by the rule of law. That is what we wish to do with you. The winds that traverse the ocean turn our eyes to the future.[3]

The vision has a prehistory. He visited Delhi on 22 August 2007 as Prime Minister of Japan. In the Indian Parliament, he delivered a speech titled 'Confluence of the Two Seas'. It is now considered the genesis of his strategic vision.[4] He quoted Swami Vivekananda and said,

> The different streams, having their sources in different places, all mingle their water in the sea.' It gives me tremendous pleasure to be able to begin my address today with the words of Swami Vivekananda, the great spiritual leader that India gave the world. My friends, where exactly do we now stand historically and geographically? To answer this question, I would like to quote here the title of a book authored by the Mughal prince Dara Shikoh in 1655. We are now at a point at which the *Confluence of the Two Seas* is coming into being. The Pacific and the Indian Oceans are now bringing about a dynamic coupling as seas of freedom and of prosperity. A 'Broader Asia' that broke away geographical boundaries is now beginning to take on a distinct form. Our two countries have the ability—and the responsibility—

to ensure that it broadens yet further and to nurture and enrich these seas to become seas of clearest transparency.

The vision started to spread globally and was appreciated by the US and various European and Asian countries. It was so influential that President Donald Trump of the US immediately embraced it and the US Pacific Command in Hawaii was renamed the Indo-Pacific Command.[5] Australia, Britain, France, Germany, the European Union and the Association of Southeast Asian Nations all followed suit by launching 'Indo-Pacific' strategic visions.

There are two reasons why his FOIP vision was so widely accepted. The first is that the vision brilliantly articulates the strategic transformation of international politics in the first half of the twenty-first century, in particular Japan and the United States growing distant strategically from an increasingly authoritarian and belligerent China while growing closer to India. The competition between great powers has started involving India.

International stability has been predicated since 1945 by the interaction of two strategic triangles. The first triangle is the predominantly maritime 'Western' framework encompassing Europe, Maritime East Asia and North America. It comprises the European members of the North Atlantic Treaty Organization at the western end of the Euro–Asian continent; the United States in the centre between the Atlantic and the Pacific Oceans; and Japan, South Korea, the Philippines, Thailand and Australia at the eastern end of the Euro–Asian continent. They are tied together by the leadership of the United States, the primary ally for these Western nations.

Within this triangle is another triangle of unique dynamism comprising the continental Eurasian powers of Russia, China and India. The United States has always tried to exploit the uneasy relationship among these three continental powers to its advantage. In World War II, it used the Soviet Union under Stalin to halt Hitler's advance and eventually defeat Nazi Germany. During the Cold War, the United States took advantage of the Sino-Soviet split in the 1960s and engaged Beijing in order to confront Moscow. The rapprochement was predicated by the cold logic of power politics that states 'the enemy of my enemy is my friend'. Japan soon followed suit in normalizing relations with the People's Republic of China. The normalization of relations between Washington and Beijing brought about the era of détente and the end of the Vietnam War.

One unexpected by-product of this diplomatic manoeuvring was that 'non-aligned' India—which was more sympathetic ideologically towards Moscow than Washington at the beginning of the Cold War—grew closer to the Soviet Union due to New Delhi's wariness of China, which had attacked Indian territory in 1962 under Mao. Isolated India sought to counterbalance China by approaching Russia. And Moscow, for its part, needed India to face the new alliance of Washington, Tokyo and Beijing. The legacy of this is that even now almost all of India's weapons are made in Russia.

As the strategic competition between the United States and China has heated up in the new millennium, India has slowly increased its distance from Russia and has come closer to the US–Japan alliance. Mr Abe did not miss the opportunity to push forward this strategic vision and to realize the strategically tectonic transformation of world politics. He said openly that the Pacific and Indian Ocean regions should be understood as a single strategic picture and it is vital to position India as an important partner of the West in it. This is because the West does share universal values and strategic interests with India, the would-be superpower of this century.

India is the hope of the liberal international order. Its population will surpass China soon, and is on average ten years younger than the Chinese demographic. India will soon surpass Japan as an economic power. Its naval fleet is becoming a truly blue water navy. India still needs Russia to counterbalance Xi's powerful China. But as India grows as a superpower of this century, it will share the responsibility to sustain the global liberal order and will become a pillar of the multipolar and more diverse liberal international order.

Dr Kissinger's framework of 'the West plus China face the Soviet Union plus India' has come to an end. The new strategic framework is now 'the West plus India face China and Russia'. Mr Abe's strategy is not at all a simple confrontation with China. He wanted to engage

China from a position of strength. He understood well that China would not listen to the weak—China would respect only strong opponents, and it too wished to be respected as a strong, leading power.

Prime Minister Abe tried to rehabilitate the shattered unity of the West. China will become stronger and wealthier, but it cannot match the size of the united West. The West could still engage China from a position of strength. China, on the other hand, has no idea as to how to lead humanity as a whole. As George Kennan predicted the fall of the Soviet Union due to its internal contradictions, so too Mr Abe believed that the West could win the long game with China. To do so, the West must be united and stand together with a rising India.

The weakness of the FOIP concept is that it is a diplomatic framework and does not have military muscle. Like-minded nations gather to uphold freedom, democracy and rule of law, but there is no strong military organization like NATO for deterrence. In comparison with NATO, the US–Pacific Alliance of Japan, Korea, the Philippines, Thailand and Australia is sadly far weaker. There is even no common perception of threat among the US–Pacific Allies.

Today's China is far stronger than the Soviet Union. To deter China from adventurism and unilateral change of the status quo, there is no other way than to think of a framework of capable nations with the US at the centre. This has led to the creation of Quad (Japan, US, India and Australia) and AUKUS (Australia, US and UK). But the nation who should worry the most is Japan. In the US–Pacific Alliance system of 'hub and spokes', the most robust 'spoke' is Japan. But the long pacifist inclination and the bitterly divided nation has not let Japan produce enough capabilities for defence so far.

Prime Minister Abe raised the consumption tax twice—from 5 per cent to 8 per cent in 2014 and then from 8 per cent to 10 per cent in 2019—securing tax revenue of around ten to fifteen trillion yen per year to secure financial resources for the government. He twice revised the National Defence Program Guidelines—in 2012 and again in 2017—and steadily increased the defence budget every year. When Mr Abe assumed office in 2006, the defence budget was only 4.6 trillion yen. Now Prime Minister Fumio Kishida's defence budget for the fiscal year

2022 is 6.1 trillion yen, including supplementary budgets. Prime Minister Kishida is now building upon Mr Abe's efforts and accelerating the enhancement of the Self-Defence Forces' capabilities to counter the build-up of the Chinese army. The purpose is to deter China from any unilateral and coercive change of the status quo, particularly in Taiwan.

The second reason for FOIP's wide acceptance is that India is a creation of Gandhi and Nehru, and a democracy since 1947. While Roosevelt teamed up with Stalin to crush Hitler, and Nixon with Mao to confront the Soviet Union, both choices were typical manoeuvring of naked power politics. By contrast, the United States is now embracing India, the democratic state birthed by Gandhi and nurtured by Nehru. Teaming up with India could bring into existence a massive democratic coalition of nations spanning the coasts of the Indo-Pacific region.

In this century, Asia and Africa will enhance their political and economic power. They are now called the 'Global South'. Asia alone will account for 60 per cent of the world population and industrial production. The Western nations could be marginalized if they do not expand into the Global South. The West should remember that while they were industrializing and democratizing themselves in the nineteenth century, they were also expanding their colonial empire globally as fierce colonial rulers. Human dignity, human rights and sovereignty were, to say the least, partially denied to the people of the colonized Asian and African nations. They were forced to work in plantation farms and mines under poor labour conditions. In the case of Malaysia, the massive induction of foreign labourers from India and China by the British even changed the ethnic composition of the country. Their national history was erased and their borders redrawn arbitrarily.

The Global South is now headed for industrialization and democracy. By the 1980s, four 'Asian tigers' had already begun their growth: Singapore, Hong Kong, Taiwan and South Korea. Today, the South Korean economy is at G7 level, while the Taiwanese economy is in the G20 category. Both are vibrant democracies. Meanwhile, Hong Kong is the financial centre of Asia, though their freedom was reduced by Xi Jinping. Now foreign investment is flooding into Vietnam. In this century, the centre of global wealth production will move from East Asia to West Asia.

Asia has a long and deep political philosophical tradition to accept Western liberal thought. Over 2,300 years ago, Mencius—a quasi-saint in the Confucian school—wrote that the people's will is Heaven's will and that the ruler who goes against Heaven's will must perish. He even wrote that a bad king can be decapitated because Heaven no longer gives him its grace and mandate to rule the world. It is well known that Mahatma Gandhi's satyagraha had a strong influence on Marin Luther King's civil rights movement in the US that brought down institutionalized racism. What the Global South lacked was the institutions that guaranteed democratic political institutions such as a parliament, free elections, universal suffrage, a free press and an independent judiciary.

The West is at an inflection point where it must decide whether to be marginalized or to expand into the Global South. In this context, the new membership of India into the West is valuable not only for India, but also for the West. The liberal international order is precious, but not robust. The West's ideas such as human dignity, human rights, democracy and rule of law will continue to shine. But we must remember that these ideas and ideals were very often trumped, denied and destroyed by cruel dictators.

China and Russia openly decline to join the West and share values with them. They still live in a state where force is the most important factor and only the fittest survive. The strongest can freely expand its territories while the weak is subjugated or eradicated. They cannot understand that the government is a mere instrument to enhance the wellbeing of the people who entrusted it with power. China and Russia believe that their influence could counter the expansion of the universal values of the Global South. With India, the West could hope to win the race for global leadership: a contest that pits individualism and liberalism against collectivism and authoritarianism.

Reshaping the Regional Security Framework

Prime Minister Abe worked hard to enact the legislation authorizing the right to exercise collective self-defence—a long-running and bitterly divisive issue in Japan's post-war politics. In all major international agreements during this period, the Japanese government made it clear that Japan, like all other nations, possesses the right to collective self-defence as identified in the United Nations Charter. It is so written even in the joint statement to normalize relationships with the Soviet Union in 1956. This statement is in fact a treaty that was ratified by both the Japanese and the Soviet Parliaments.

However, the second paragraph of Article 9 of the Japanese constitution—written in 1946 by General Douglas MacArthur of the Occupation Forces and promulgated in 1947 under the Occupation—prohibited the possession of land, sea and air forces. This paragraph was inserted into the constitution in the early period of the Occupation. It was a pre-Cold War decision by the General Headquarters of the Allied Forces (GHQ) to completely demilitarize Japan. Even after the Korean War started in 1950 and the Occupation ended in 1952, the constitution was not rewritten as the procedure for amendment was cumbersome.

In the Sunagawa case of 1959, the Supreme Court of Japan declared that Japan has the right of self-defence under the constitution, for no constitution can deny the people's inherent right to exist. Following this critical judgement, the government concluded that it was its duty to protect the security of innocent Japanese people through the deployment of 'minimal force'. This is how the Japanese Self-Defence Forces came into being.

However, the government continued to tie its own hands with a narrow interpretation of the constitution that denied Japan the right to collective self-defence. Japan's internal politics at the time was structured by the Cold War tensions and divisions. The ruling Liberal Democratic Party wanted to strengthen the US–Japan alliance, while the Japanese Socialist Party advocated 'unarmed neutrality'—which involved ending the alliance with the US and not militarily threatening the Soviet Union. The socialists and communists could not accept Japan using the right to collective defence in alliance with the US.

During the Cold War, the issue of Japan exercising its internationally recognized right to collective self-defence was a subject of highly politicized and heated debate within the Japanese Parliament. The government eventually caved in and renounced the right to self-defence, severely restricting the scope of military cooperation with the United States. This interpretation was a political compromise with the socialists that was necessary at the time.

Mr Abe corrected the mistake of previous governments by creating a new legal authority to enable the SDF to use the right to self-defence. This was a reversal of the post-war conventional and constitutional interpretation that Japan could defend itself but could not help the US in any warlike activity. Mr Abe fixed the confused strategic direction that Japan followed during the Cold War period and made it clear that Japan stands with the West, not only economically but also militarily. This was a great contribution not only to the national security of Japan but also to the regional security of the North Pacific region.

It is interesting and important to examine how the regional security of the post-war period was constructed and with what kind of vision and framework. The US–Japan Security Treaty was revised in 1960 by Prime Minister Kishi to contain the 'Far East' Clause (Article 6) in addition to Article 5, which stipulates an American obligation to participate in the joint defence of Japan. Article 6 allows the United States to use Japanese territory as a support base for protecting South Korea and Taiwan (both former territories of the Japanese empire) as well as the Philippines (a former US territory). Japan was relieved from the heavy burden to protect the Korean peninsula.

Japan refrained from entanglement with Asian continental affairs for more than a thousand years, with only a few exceptions. The Japanese knew that historically only the issues concerning the Korean peninsula brought Japan to confront the continental powers. After the devastating defeat in World War II, Japan had no power to sustain the imperial sphere of influence. The US took over this sphere, which was a welcome move for Japan.

The United States needed Japan's help during the long Cold War, but also feared the resurrection of the Japanese Imperial Army. At the beginning of the Occupation, the American military force in Japan was considered the 'cork of the bottle' to contain the genie of Japan's militarism. Thus, even when Japan created the SDF in 1954, its scale was kept modest. The responsibility to defend the former Japanese imperial territories was shouldered by the US, with Japan's role limited to allowing the American forces to use their territory for bases.

By the 1990s, the Cold War had ended and the Soviet Union had been dismantled. The strategic focus was now on North Korea, who had decided to develop nuclear weapons. When the United States imposed severe sanctions on North Korea in response to their nuclear ambitions, fears of a second Korean War increased. The dissipation of the military threat from Moscow in Japan's north meant that there were raised expectations from the United States for Tokyo to help the American forces as it had done during the first Korean War.

Prime Minister Ryutaro Hashimoto revised the US–Japan defence guidelines in 1997, with his successor, Keizo Obuchi, passing the Major Influence Situation Act in 1999 that enabled Japan to provide logistical support to American forces in the event of another Korean War or other regional contingencies. However, what remained unchanged was the legal position that Japan was constitutionally prohibited from exercising its right to self-defence and engaging its forces in combat operations abroad.

The Abe administration's new interpretation of the constitution allowed Tokyo to exercise this right and led to more powerful coordination between the SDF and the US military forces. The new interpretation of the constitution allowed the Japanese forces to engage in overseas combat operations in conflicts where there was a possible threat to Japan even if Japanese territory had not yet been attacked. Mr Abe's constitutional reinterpretation and the resulting legislation therefore increased the deterrent power of the US–Japan alliance. In theory, both Japan and the United States now hold equal responsibility for regional defence in the North Pacific. However, in practice this institutional change is not yet reflected in the revision of the US–Japan defence guidelines nor in military planning.

The First National Security Strategy and Taiwan Contingency

In 2013, Prime Minister Abe wrote the nation's very first National Security Strategy. This strategy gave directions for the national defence program guidelines and the midterm defence plan, which were revised in 2013 and 2018 respectively under Mr Abe's guidance. In addition to the existing strategic focus on Hokkaido to defend against a possible Russian invasion as well as on any Korean peninsula contingency, the new documents placed emphasis on the defence of Japan's Nansei Islands at the southwestern end of the archipelago. These islands spread across 1,000 kilometres from the East China Sea to the Pacific Ocean.

The focus was on Taiwan, as it is only 110 kilometres away from the Japanese territory of Yonaguni Island. Defending Japan's islands in the vast East China Sea region against China and providing support to the US forces in the event of a Taiwan contingency would be an extremely difficult task. Japan would have to shift its strategic focus from the north to the south for the first time in its modern history. To this end, the Abe administration set up a 3,000-strong amphibious task force and expanded SDF responsibilities into the cyber, electromagnetic and space warfare domains.

During Prime Minister Abe's time in office, China's economy grew to become three times the size of Japan's and three-quarters the size of the US economy. Chinese military spending skyrocketed at an even greater pace to five times Japan's defence budget—which is roughly the same as the UK, France or Germany. At the twentieth convention of the Chinese Communist Party (CCP) in October 2022, Xi Jinping started an unprecedented third term as the leader of China, scrapping Deng Xiaoping's ruling that the maximum term of office for the Chinese leader is ten years and two terms. He eliminated all the political rivals from the polit-bureau of the party and is now the absolute dictator of China and has set his eyes on the free island of Taiwan. Reconquering Taiwan seems to be the only purpose of Xi's long rule, as it will give him a chance to declare himself a greater leader than Mao Zedong.

When Tokyo and Washington normalized relationships with Beijing in the 1970s, the understanding was that China is one nation and that Beijing is the legitimate capital. But neither Tokyo nor Washington accepted the Chinese assertion that Taiwan is a part of Chinese territory and that China has a legal right to annex Taiwan by force if necessary. Yet, because both Mao Zedong and Chiang Kai-shek insisted that there was only one China and that their respective capitals of Beijing and Taipei were the only one legitimate government of China, Tokyo and Washington accepted the 'One China' theory. But neither capital accepted that Beijing could unilaterally change the status quo by force.

The understanding of Tokyo and Washington at the time of resuming relations with Beijing was that the status quo of the Taiwan Strait would be preserved. That is the reason why Tokyo and Washington repeated that the peace and stability of the Taiwan Strait is vital for regional stability. In 2021, President Joe Biden of the US and Prime Minister Yoshihide Suga of Japan stated the same in their joint communique. It was the first time such a statement had been released since the rapprochement between Tokyo, Washington and Beijing.

Prime Minister Abe had made every effort to keep peace and stability in the Northeastern Pacific. He is to be credited with the concept of FOIP, the creation of Quad as well as establishing a new legal authority for the SDF. His efforts led to an increase in the Japanese military budget and stronger ties with the US. A creation of a new compensatory fund for the wartime 'comfort women' led to an improvement in the relationship with South Korea, and Mr Abe also fostered close personal ties with the Australian and British Prime Ministers. He held several summit meetings with ASEAN leaders and had a strong relationship of mutual trust with Prime Minister Modi.

Perhaps his achievements would only be truly tested if Taiwan were to come under attack from China. But one thing is very clear: if Prime Minister Abe had not served his second term, Northeast Asia would now be a much more dangerous and precarious place.

Expanding Free Trade Zones

A free market is a splendid creation of humanity from the days of old when people travelled long distances to exchange goods and produce. Prime Minister Abe had great success in his efforts to expand free trade zones by pushing back the anti-free trade trends of the world. Presently, the World Trade Organization (WTO) is picking up steam again under the new leadership of Dr Ngozi Okonjo-Iweala. But for a long time, the WTO had lost its ability to enhance the worldwide free trade system. Free trade was under attack. In many advanced industrial nations, factories were moved abroad and industry was hollowed.

New billionaires emerged with the spread of the internet industry, but the wages of ordinary workers of the traditional industries did not increase. A new social wealth gap had formed, and this issue became the subject of political agendas and heated debates in many countries. A typical example of a response was the 'America First' slogan of the former US President Donald Trump. He raised tariffs and shut the border with Mexico by building a wall. Prime Minister Abe had a different approach.

In the industrial era, the beauty of free trade is that the investment flows to the places where there is the biggest possibility for profit. Japan itself has become one of the major investors internationally, with wealth moving from the industrialized nations to the Global South. The world's economy spread from Europe to the US, Japan, Korea, Taiwan and the ASEAN nations—it will probably soon include India and eventually, Africa. The industrial revolution changed the face of this planet, and it will not end until all nations—including those in Africa—become industrialized. This could even happen in the latter half of this century, thanks to the power of free markets and free trade.

Prime Minister Abe created the Comprehensive and Progressive Trans-Pacific Partnership (CPTPP). It is an agreement for free trade between Japan, Singapore, Vietnam, Brunei, Malaysia, Australia, New Zealand, Canada, Mexico, Peru and Chile. These nations represent 14 per cent of the world GDP. Initially, the US was leading the negotiations under President Barack Obama. At that time, the agreement was called Trans-Pacific Partnership (TPP). But President Obama could not get approval from the Congress and his successor, Trump, just scrapped it. Mr Abe then showed strong leadership to push forward the agreement so that it could come into effect.

Mr Abe also signed the Japan–EU Economic Partnership Agreement. The total population of Japan and the European Union adds up to 640 million, their combined GDP is 28 per cent of the world GDP and together they account for 28 per cent of world trade. This is one of the biggest free trade zones among advanced industrial nations. Mr Abe and the leaders in Brussels wished to show that even as support for free trade may be receding in some countries, it is still thriving globally—and that Japan and Europe would take the lead in spreading it further.

Japan was instrumental in the creation of the Regional Comprehensive Economic Partnership Agreement (RCEP). This is a trade framework comprising the ASEAN nations of Japan, China, South Korea, Australia and New Zealand. They represent almost 30 per cent of both the world population and the world GDP. Japan invited India to join the RCEP, but India withdrew from the negotiations at the last moment.

Towards the Future

The industrial revolution of Great Britain changed history forever. Since then, people have struggled to create a modern industrial society in the industrial age. The answer was not communism nor any other form of dictatorship, but democracy and a free market. During the twentieth century, we also struggled to eliminate colonial rules and racial discrimination. The answer was in the establishment of a liberal international order.

Now the liberal order should expand into the Global South and become much more diverse, colourful and universal. This was Prime Minister Shinzo Abe's message.

4

THE POLITICAL SIGNIFICANCE OF SHINZO ABE

Robert Ward

THE LATE SHINZO ABE was Japan's most important post-WWII Prime Minister. This partly reflects his significant contribution to Japan's foreign and security policies, which is described elsewhere in this volume in more detail and which marked a structural shift in Japan's ability to project power in the Indo-Pacific. Abe's record in these areas included institutional, legal and other reforms that were groundbreaking by Japan's post-WWII standards and mark him as one of the country's most strategically alert leaders of recent times.

But Abe's political longevity and dominance also inevitably left its imprint on Japan's domestic political scene. His second administration, which ran from 2012 to 2020, made him Japan's longest-serving premier. During this period, he also led his party, the Liberal Democratic Party (LDP) to six consecutive wins in national elections—a record for a single leader of the party. Other than Shigeru Yoshida—who was Prime Minister from 1946 to 1947 and again from 1948 to 1954— Abe is also to date the only Prime Minister to have returned to power for a second term and, like Yoshida, to have been accorded a state funeral. However, to understand the nature of his domestic political legacy, it is important to first consider the context of his second term, not least the

41

factors that facilitated his rise to power and the lessons that he learned from the failure of his first term.

Centralizing political reforms in the 1990s

The 1990s in Japan was a period of intense political upheaval and reforms that centralized power within the LDP and increased the power of the Prime Minister. Shinzo Abe entered national parliamentary politics in 1993, when he won his late father's Diet (Parliament) LDP seat in the general election in June that year. This election also triggered the party's fall from power for the first time since its formation in 1955.

The two non-LDP governments that followed were short-lived and unstable, and the LDP was able to return to power in mid-1994, albeit in coalition.[1] But the first of these non-LDP administrations, under Prime Minister Morihiro Hosokawa, was able to implement an important electoral reform in the lower house of the Diet. The reform replaced the old multi-seat 'medium-sized electoral districts' (*chūsenkyokusei*)—in which constituencies were represented by up to five Members of Parliament (MPs)—with a mixture of single-seat and proportional representation constituencies. This reform was designed to satisfy voters' clear desire for political change—after a slew of scandals that discredited the LDP—and to foster the development of a two-party system.

The emergence of the centre-left Democratic Party of Japan (DPJ) as the largest opposition party in 1998 was one result of the change. But the most important impact was felt within the LDP itself. Under the multi-seat system, LDP factions had competed against each other in the same constituencies even in terms of policy, giving them sway at the expense of the party leadership over candidate selection and fundraising. The pressing need for financing by the factions was also cited as a source of corruption. The collapse in the income of the three largest factions—Heisei Kenkyūkai, Kōchikai and Seiwa Seisaku Kenkyūkai— since the first election under the new system in 1996 again evidences the impact of the reform.[2] Thus this electoral reform greatly centralized the authority of the LDP's central executive within the party, increasing its potential for control over funding and patronage.

Similarly important were the administrative reforms of Prime Minister Ryutaro Hashimoto of the LDP, who was in power from 1996 to 1998. His changes were designed to improve the efficiency and quality of Japan's political decision-making, which was seen as deficient after the various traumas earlier in the decade: including Japan's fumbled responses to the first Gulf War in 1990–91 and the twin domestic shocks in 1995 of the Kobe earthquake and the sarin gas attack on a Tokyo subway train by the Aum Shinrikyo cult. As well as reducing the number of ministries by half, *inter alia* the reforms established a cabinet office to be administered by a newly empowered chief cabinet secretary and the deputy chief cabinet secretaries, expanded the staffing of the cabinet secretariat and set up advisory councils to enable the Prime Minister and the cabinet to better deliberate and coordinate policy, a function that had hitherto been largely the preserve of the LDP's Policy Research Council.

These reforms also revised the cabinet law to boost the Prime Minister's power, for example by clarifying his or her right to initiate policy on 'basic principles on important policies' in the cabinet.[3] The changes took effect in 2001 and were exploited by Prime Minister Junichiro Koizumi, also of the LDP, from 2001 to 2006 to bypass the opposition to his structural reforms from various interest groups inside his party. The reforms sought to deal with the large stock of non-performing loans sitting on the books of Japan's banks following the bursting of its economic bubble in the early 1990s as well as the push for the privatization of the postal system.

Prime Minister Abe's resignation in 2007 was followed by two short-lived LDP administrations and then, in 2009, by the party's comprehensive general-election defeat by the DPJ. The DPJ's emphatic win raised hopes of political change again in Japan—witness *The Economist*'s leader just after the election: 'The vote that changed Japan/ The electorate has thrown out not just a party but a whole system.' However, the DPJ's genesis as an amalgam of smaller centre-left parties and disgruntled ex-members of the LDP—many of whom were refugees from the upheavals of the 1990s mentioned earlier—suggested from the start that it would struggle to articulate a coherent policy platform.[4]

Eventually, a mixture of poor policy, weak leadership, intra-party fissures, lack of networks in Japan's bureaucracy and bad luck—in the form of the Fukushima nuclear disaster in the wake of the Great East Japan Earthquake and tsunami—eviscerated public support for the DPJ government. The frequently changing leadership—there were three Prime Ministers in just over three years of the DPJ government—was emblematic of the party's inability to assert its grip on power. It is hard to overstate the impact that the comprehensive failure of the progressive left in this period had on Japanese voting patterns in the 2010s, not least in creating a strong tailwind for the string of national election wins by Abe in his second term. The dire performance of the Constitutional Democratic Party (CDP)—the DPJ's successor as the largest opposition party—in the 2021 general election and the 2022 upper-house election under Fumio Kishida shows how weak the centre-left remained nearly a decade after it fell from power.[5]

Abe's Wilderness Learnings

Although seen by many as a spent political force after his resignation as Prime Minister in 2007—ostensibly owing to health issues—Abe used the period in the political wilderness—both within the LDP, where he was held responsible for the party's 2009 election failure, and externally—to reflect on the mistakes of his first term. From the point of view of identifying the drivers of the success of his second term, his lessons learned can be broken down into three broad areas. These were the need for: greater attention to voters' concerns; greater control over the levers of power; and prioritization of administration stability. The first found form as his signature economic programme, 'Abenomics'—which was announced in late 2012 with its three 'arrows' of unorthodox monetary policy, flexible fiscal policy and economic structural reform.

Although it eventually delivered only mixed results—particularly in terms of structural reform and a failure to boost wages—at the time

Abenomics and its optimistic message of growth and activism were a welcome change of pace and mood after the vacillation of the DPJ government, the shock of the 2008 global financial crisis and even the fiscal conservatism of the Koizumi administration. The attention given to domestic economic reform almost immediately into Prime Minister Abe's second term contrasted with his first term, when he overfocused on his own ideological issues—such as security reform and promotion of patriotic education—at the expense of pocketbook issues. This was one reason why the LDP lost control of the upper house of the Diet in a crushing defeat at the 2007 election to the chamber.

The second lesson drove a series of institutional changes that built on the centralization of power since the 1990s, again early into his second term. One of the most important of these was the creation in 2013 of Japan's first inter-agency National Security Council (NSC) and in 2014 of its coordinating body, the National Security Secretariat (NSS). The NSC replaced the Security Council—which had been set up in 1986 by Prime Minister Yasuhiro Nakasone and was mainly concerned with the deployment of Japan's military (the Self-Defence Forces) and budgetary issues rather than bigger issues of strategy. Chaired by the Prime Minister, the NSC gives Japan an integrated foreign and security policy 'control tower' (*shireitō*) and increases the Prime Minister's control over these policy areas.

Abe made considerable use of the NSC's so-called 'Four-Minister Meeting' (*Yon Daijin Kaigō*), a core grouping within the NSC that the defence and foreign ministers and the chief cabinet secretary attend along with the Prime Minister.[6] The inter-agency NSS was partly designed as a means of forcing information exchange between Japan's notoriously turf-conscious ministries. Its secretary-general reports directly to the Prime Minister, thus boosting its political authority within Japan's bureaucracy.

Abe's recognition of the need for the Prime Shinzter to control strategically or politically important posts in the bureaucracy also led to the creation in 2014 of the cabinet Bureau of Personnel Affairs (CBPA). The CBPA thus became for Prime Minister Abe a critical tool for extending his remit further into the ministries and for overcoming often fierce inter-ministry turf conflicts. His top-down approach to policymaking was also evident in his setting up in 2015 of a special unit in the cabinet Secretariat Office to serve as the government headquarters for the Trans-Pacific Partnership (TPP) mega trade deal. The unit was tasked with advancing negotiations on the TPP, and allowed him to bypass vested interests and lobby groups in the various ministries and those within his own party who feared losing out from the opening of Japan's markets as a result of the deal.

Prime Minister Abe's tight-knit group of core allies—including Yoshihide Suga, in the key chief cabinet secretary role; Kazuhiro Sugita, deputy chief cabinet secretary for administrative affairs; and Taro Aso, who served as deputy prime minister and finance minister—reinforced this central control. Suga, Sugita and Aso each served in their positions for the entirety of Abe's second term, with the former two becoming record holders for length of tenure in their respective roles.

The third lesson manifested itself partly in the form of a willingness to be pragmatic where politically expedient. This is clearest in Prime Minister Abe's signature policy of constitutional reform—particularly of Article 9 of the constitution, in which Japan renounces war as a 'sovereign right' and forswears maintenance of 'war potential'—which was considered central to his wish to restore the 'autonomy' (*dokuritsu no kaifuku*) that Japan had lost as a result of its defeat in World War II.[7] Notwithstanding its centrality to his personal policy platform and, in the latter part of his premiership, the government's holding of the parliamentary numbers needed to initiate the constitutional reform process, he was unwilling to destabilize his administration in pursuit of this goal, calculating that public opinion was still not yet sufficiently supportive to guarantee success.[8]

Record-low turnout rates in national elections in his second term will also have reinforced this caution.[9] Rather he opted in 2015 for legislatively easier—although still politically controversial— constitutional reinterpretation allowing Japan to engage in collective self-defence, albeit only under certain circumstances. Abe's pragmatism was also evident in his single visit in December 2013 to the controversial

Yasukuni Shrine in Tokyo—which honours Japan's war dead, including convicted war criminals—during his second term. The subsequent reticence from further visits to the shrine partly reflected concern for the impact such actions would have on relations with South Korea and China—and came despite his previous defence of visits to the shrine.[10] Similarly, despite his domestic political dominance, he was reluctant to push on political hot-button issues such as the reprioritizing of Japan's nuclear power industry—largely mothballed since the Fukushima disaster—to meet Japan's energy needs. For Abe, therefore, the longevity of his second administration and a resulting careful selection of issues often trumped his ideological drive.

The Balance: A Culmination of the 1990s Reforms and 1955 Redux

Abe's success in his second term owed much to his ability to harness and build on the centralizing trend in Japanese politics that arose from the political upheavals of the 1990s. Indeed, his second administration may be seen as the apogee of the 1990s reforms in terms of increasing the power of the executive at the expense of the bureaucracy and vested interests in the LDP. But his administrative and political success has also, paradoxically perhaps, contributed to turning Japan's political clock backwards to what might be called a '1955-like system'. The original '1955 system' (*55-nen taisei*) describes the period between the LDP's creation in 1955 and its first fall from power in 1993, in which changes of power at the national level occurred not between parties but between factions in the LDP—as has, indeed, happened since Abe's resignation with the successive appointments of Suga and then Fumio Kishida as Prime Minister.

In part, of course, this reflected the discrediting of the centre-left after the DPJ's turbulent period in office from 2009 to 2012, the 'nightmare' memory of which Abe worked hard to keep alive till the end of his second premiership.[11] But Abe was also ruthless in exploiting opposition weakness by repeatedly using the Prime Minister's power to call lower-house elections.[12] This also explains his strategic and persistent focus on maintaining his public support levels at above what he considered a defensive line of 30 per cent approval—although in his second stint in office he averaged a respectable support rate of over 40 per cent.

Thus, Abe fought and won two lower-house elections after his return to power in 2012 in addition to the three upper-house polls held during his second term, thereby draining the opposition of organizational energy and financial resources. The combination of Abe's ability to control the political agenda and the centre-left's lingering weakness has left the LDP as the overwhelmingly dominant force in Japanese politics—a phenomenon known as *Jimintō ikkyō* ('strong LDP', or 'LDP on top')—with little prospect in the near future of a return to a two-party system.

This return to a '1955-like system' has also seen a rise in the influence of the LDP's factions. Although the 1990s' electoral reforms reduced the financial clout of the party's factions, their political importance rose over the period of Prime Minister Abe's second term. In part this may have reflected the longevity of the term and Abe's position as the leader of the largest faction, the Seiwa Seisaku Kenkyūkai. One illustration of this rise is data from the *Asahi Shimbun* daily newspaper from early 2022, which shows an increase in the percentage of LDP MPs belonging to party factions. Towards the end of Prime Minister Abe's second term this figure was around 80 per cent of MPs, an increase from a figure of around 65 per cent immediately before Abe returned to power—although this was still lower than the 1990s, where the figure was over 90 per cent.[13] Abe's decision to remain as leader of his faction even after resigning as Prime Minister in 2020 was unusual by the standards of his predecessors and an indication of the importance that he attached to faction control as a tool of political influence.

Abe refashioning himself into a disruptor of the status quo during his second term was due to his overwhelming dominance over the opposition. This was an extraordinary feat for a party that, as of late 2022, had been in power for nearly sixty-two of the past sixty-seven years and whose leadership remains dominated by long-standing political dynasties. But Abe challenged the boundaries of Japan's political thinking with his call for constitutional change (even if unfulfilled), his pushing aside of vested interests in pursuing projects such as the TPP and CPTPP, his willingness to overturn consensus in controversial areas such as Japan's exporting of arms and even his abandoning of orthodox monetary policy in his Abenomics economic programme. This contrasted with centre-left and left-wing opposition parties such as the DPJ, its successor, the CDP, and the Japan Communist Party, who generally favoured preserving the status quo.

This, coupled with a campaigning focus on young voters and near full employment for this demographic segment during Prime Minister Abe's second term, was perhaps a major reason for the LDP's popularity with those in their twenties and thirties during this period—significantly exceeding its popularity among those in their sixties.[14] The development of the youth vote made strategic sense for the LDP given the demographic decline in traditional voter strongholds such as agriculture and construction and a similar tailing off in the support bases of the centre-left and left-wing parties.

Demonstrating Capacity for Change

Perhaps one of Prime Minister Abe's most important domestic political legacies may be his embedding of foreign and security policy issues into Japan's domestic political debate. He achieved this by understanding the political levers needed to bring about a step change inside Japan in terms of the awareness of the threats to it from its external environment, and by nudging public opinion towards an appreciation of the domestic decisions needed to ensure the country's security and prosperity.

This partly sprang from Abe's early understanding of the implications of China's rise for Japan and his recognition that Japan needs to deal with China from a position of strength. He thus sought agency within the US–Japan alliance while also developing Japan's own resilience and ability to project power. This found striking expression in the campaign for the 2022 upper-house election, in which Prime Minister Kishida led on defence and foreign policy. This would have been unthinkable but for the policy priorities and successes of Prime Minister Abe's second term in office.

Similarly, Kishida's persistent articulation to voters on the need to preserve the rules-based order following Russia's invasion of Ukraine in February 2022 builds on Abe's own foreign-policy emphasis on the stability of the international order—see for example his keynote speech in 2014 at the International Institute for Strategic Studies's Shangri-La Dialogue, which is subtitled 'Japan for the rule of law, Asia for the rule of law, and the rule of law for all of us'.[15] Broad public support for an increase in defence spending to 2 per cent of GDP—which Kishida has promised to implement—should also be seen in this light.

Finally, Prime Minister Abe's second term also demonstrated through his understanding of the effectiveness of executive power that Japan's political system was capable of initiating and executing significant reforms. He bequeathed his successors an array of powerful institutional tools to do this, whose creation was in turn underpinned by an urgency deriving from Abe's experience of the failure of his first term. How potent these tools will remain depends on the political will of successor administrations to deploy and supplement them. In this regard, the LDP's current overwhelming dominance in the Diet reflects Abe's domestic political success from 2012 to 2020. But it also suggests reason for caution for those with memories of Japan's political history over recent decades.

Shinzo Abe's absence from Japan's political scene deprives the country of an important strategic voice ready to raise difficult issues—particularly on matters of foreign and defence policy—at a time of increasing external threat to its prosperity and security. His absence also leaves a significant power gap in the LDP, at least for the near term, which may complicate policy coordination between the government and the party. Prime Minister Abe's second term raised expectations outside Japan of the country's capacity to support the rules-based order. Rising tensions around Taiwan as China presses its claim on the island with increasing shrillness and the geopolitical shock of Russia's invasion of Ukraine in 2022 have further increased the importance of Japan as a global player. How Abe's domestic political legacy evolves is thus of concern outside as well as inside Japan.

5

REMAKING JAPAN: THE ABE WAY

Titli Basu

SHINZO ABE WAS ONE of the sharpest strategists in post-war Japan. He emerged as a transformative thought-leader who was bold enough to elevate Tokyo's global profile and was seen as the foremost flagbearer of a rules-based international order. He became a pivotal name in the power corridors of Indo-Pacific capitals. An international statesman of Abe's intellectual stature, strategic value and towering political might is a rare quality in Japanese political culture.

Abe's strategic foresight enabled him to foresee the eventual clash between Beijing and Tokyo as a result of their competing visions of regional order. His ascent to power coincided with the arrival of Beijing as a major actor in the international system, prompting structural shifts in the distribution of power and challenging the core principles of the US-led liberal international order. The power disequilibrium in US–China–Japan dynamics meant that Abe detested the potential emergence of a Sino-centric regional order. Therefore, he invested in an intense national debate to revisit the guiding principles of post-war Japan's security orientation. Abe had worked towards a grand strategy aimed at managing the changing balance of power, political values and ideology.

Putting Japan back on the map of international power politics required the undoing of the limitations that were forced onto Japan in the post–war period, such as the constitutional restrictions brought by the pacifist clause—Article 9. Japanese post-war security identity is defined by Article 9 of the country's constitution, which influences the scope of engagement and terms for use of force. The domestic debate on security is as old as the constitution itself, and in post-war Japan, fault lines on the issue of Article 9 are well established between the pacifists, the revisionists and the pragmatists. Analysing post-war security discourse reveals that over the decades Japan witnessed several waves of the discussion regarding the exercise of the right to collective self-defence.

It was Prime Minister Shinzo Abe who transformed the core of Japan's security policy by undoing the long-standing narrow reading of Article 9 that denied the nation the right to collective self-defence. When Abe opted to reinterpret the essence of the pacifist clause in 2014 through a cabinet decision instead of a constitutional amendment— and employed the cabinet Legislation Bureau for his cause—he drew criticism for his boldness. But this did not deter him in decisively putting limited use of the right to collective self-defence into concrete legislation in 2015. This action considerably redefined how Japan contributed to international security. Abe spun the 'reactive Japan' narrative and boldly redefined the latitude of Article 9 with a carefully crafted concept of 'Proactive Contributor to Peace' anchored on 'positive pacifism'. This infused clarity into Japan's evolving character as a security actor.

Abe dedicated his political career in restoring international confidence in Japan and in rebuilding Tokyo's standing in the international community. To achieve his goals, Abe steered Japanese politics away from the culture of ever-changing Prime Ministers and leadership deficit, instead centralizing political power and administration on the Kantei (Prime Minister's Office). He consolidated his political capital by securing a third term as the Liberal Democratic Party (LDP) president in 2018 with support from five intra-party factions. This yielded political stability to pursue the goal of redefining Japanese post–war security identity and to create a greater role for Japan in the regional security architecture.

This essay deconstructs the influences, ideas, values and vision that shaped the Abe phenomenon. The next section takes a deeper dive into the roots of Abe's aspirations and ambitions to elevate Japan's global standing amongst the comity of nations. It traces the conversations he had growing up in a political family, especially with his grandfather, former Prime Minister Kishi. The early political influences came while serving his father, and subsequently his political guru, former Prime Minister Koizumi.

In subsequent years, as he rose in rank, the key advisors fuelling his intellectual pursuit—including Hisahiko Okazaki, Shotaro Yachi, Nobukatsu Kanehara and Shinichi Kitaoka—also played a decisive role in the shaping of Shinzo Abe. In the second section, the essay delves into how these influences shaped Abe's visions and values. Finally, the essay reflects on some key areas in the security conversation where the trends set by Prime Minister Abe will outlive him.

Deconstructing the Abe Phenomenon

Ideas and Influences

Shinzo Abe had many labels. While for many of us he was a pragmatic realist, for Japan's neighbours, he was a 'revisionist' and 'ultra-nationalist'. Abe defined himself as a 'conservative with [an] open mind'. As he writes in his book *Utsukushii Kuni E (Towards a Beautiful Country)*, Abe envisioned himself as a political leader who is willing to fight for his beliefs without getting deterred by challenges and criticisms. As a flagbearer of the conservative plank of politics, his contributions, contradictions and controversies make for a central chapter in Japanese history. However, one thing is certain: he had colossal success in re-engineering Japan's position in the international system.

A Family Affair

Shinzo Abe hails from a political dynasty that played a decisive role in determining post-war Japan's strategic choices and security roles. During his formative years, he was influenced by his maternal grandfather, the former Prime Minister Nobusuke Kishi. Kishi's ambitions for Japan included reclaiming the country's place amongst the great powers through constitutional revision and rearming. This considerably shaped the young Abe's outlook. In contrast, it is notable that Abe's paternal grandfather, Kan Abe—whom he rarely talked about—belonged to the other side of the spectrum and opposed Japan's wartime aggression.

The polarized domestic politics during the revision of the US–Japan treaty in the early 1960s and Kishi's vision for Japan both made deep impressions on Abe. Amid massive protests against the security treaty, young Abe often spent time with Kishi, either in his residence or on weekend trips to Hakone. More importantly, at a tender age, Abe's conversations with Kishi demonstrated his curiosity and inquisitiveness about the protests related to the security treaty. Kishi would often engage in explaining his position on the contentious subject. There are accounts indicating instances where Abe and his brother imitated the Anpo protesters, much to the family's amusement.[1]

Early impressions gathered from these conversations with Kishi loomed large in the making of Shinzo Abe. As a mark of his deep respect, Abe often cited Kishi in his landmark speeches, be it the 'Confluence of the Two Seas' or the historic address to the US Congress. During his visit to India in 2007, Abe met the son of Radha Binod Pal, who had served on the Tokyo War Tribunal. Kishi—who had been part of the Tojo cabinet during WWII and was later projected as a war criminal—had in his prison journal articulated great regard for Pal for his 'sense of justice' and 'courage'.

Shinzo Abe's father, Shintaro Abe, was the foreign minister from 1982 to 1986 and known to be a pragmatist. However, it was Kishi who Shinzo drew motivation from. In post-war Japan, Kishi was a formidable force in the constitutional revision movement. In 1955, he pushed to embrace constitutional revision as a founding mission of the LDP with the aim of undoing the 'weakening of the nation'. As Prime Minister, Kishi chased this objective with the institution of a research commission on the constitution.[2]

However, political instability in 1960 following the revision of the US–Japan Security Treaty compelled Kishi to give up office before the report of the research commission came in 1964. Kishi's zeal reflected in his arguments. He suggested that for Japan to recuperate its standing as a 'respectable member (of) the community of nations it would first have to revise its constitution and rearm: if Japan is alone in renouncing war … she will not be able to prevent others from invading her land'.

Prime Minister Eisaku Sato—who was Abe's granduncle—was also a pivotal figure in the post-war security discourse in Japan. Though it is not clear how much Abe drew motivation from his granduncle, Prime Minister Sato was just as consequential in the Japanese security landscape as Kishi. He steered the Okinawa reversion and enunciated Japan's famous 'Three Non-nuclear Principles' in the Diet in 1967. Interestingly, at one point around 1964, he had professed a pro-nuclear ideology.[3]

Prime Minister Sato is important in the Japanese nuclear discourse. Though he was awarded the Nobel Peace Prize, he established the 'Study Group on Democracy' with the objective of conducting research on the cost-benefit analyses of Japan's nuclearization after Beijing's maiden nuclear test. Moreover, declassified documents present the details of the 'Agreed Minute' between US President Nixon and Prime Minister Sato and the 'Okinawa Package' during the Cold War.[4]

Two decades later, the beginning of Abe's political career started taking shape as he became political secretary to his father. He rose in seniority within the party's factional dynamics and was eventually appointed as deputy chief cabinet secretary and later as the chief cabinet secretary during the Kozumi administration. Once arriving at the centre stage of Japanese politics, he went on to lead the largest faction of the LDP before becoming the youngest Prime Minister of Japan. He remains the longest-serving—and perhaps the most consequential—Japanese premier.

Though Koizumi was not family, he also shaped Shinzo Abe's ideology significantly. When he was part of the Koizumi administration, Abe was mentored as Koizumi's successor. In December 2004, Koizumi instituted an LDP task force to outline a revised constitution. The party's pro-revisionist group gathered momentum under Koizumi alongside the

Mori faction. The LDP constitution drafting committee comprised ten subcommittees with Yasuo Fukuda and Yasuhiro Nakasone leading the subcommittees on Article 9 and the Preamble.

In 2005, the party's draft constitution was presented. It stressed the amendment of Article 9, advocated authorizing the armed forces in the second paragraph of Article 9 and firmly summarized that Japan must exercise the right to collective self-defence just like other nations. During this time, Abe argued that the official reading on collective self-defence had arrived at its limit and 'one of the duties of our generation is to change this government's interpretation so as to enable Japan to exercise that right'.

Intellectual Anchors

As Abe matured as a politician, he not only drew from his family's legacy but also gathered a cohort of intellectuals as his advisors. Some argue that Abe's Kantei-led political decision-making style led to empowering informal actors in contributing towards the strategic thinking behind Japanese foreign and security policy. Among these, one of the most influential names was Hisahiko Okazaki. Abe developed a close intellectual association with him and the two co-authored a book titled *Determination to Protect This Country* when Abe was the secretary-general of the LDP. Okazaki backed Abe's ideas on foreign policy and further strengthened his opinion that Japan should exercise the right to collective self-defence.

Okazaki subsequently became a key member of the Abe administration's roundtable on rebuilding the legal foundations of security. His influence was so strong that Abe paid his respects to Okazaki along with his grandfather and father after the security related laws were enacted in 2015 enabling Japan to exercise the right to collective self-defence.

Abe also heavily relied on the powerful duo of Shotaro Yachi and Nobukatsu Kanehara. When Abe assumed office for the second time, Yachi became involved in the administration as a cabinet secretariat counsellor, and became the first director general of the

National Security Bureau. Abe then completed the team by bringing in Kanehara—who had been deeply involved in creating the foreign policy of the first Abe administration—to be his deputy chief cabinet secretary. Kanehara is often credited as one of the chief architects of Abe's value-based strategy. In his writings, he argued the case that in the twenty-first century, Japan would not just pursue power alone but also justice based on universal values.

Japan was quiet on values in the nineteenth century as well as the first half of the twentieth century, and the primacy of pacifism was the only value in post-war Japan. That changed considerably as Abe anchored Japan's evolving role in the global theatre on 'value-oriented diplomacy', denoting a commitment to such universal values as freedom, human rights, democracy and the rule of law.

Another intellectual who cast a strong influence on Abe but is not talked about often is Shinichi Kitaoka. His most distinguished contribution was helping Abe shape and fine-tune the idea of 'Proactive Contribution to Peace' (*sekkyokuteki heiwashugi*), which became a buzz phrase of the Abe administration's maiden National Security Strategy. The idea implied that Japan's contribution to the 'peace, stability and prosperity of the international community' is commensurate with its international political and economic standing. This is anchored in the concept of 'positive pacifism' encapsulating the principle of international cooperation as opposed to 'passive pacifism'.

Drawing from the political capital of his family—especially Kishi's ideas—and the hands-on experience gained while serving in the Koizumi administration, Abe carefully crafted the right tone for positioning Japan on the global stage. In this pursuit, he created an effective ecosystem of advisors. To translate his vision into action, Abe brought instability in Japanese politics by navigating the dense factional politics of LDP—keeping the old guard of Toshihiro Nikai and Aso on his side while keeping potent political rivals like Shigeru Ishiba at bay. He also centralized the power of Kantei. Winning successive elections gave him the mandate to usher in an irreversible shift in the Japanese security identity.

Vision and Values

Abe was not convinced by the 'Yoshida Doctrine', which is often referred to as post-war Japan's grand strategy. In his account in *Atarashii Kuni-e,* Abe argued that while post-war Japan's grand strategy of delegating security to Washington and solely focusing the nation's energy on economic advancement may have led to material gains, it also led to losing out spiritually. Abe was not alone in this thought. There were a few intellectual voices echoing that the Yoshida Doctrine—which advocated 'economic growth and the lightly armed line' and essentially relied on others for security—had led to the 'spiritual decay' of Japan. For instance, Masataka Kosaka argued that 'the biggest problem is that the pursuit of freedom without being held responsible for the consequences corrupts the spirit of a person'.

Japan's limited international role and responsibility was unacceptable to Abe. In his writings, he has articulated that 'Japan has humbly committed to nation-building' and contribution to international liberty, democracy and fundamental human rights for sixty years while never showing 'a belligerent attitude'. 'Nevertheless, when something goes wrong in relations with other nations,' he wrote, 'we have assumed a stance of standing still and waiting for the storm to pass, due to our guilt over past wars. As a result, it has given the world the impression that the fault lies with us.'[5]

Abe's vision gained from the traditions and influences of an elite political dynasty can be seen in his political philosophy, writings and a series of historic speeches delivered over the last two decades. It demonstrates a leader on a definitive mission: rewiring Japan's prestige and standing in the international system as a respected, trusted and strong power ready to step up as a foremost 'promoter of rules and guardian of the global commons'. This is one of the key messages articulated in his vision.[6]

In his political career, Abe succeeded in not just positioning Japan as the biggest champion of liberal international order but also as a decisive player in twenty-first century rulemaking: be it on free trade, data governance, high-technology or quality infrastructure.

The primary pillar of the 'Abe Doctrine' remained rooted in his conviction and confidence that Japan must be a 'tier-one power' that resolutely determines international relations. This is enunciated in his 'Japan is Back' speech at the Centre for Strategic and International Studies (CSIS), Washington DC.[7] At the start of his second term in office, Abe received a provocative query from Richard Armitage, a former US assistant secretary of state: 'Does Japan desire to continue to be a tier-one nation, or is she content to drift into tier–two status?'[8] Abe responded, 'Japan is not, and will never be, a tier-two country.'

Abe kept international rules and norms as a guiding force in pursuit of Japan's national interests and power. From Shangri-La to Davos, he struck the right chord by putting up a banner that read: 'Japan for rule of law, Asia for rule of law, rule of law for all of us'.[9] Making a clear departure from the Yoshida Doctrine, Abe mainstreamed value-based strategy driven by a sense of mission that Tokyo should become the defender of the values of liberty and democracy. Abe anchored Japan's evolving role in the global theatre on 'value-oriented diplomacy', denoting a commitment to such universal values as freedom, human rights, democracy and the rule of law. This value-based foreign policy was fresh and new for Tokyo.

Abe emerged as a pivotal thinker in the global stage as he skilfully balanced values, interests and strategy by conceptualizing innovative frameworks. His 'Confluence of the Two Seas' speech referred to the 'dynamic decoupling of the Pacific and the Indian Oceans as seas of freedom and of prosperity'—this germinated into Abe's most consequential contribution to international relations: the Free and Open Indo-Pacific (FOIP). Abe was way ahead of his peers both in the domestic political space as well as globally, and received international acclaim for his FOIP strategic construct. He envisioned and put a premium on engineering a 'Democratic Security Diamond', which today has matured into the Quad and emerged as a force for global good amid the deterioration in the US–China relationship. Abe pushed Japan's global influence by doubling down on cooperation with an alliance of democracies.

Setting the Stage

Shinzo Abe's work remains consequential for change in the Japanese security conversation. While he may not have succeeded in his most cherished goal of formally amending the post-war constitution—despite having super-majority in the Diet for most of his tenure— he did realize his primary objective of expanding the scope of the right to collective self-defence. However, it is also important to understand that Abe's achievements were not restricted to the amendment of Article 9 of Japan's constitution. Whether in or out of office, Abe was a rare force in Japanese politics—one who set the course of the country's security debate for decades to come.

One of Prime Minister Abe's greatest accomplishments was the ambitious and effective institutional change achieved with the setting up of the National Security Council (NSC) in 2013. This was aimed at easing competing inter-ministerial influences involving the Ministry of Defence, Ministry of Economy, Trade and Industry (METI) and the Ministry of Foreign Affairs (MOFA), loosening bureaucratic control and better coordinating national security matters. It was also about boosting the Prime Minister's powers. Abe's idea of letting the NSC— often considered to be the 'control tower'—set the basic direction of security policy has worked successfully and has produced the results he had hoped for.

Prime Minister Abe fleshed out Japan's maiden National Security Strategy (NSS) in 2013, imparting clarity on Japan's long-term security outlook. Later, in 2020, it was Abe who gave the orders to revise the NSS—keeping in mind the need to deliberate on realistic options in pursuit of national security goals—as the strategic environment had changed drastically since the first NSS was conceived. The current NSS of 2013 predates the intense US–China strategic competition, FOIP, the resurrection of Quad, the Covid-19 pandemic and the Russian invasion of Ukraine. Some in Japan believed that the review should have happened as early as 2018, when former President Trump of the US had identified China as a primary strategic competitor.

In addition to institutional restructuring, another domain where Abe's footprint is deep is defence spending. Today as Japan is revising the NSS, the domestic conversation on doubling defence spending has emerged as one of the dominant themes in the debate. LDP's research commission on security formally submitted recommendations to Prime Minister Fumio Kishida in April this year. It suggests increasing defence spending to at least 2 per cent of GDP within five years. The recent LDP election manifesto also referred to the NATO defence spending goals. While one of the central discussions in Tokyo today is how to garner resources in an already severe fiscal space with unsustainable public debt, the government is weighing up options such as issuing bonds and raising taxes.

Back in 2017, it was Shinzo Abe who told the Diet that he does not intend to cap defence spending below 1 per cent of GDP given the fact that Japan sits on the frontline of a severe regional security environment. During his time in office, Prime Minister Abe sent the defence budget on northward trends over the last decade. While regional powers often critically analyse the discussion on increasing the defence budget through the lens of Japan's return to militarism, the debate itself is an old one. The US has long pushed Japan towards equitable burden sharing. For instance, in the late 1980s, former US defence secretary Frank Carlucci had advocated in his report to the Congress that Japan must significantly bolster its self-defence capability. There was resolution calling on Japan to spend around 3 per cent of its GDP annually on defence.[10]

With the ever-present possibility of a Taiwanese contingency in mind, Abe remained a strong advocate of good relations with Taiwan for decades. In the wake of the Ukraine War, there is global attention on Prime Minister Kishida's narrative of 'Ukraine today may be East Asia tomorrow'. But even before the Russian invasion of Ukraine, stabilizing the situation surrounding Taiwan had been a central issue for defence planners in Tokyo since it is intrinsically linked to Japanese security. This is evident from Japan's conversations with the US and from the appearance of the subject in defence white papers. Abe was one of the leading names in the LDP—along with Yasuhide Nakayama, Taro Aso, Takaichi Sanae and Nobuo Kishi—who believed that, given Taiwan's proximity to the southern Japanese island of Okinawa, a Taiwanese emergency is in fact a Japanese emergency. The LDP has established its own Taiwan project team, intensifying discussions on how Japan can coordinate with the US effectively in such an event.

Abe, staying true to his character, penned a powerful piece for *Project Syndicate* arguing in no uncertain terms that the US's strategic ambiguity over Taiwan must end.[11] Abe was also central in advancing the LDP's relationship with Taiwan's ruling Democratic Progressive Party (DPP), especially on the economic security vertical. He valued Taiwan's potential on matters regarding economic security. In a speech titled 'Rise up Taiwan' delivered at the US–Japan–Taiwan Trilateral Indo-Pacific Security Dialogue, Abe had advocated deeper technological cooperation across domains.

Abe also had a keen understanding of economic security given the high politics over technology and its impact on geopolitics and national security. This is why he set up an economic unit at the National Security Secretariat while in office. Even when he was no longer Prime Minister, he worked closely within the party to set up a Diet group on semiconductor strategy led by Akira Amari. The group was supported by Abe and Aso, the trio being referred to as the '3As' in LDP circles. They worked to achieve the aim of controlling the choke points in the global semiconductor ecosystem and focused on areas where Japan is internationally competitive—for instance, advanced materials and production equipment.

Till the end, Shinzo Abe remained true to his character, never shying away from debating provocative ideas and testing the mood of the nation—be it urging a discussion on nuclear sharing arrangements or rebooting counterstrike capabilities. He made headlines for his comments on nuclear sharing in the wake of the Ukraine crisis, but his thinking on nuclear issues can be traced back to his days as Japan's deputy chief cabinet secretary. Then, he had argued that 'possession of nuclear bombs is constitutional, so long as they are small'. Each of these themes in the security debate predates the Russian invasion of Ukraine, which has accorded a sense of urgency and accelerated some of the already present trends in the national conversation in Japan. Similarly, his push to discuss counterstrike capabilities can be traced back to his days as chief cabinet secretary.

Abe has left the stage at a time when Japan is at an inflection point. An assassination that stunned the world has abruptly ended the phenomenon of Shinzo Abe. His demise has left a sudden void in the national security conversation in Japan, but the direction and high standards of fearless debate on national politics and grand strategy that he has set will guide Japan's next generation of leaders.

6

SHINZO ABE AND JAPAN'S NUCLEAR DILEMMAS

Manpreet Sethi

COUNTRIES CAN HAVE RATHER straightforward positions on nuclear weapons and nuclear energy: they either like them and want to have them, or they don't. However, Japan's position on these matters is a complex one. This is not surprising given that it is the only country in the world to have suffered two atomic bombings as well as a nuclear accident at a civilian nuclear reactor. The atomic bombings of Hiroshima and Nagasaki in 1945 have resulted in an abhorrence for nuclear weapons, while the accident at the Fukushima nuclear plant in 2011 has led to concerns about the safety of nuclear reactors.

While these tragedies have scarred the psyche of the Japanese people, they have not made Japan completely turn its back on either nuclear weapons or energy. Rather, national and energy security concerns have necessitated keeping the nuclear options alive. In the security dimension this has translated into Japan accepting protection under the American nuclear umbrella. However, on the nuclear energy front, the country—not well-endowed with energy sources—finds it difficult to get by with zero reliance on nuclear electricity.

There is a divided domestic view on these issues. While on the one hand, the country is acutely conscious of an increasingly nuclearized neighbourhood—where the hostile attitudes of China and North Korea have grown in the last decade—it, nevertheless, finds its ability to enhance its nuclear deterrence posture constrained by a staunchly anti-nuclear public sentiment. Meanwhile, though the logic of restarting the nation's nuclear reactors not long after the Fukushima disaster—to reduce high dependence on imported fossil fuels and to meet climate change commitments—is widely understood, governments have still been inhibited by overall public sentiment on the issue. The ongoing conflict in Ukraine has resulted in fuel supply disruptions, which have only sharpened the focus on Japan's energy predicament.

Japanese political leaders have struggled to find balanced answers to these challenges. Their solutions have been influenced by their party leanings and personal convictions. Ambivalence on both nuclear issues has been high. Amid all this, Shinzo Abe distinguished himself by taking clear positions on the nuclear issues, including those that were contrarian to the majority view. As Japan's youngest Prime Minister, albeit for a year in 2006–2007, and then returning to the position in December 2012 to remain Prime Minister until 2020, when he resigned for reasons of personal health, he has left a distinct imprint on the nation's nuclear policy.

Abe was extremely concerned about national security, especially after China's increasingly aggressive behaviour towards the Senkaku Islands from the early 2000s and North Korea's growing nuclear and missile capabilities since its first nuclear test in 2006. He encouraged Japan to debate its stand on defence and nuclear weapons, and in 2007, during his first term at Prime Minister, he established the Ministry of Defence. Until then, Japan only had a 'defence agency'.

During his second term, Prime Minister Abe supported legislation to strengthen the Ministry of Defence and revise Article 9 of the country's constitution.[1] This article—titled 'Renunciation of War'—outlaws war as a means to settle international disputes involving the state and, in fulfilment of this objective, it disallows Japan from maintaining land, air and sea forces or other war potential. The Self-Defence Forces (SDF) military unit was established in 1954 only for defensive purposes. Abe sought to make the SDF more capable.

Though he did not completely succeed with the amendments[2] he proposed, his positions did lead to serious thinking on threat perceptions in Japan. On the issue of nuclear energy, Abe was convinced that, despite the Fukushima disaster, there was no other sustainable solution to Japan's energy needs. He stood steadfast in favour of an energy plan that would include nuclear reactors.

Through his various positions and actions, Shinzo Abe has left a mark on the country's nuclear debates. Whatever be the policies of future governments, there is little doubt that he forced Japanese people and leaders to think practically about nuclear matters in the context of real-world challenges that the country faces.

What challenges did Abe flag? How and where did he leave his imprint? Will his legacy last? This essay explores Abe's positions on the two nuclear issues in some detail and places them in context of the country's political and sociocultural landscape.

Japan's Stance towards Nuclear Weapons

Having suffered the unprecedented short- and long-term consequences of the atomic bombings on Hiroshima and Nagasaki, it is not surprising that Japan became—and remains—a staunch advocate of nuclear non-proliferation and disarmament. Of course, it also needs recalling that during a visit to Washington, D.C. in January 1965—soon after the Chinese nuclear tests the previous year—Prime Minister Eisaku Sato of Japan had told US President Lyndon B. Johnson that he personally thought that if China had nuclear weapons, Japan should too. Concerns over Japan's possible nuclear armament prompted the Johnson administration to provide clear nuclear guarantees to Japan.

With these guarantees in place, Sato decided to give up the idea of Japan possessing nuclear weapons and accepted the policy of the 'Three Non-Nuclear Principles' in December 1967. These included the commitment to 'not possess, not produce and not permit the introduction of nuclear weapons'. They were adopted as a resolution by the Japanese Diet in November 1971 and have been national policy ever since.

However, Japan has struggled to reconcile its broad acceptance of pacifist values with its desire to become a 'normal country'. A resurgence of nationalism in the face of growing security challenges has strengthened a desire to build more military capabilities. Accordingly, Japan has stepped up its military initiatives and strengthened its security relationship with the US—including working on the procurement of ballistic missile defences (BMD) and active involvement in the global war on terror. Being 'normal' has also sometimes been associated with possession of nuclear weapons.

Many Japanese conservative leaders have emphasized that the Three Non-Nuclear Principles are policy, not law. If security conditions so warranted, Japan had the option of possessing nuclear weapons. In 2004, Prime Minister Koizumi stated at a press conference that it would be constitutionally possible for Japan to possess nuclear weapons if they are for the defence of the country. He said, 'It all depends on how you interpret the constitution but I think having small nuclear arms solely for defence purposes is not banned under the constitution.'[3]

Over the last two decades, the regional security climate for Japan has worsened, leading to attempts at innovative interpretations of the non-nuclear policy by the leaders of the LDP. North Korea's repeated nuclear tests and unrestrained missile testing between 2006 and 2017 as well as China's nuclear expansion coupled with aggressive behaviour have been a source of concern for Japan. Concurrently, South Korea's growing missile capabilities, a weak US/NATO response to the Russian annexation of Crimea in 2014 and a perceived weakening of extended deterrence from the US under the Trump administration have also exacerbated Japan's threat perceptions. As these developments unfolded, Shinzo Abe was at the helm of the LDP and thereby the nation. Confronted by an increasingly hostile regional environment, he advocated a reassessment of Japan's thinking of its security—including whether it might be better protected by having its own nuclear weapons.

Abe's radical views on nuclear weapons go as far back as 2002, when he was deputy chief cabinet secretary. While addressing university students on one occasion, he then said, 'The possession of nuclear bombs is constitutional, so long as they are small.'[4] These remarks were not well received by the public. Despite this, he continued to believe in the value of nuclear weapons.

In 2012, when he was elected Prime Minister for the second time, he introduced a National Security Strategy document for the first time, along with updated guidelines for the National Defence Program that outlined five- and ten-year targets for Japan's defence policy.[5] The main focus of the strategy was a major augmentation of Japanese conventional naval and air capabilities and a first revision of the guidelines for Japan–US defence cooperation since 1997.

Abe also made a strong push to revise Article 9. However, a poll by *Asahi Shimbun* showed that 59 per cent disapproved of the move and only 27 per cent agreed with it. Bowing to the public mood, the LDP backed down from pursuing a revision of the constitution and settled instead for a milder reinterpretation of the clause to allow the SDF to engage in collective self-defence. While the SDF was still prohibited from conducting missions alongside its allies in combat zones (with the exception of humanitarian search-and-rescue missions[6]), this change—coming into effect on 1 July 2014—was still an important milestone for Japanese security policy.

Cognizant of the sensitivities of the Japanese public to a more militaristic position or possession of nuclear weapons, Abe appeared to follow a two-pronged approach towards Japan's security. On the one hand, he insisted that the US maintain a nuclear posture that credibly supported extended deterrence. On the other hand, he also kept making attempts to push the envelope of thinking at the domestic level.

Two instances illustrate how Abe implemented this approach. His insistence on a firm US–Japan relationship strongly anchored under the nuclear umbrella was clear when he expressed concern about US President Barack Obama's support for 'no first use' and the desire for a world free of nuclear weapons that Obama expressed in his speech at Prague in April 2009. Subsequently, in the wake of heightened tensions in the region, Prime Minister Abe sought firm nuclear commitments from the US.

Some years later, when President Donald Trump cast aspersions on American spending on security for allies, Abe ensured an end to such an attitude by getting Trump to reiterate his commitment to defend Japan with 'the full range of US military capabilities, both nuclear and conventional' during the latter's visit to Japan in February 2017.[7] One year later, when the Trump administration brought out its Nuclear Posture Review, Japan was quick to express appreciation of the American resolve 'to ensure the effectiveness of its deterrence and its commitment to providing extended deterrence to its allies including Japan'.[8]

At the domestic level, Abe had often expressed his conviction that Japan should seriously reconsider its nuclear policy. He knew that until the Japanese public could be convinced on this matter, the country had to seek protection under the US nuclear umbrella. But Abe was not sure if this protection would continue to suffice in the future, especially as threats grew. Therefore, he kept trying to change public thinking on the issue. For instance, in the official commemoration ceremony in 2015 on the seventieth anniversary of the atomic bombing of Hiroshima, Prime Minister Abe omitted to mention the Three Non-Nuclear Principles. A public outcry followed.

Accepting the public sentiment, Abe then mentioned the principles in his speech at the ceremony at Nagasaki three days later. In 2020, at the Hiroshima Peace Memorial Park on the seventy-fifth anniversary of the atomic bombings, Abe acknowledged Japan's 'unceasing mission of advancing steadily, step by step, the efforts of the international community towards realizing a world free of nuclear weapons'.[9] He also reiterated Japan's unwavering commitment to the Three Non-Nuclear Principles.

But in 2022, soon after the invasion of non-nuclear Ukraine by nuclear Russia, he was quick to resurrect the issue of Japan's need for nuclear weapons. He was one of the first leaders to publicly acknowledge that the action by Moscow could lead to a reappraisal of security strategies by non-nuclear weapon states, including Japan. For the immediate term, Abe recommended that Japan should discuss the option of a NATO-style nuclear-sharing arrangement with the US.[10] He called for Tokyo to cast off taboos around its possession of nuclear weapons and consider hosting them like NATO members do in Europe. He encouraged an open discussion on how Japan could best secure itself.[11]

Abe's approach can be seen as a hedging strategy that grappled with Japan's deteriorating regional security environment and a possibility of the fraying of the American nuclear umbrella. He kept trying to prepare the public for a time when Japan's nuclear policy may require a change, but also realized that this could not be done easily given the deep influence the *Hibakushas* (the surviving victims of the atomic bombs dropped on Hiroshima and Nagasaki) have on his countrypeople's thinking. He also understood the political, legal and structural constraints he faced.

While the country did possess a stockpile of plutonium that could be used to make nuclear weapons[12], much more was needed to build credible deterrence—most important of which was political will. And this, Abe knew, was missing, given the majority public opinion and the opposition to his views within his own party. For instance, the present Prime Minister Fumio Kishida, also from the LDP—and hailing from Hiroshima—maintains an unwavering commitment to nuclear disarmament and has dismissed any pursuit of nuclear weapons by Japan, including placement of US nuclear weapons on Japanese soil.

Abe's support for nuclear weapons for Japan's security served three purposes. First, it kept the domestic debate alive and made more people consider the potential deterrent role of these weapons. Second, it signalled a nuclear ambivalence to China to keep it unsettled. As also expressed by some other conservative leaders, Japan's flaunting of the bomb option could help it gain 'diplomatic clout'[13]. Third, it helped to gauge the US response. As explained by an analyst,

> Even though the US does not want to see Japan develop nuclear weapons, its reaction to this would be more about how it affects US security policies in Northeast Asia than about proliferation concerns and damage to the NPT regime. Already having the

technological capability and the plutonium, and with the political dynamics of a normal state continuing to evolve, there is the possibility—albeit slim at the present time—that Tokyo could begin pushing for the inclusion of the possession of nuclear weapons into Japan's security identity.[14]

Shinzo Abe has left behind a legacy that will encourage his country to continue thinking about its security challenges and options. It remains to be seen whether this leads to a dilution of the three principles to the extent of accepting American nuclear weapons on Japanese territory as an interim compromise solution. China's behaviour will have a lot to do with how Japan assesses its threat environment and the policies it adopts.

Abe on Nuclear Energy in Japan's Energy Mix

Japan's tryst with nuclear energy started in the 1950s when it set up a nuclear power programme with US help. In 1966, commercial use of nuclear electricity began. Rapid industrialization, increasing energy demands and a lack of natural resources were the primary drivers for Japan's pursuit of nuclear energy. The biggest push to increase the reliance on nuclear energy came with the oil crisis of the 1970s.

At the time, Japan was importing 66 per cent of its oil from the Middle East, and only five nuclear reactors were operational. In a move to readjust the energy mix, Tokyo undertook rapid deployment of nuclear reactors. Japanese companies purchased plant designs from the US and received licenses to build them at appropriate locations around the country. The Japanese nuclear industry matured over the years to develop its own designs and manufacturing technologies.

Over the next three decades, Japan installed fifty-four nuclear reactors. By the start of the new millennium, it was drawing 30 per cent of its electricity from nuclear energy. It became the world's third-largest producer of nuclear power, and had ambitious plans to ramp up nuclear energy to 50 per cent of the national energy mix in the future. However, a serious accident at the Fukushima Daiichi nuclear power plant in 2011 unravelled these plans.

The jolt came in 2011 when an earthquake and tsunami of unprecedented proportions rocked six nuclear reactors stationed at Fukushima. The accident made a huge impact on the nuclear industry as well as on public confidence in nuclear safety. After the Fukushima accident, 31 per cent of the population wanted the government to abandon nuclear power immediately, while 54 per cent wanted a gradual phaseout.[15]

The government of the time was led by Prime Minister Naoto Kan of the Democratic Party of Japan (DPJ). He decided to suspend operations at all nuclear reactors and ordered elaborate safety audits. To cope with the electricity deficit created by the loss of reactor operations, the government appealed to citizens for 'voluntary reductions' of electricity usage around the country by applying 'simple measures to conserve electricity'.[16] Half the deficit could be covered through these reductions. The other half was met from increased use of thermal sources.

In 2012, LNG imports by Japan had increased by 14.9 per cent and petroleum imports had risen by 5.3 per cent. Energy imports constituted one-third of Japan's total imports in 2012.[17] By 2013, Japan had become the world's largest importer of LNG and the second-largest importer of coal.[18] Expensive fuel imports also increased the cost of producing electricity, leading to combined annual losses to power companies of USD 16 billion in FY 2012–13.

The horrendous experience of handling the aftermath of the nuclear disaster made Prime Minister Kan turn against nuclear energy. In a book written to record his experience, he writes, 'Personally, at all costs, I want to see an end to the use of nuclear power.'[19] He advocated a move towards renewables. At a press conference in May 2011 he said, 'Where electricity is concerned, nuclear power and fossil fuels have functioned as two large pillars, but in light of the Fukushima accident and global warming, we must add renewable, natural energies such as solar, wind and biomass … as energy mainstays …'[20]

Kan recommended that Japan's energy planning return to the drawing board to reassess the targets for 2030, which had the ambitious target of 50 per cent for nuclear energy and of only 20 per cent for renewable energy.[21] He clearly sought a reduction of the nuclear share in favour of renewables. By July 2011, he had managed to get the approval of his cabinet to start a debate among the Japanese government, experts and the public on reducing the role of nuclear power. With this in mind, Kan's successor Yoshihiko Noda set up the seventy-member Committee for the Consideration of a Roadmap for a Non-nuclear Japan in April 2012. The debate continued until September 2012, when the DPJ decided on committing to eliminate nuclear power by the 2030s.

This position, however, was not shared by the LDP. In fact, Kan alleges that the LDP was under the hold of the 'nuclear village'[22]—a vast and powerful network of vested interests consisting of pro-nuclear advocates in the bureaucracy, Diet, business community, utilities corporations, vendors and lenders. The general elections in 2012 saw polarized positions on the issue of nuclear power. However, the results showed the dilemma in the mind of the Japanese public. According to Kan, 'While public opinion polls showed that approximately 70 per cent of the people wanted a nuclear-free society, in the general elections, voters showed strong disappointment with the highly factional Democratic Party…. The nuclear-tolerant LDP took back a large number of parliamentary seats and enjoyed a major victory.'[23]

Abe emerged as the victor in these elections. Once appointed Prime Minister, he announced that he would do away with the nuclear-free approach the Democratic Party had been pursuing. He would develop 'a new basic plan for Japan's energy'.[24] While Abe started his second term in office by putting up a brave front and backing the Tokyo Electric Power Company's efforts to bring the Fukushima situation under control, he had to change his stance after mounting troubles in the following months. As media reports on dangerous radioactive water leaks continued into 2013, he announced that the government had lost faith in the company's ability to manage the ongoing crisis[25] and that it would take over the situation to address issues that were harming public opinion on nuclear energy and getting in the way of restarting other nuclear reactors.

Keen to get the Japanese economy into high-growth mode, Abe wanted to restart the nuclear reactor operations so that he could put an end to the expensive fuel imports that were draining the economy.

Facing rising energy imports, high electricity prices, plunging factory production and a widening trade deficit with a 30 per cent decrease in exports[26], Abe realized that if he wanted to keep his electoral promise of putting the Japanese economy on track, he had to take the politically risky decision of restarting the nuclear reactors.

As part of his efforts in this regard, he announced a new energy plan on 11 April 2014. While the plan envisaged reduced dependence on nuclear energy, it recognized nuclear power as an important baseload energy source and allowed the construction of new reactors.[27] On the fifth anniversary of the Fukushima disaster, Abe reiterated at a press conference, 'Our resource-poor country cannot do without nuclear power to secure the stability of energy supply while considering what makes economic sense and the issue of climate change.'[28]

Abe's efforts to revive Japan's nuclear energy industry were driven by several factors, the most important of which was the conviction that nuclear energy was the most cost-effective way to generate electricity and thereby hasten economic recovery. A second motivation was to see Japan emerge as a major nuclear exporter to tap the lucrative international market. A sense of return to nuclear normalcy within Japan was critical to enable exports. Thirdly, Abe was aware of the hold of the nuclear industry on the Japanese political system.

During the 2013 upper-house election campaign policy debate, the LDP was the only party to oppose phasing out nuclear energy. The narrative of this position was built around it being one of responsibility, but substantive financial interests were also behind this pro-nuclear stance. Even the Kan-led DPJ failed to approve a cabinet endorsement for phasing out nuclear energy owing to the pressure from the 'nuclear village'.[29]

Lastly, there is an argument that the US too has insisted that Japan should keep its nuclear reactors running. In September 2012, the *Tokyo Shimbun* reported that the US government demanded that no cabinet decision endorsing a phasing out of nuclear power be made in Japan.[30] If that were to happen, the US would have to retract permission for Japan to reprocess spent nuclear fuel that had been sourced in the US.[31]

This ability to reprocess nuclear fuel to extract and reuse plutonium in mixed oxide fuel keeps alive, even if only notionally, the option for Japan to go down the route of nuclear armament if the security situation deteriorates.

Abe tried to revitalize the nuclear sector with his efforts to rebuild a consensus in favour of nuclear energy. As noted by an analyst, Abe attempted to adopt policies that would shift the governance of the Fukushima disaster 'from a situation of crisis to a situation of revitalization'.[32] This included the revival of Fukushima prefecture with socioeconomic incentives on promoting tourism, agriculture and employment. He also announced that the Olympic torch relay for the 2020 Tokyo Games would start from Fukushima as a symbolic gesture.

However, he did not enjoy wholehearted public support on these decisions. The emphasis on revitalization was criticized for ignoring the still-present risks of radioactive contamination. Indeed, despite Abe's efforts, the rapid restarting of nuclear reactors turned out to be difficult owing to local opposition and lawsuits against the move. In fact, even by the time of his untimely death in mid-2022, only fourteen of the fifty-four nuclear reactors in Japan had been granted the go-ahead to restart, of which only four had actually become operational. Of the forty reactors without permission to restart, twenty-one had been decommissioned.

Japan's vulnerability to large-scale fuel imports has once again surfaced in the context of the Russia–Ukraine conflict. A surge in energy prices has impacted an already hurting economy. Given Japan's geographical isolation, the island nation also does not have the luxury of accessing 'transnational electricity transmission systems'.[33] Also, given the nature of geopolitics in the region, there is little hope for a shared vision on energy security through regional collaborations. Therefore, the country has to find its own individual answers to its energy challenges.

Adding to these woes is another dilemma which is common to Japan and the rest of the world. This emanates from the need to move towards low-carbon sources of electricity production. While there is an emphasis on greater deployment of renewables, Japan certainly does not want to lose the costs already sunk into the constructed nuclear reactors, nor the human resources and expertise it has in the nuclear sector.

Despite Abe's conviction in favour of nuclear energy, Japan is still trying to find its way on how much to rely on this source. A clear and bipartisan support for nuclear energy is not yet evident, including on how to meet the country's climate commitments.

Conclusion

Shinzo Abe was a staunch nationalist and had a realistic, security-oriented view of how to handle Japan's challenges. Having been 'raised from birth in the ultra-conservative nationalist environment of his maternal grandfather, Nobusuke Kishi, his uncle Eisaku Sato and his father, senior LDP politician Shintaro Abe'[34], he professed a right-wing ideology and had a clear intent to revive Japanese national pride. His position on nuclear issues also reflected this. He took strong stands, even when they were contrary to majority views. This encouraged debate on Japan's nuclear dilemmas. How these are settled in the future will be shaped as much by Japan's leaders as by the actions of China and North Korea.

Interestingly, in some ways Japan's nuclear dilemmas have also been mirrored in India's positions on nuclear weapons. It may be recalled that when India tested nuclear weapons in 1998, Japan took a harsh position against India, suspended all economic assistance, placed sanctions and strongly criticized the move for its impact on non-proliferation. Yet, at the time Japan was also confronting its own fears of the 'fraying' of the nuclear umbrella and other growing security concerns.

Tokyo has often faced criticism for its apparent dichotomy in opting to keep Japan protected through American nuclear weapons while maintaining a strong cultural opposition to these weapons. These have been described as 'antithetical objectives'[35]. India too has been criticized for taking contradictory positions on advancing its nuclear deterrent capabilities while continuing to campaign for nuclear disarmament.

Like Japan, India, too, has maintained that there is no contradiction in having nuclear weapons (in India's case) or nuclear protection (in Japan's), while at the same time seeking a world without nuclear weapons. As articulated by Japan's foreign minister, Toshimitsu Motegi, in a Diet session in April 2020, there is 'no contradiction' between nuclear deterrence as a practical necessity and nuclear disarmament as a future direction.[36]

Abe supported this school of thought. Undoubtedly, he has had a profound influence on his country's efforts to evolve a coherent security vision. As the architect of the concept of the Quadrilateral Security Dialogue, he also forged strong, comprehensive relations with India and Australia. Whether Abe was right or wrong on his stands on nuclear weapons and nuclear energy for his country will be judged by history. However, what is significant is that he advocated clear choices for a country that has been characterized by ambivalence and contradictions.

Shinzo Abe went by his conviction and tried to make a difference when he was in a position of power. Irrespective of how his policies fare, he will be remembered as a leader who had clarity of thought and vision for a security-challenged country, which, unfortunately, has no easy nuclear choices to make.

ABE AND JAPAN–INDIA RELATIONS

7

ABE AND THE EVOLUTION OF INDIA–JAPAN RELATIONS

Sanjaya Baru

READING CONTEMPORARY COMMENTARY AND much of the recent academic work on India–Japan relations one may imagine that the timeline defining this bilateral relationship over the seven decades of diplomatic engagement is best divided into a 'pre-Abe' and a 'post-Abe' era. Many then insert China and the United States into this equation and suggest that India–Japan relations have been shaped during the Abe era by the global context of 'Big Power' rivalry.[1] While there is no doubt that China looms large on the horizon and has shaped the bilateral relationship—especially since 2000—the importance of Prime Minister Shinzo Abe derives from the belief that he sought to make the relationship stand on its own without being defined entirely by 'big power' rivalry.

In seeking a balance between bilateral interests and values on the one hand and regional and global interests and concerns on the other, Abe sought to reinvigorate the roots of the India–Japan relationship, which had been originally nurtured by his grandfather, Prime Minister Nobusuke Kishi, and Prime Minister Jawaharlal Nehru in the 1950s. Kishi and Nehru laid the foundations of a new post-WWII and post-colonial relationship between Asia's two democracies, independent of

81

their relations with major powers. Abe revisited this relationship in a different geopolitical context.

The initial efforts made by leaders of both countries in the 1950s shaped what has been called 'the post-war golden age' in the relationship. Abe's importance lay in his ability to revive the bilateral roots of the relationship. The 1950s is best described as the 'decade of engagement' between India and Japan. This was followed by a long period of neglect, if not dis-engagement, with a variety of regional and global factors distracting the two away from each other. It was only in the 1980s that the two countries tried to re-engage each other, more because of mutual economic interests than regional or global geopolitical factors. This period may be described as a period of 'courtship' in which India tried hard to secure Japanese interest in its industrialization effort and Japan viewed India as a source of raw materials and an emerging market for industrial products.

This period of courtship came to a gradual end when Japan was seduced by the more attractive business opportunities in China. The 1990s was a decade of neglect that ended with sharp disagreement when India tested nuclear weapons and declared itself a nuclear weapons power. However, in 2005, Prime Minister Junichiro Koizumi began efforts to engage India, which opened up a new era of 'partnership'.

This essay will try to explore this long relationship between the two nations and answer why the engagement of the 1950s took half a century to translate into the twenty-first century partnership, despite the intervening period of active courtship.

Engagement

The first post-WWII Prime Minister of Japan to visit India was Abe's grandfather, Nobusuke Kishi, who travelled to New Delhi in May 1957 soon after becoming Prime Minister. Prime Minister Jawaharlal Nehru reciprocated by paying a return visit within months, visiting Tokyo in October 1957. These visits in fact culminated a decade of partnership. After Independence, India had reached out to a beleaguered but industrially advanced Japan and received their support for India's quest for development. Kishi and Nehru painted not just on an empty canvas but also on a wide one. Their joint statement read: 'The Prime Ministers consider that the economic development of Asian countries, which had been neglected during past centuries, is essential for the peace and stability not only of Asia but of the whole world.'[2]

It was Mikio Kato, director of the International House of Japan in the 1980s, who referred to the 1950s as 'the post-war golden age' in the bilateral relationship. 'When we look back over Indo–Japanese relations of the post-war period,' Kato told a semi-official conference on bilateral relations held at the India International Centre in New Delhi in 1986, 'the fifties and sixties stand out as an era of enthusiasm, a quality which existed on both sides, particularly perhaps on the Japanese side.' [3]

Three factors defined the early and great optimism of the 1950s in the bilateral relationship generated by the Nehru–Kishi partnership. To begin with, an immediate consideration was that India had established a bond with post-WWII Japan by distancing itself from the victors of WWII. An Indian judge, Justice Radha Binod Pal, submitted a dissenting judgement at the Tokyo War Crimes Tribunal and India signed a separate peace treaty with Japan. India also became one of the first countries to extend diplomatic recognition to Japan. Prime Minister Kishi was also grateful to India for Nehru's ready willingness to accept Japanese official development assistance, signalling Indian regard for Japan.

The early post-Independence Indian enthusiasm towards Japan was shaped not just by the fact that Netaji Subhas Chandra Bose had allied himself with Japan and established the Indian National Army with Japanese assistance but also by the even more enduring fact that as Asia's first industrial and modern nation, Japan had inspired Indian national leadership.

One of the first Indian nationalists to draw attention to Japan's rapid rise was Swami Vivekananda. On his way to Chicago in 1893 to deliver his historic address to the Parliament of Religions, Swami Vivekananda opted for the Pacific route. Stopping in Japan enroute to Vancouver, Swamiji became fascinated by what he saw. 'The Japanese seem now to have fully awakened themselves to the necessity of the present times,' Swamiji said in an interview after his visit. 'They have now a thoroughly organized army equipped with guns that one of their own officers has invented and which are said to be second to none. Then, they are continually increasing their navy. I have seen a tunnel nearly a mile long, bored by a Japanese engineer. The match factories are simply a sight to see, and they are bent upon making everything they want in their own country.'[4] Swamiji wanted young Indians to be sent to Japan to be educated in modern technology and manufacturing.

On his onward journey from Yokohama to Vancouver, Swamiji travelled with the industrialist Jamshedji Tata. In conversations on the ship, the two shared their admiration for Japan's industrial development and modernization. On his return to India, Tata wrote to Swamiji that having been inspired by their conversation, he was going to fund a science research institution. The Indian Institute of Science in Bengaluru was that institution.[5]

Mokshagundam Visvesvaraya, an engineer and a promoter of industrialization, visited Japan in 1898. Visvesvaraya was one of the founders of the Institution of Engineers and the Mysore Chamber of Commerce. He gave the Indian national movement the slogan 'industrialize or perish'. After his tour of Japan, Visvesvaraya wrote extensively on the lessons India must learn from the modernization of Japan. He was impressed by Japan's development of schools, transport and communication and their role in Japan's industrial development. He was convinced that investment in education was the key to economic development. In 1916, Rabindranath Tagore travelled to Japan and was equally impressed by its modernization as well as its preservation of tradition.[6]

Finally, Jawaharlal Nehru himself wrote eloquently about Japan's victory over Russia in the 1905 Russo–Japan war, noting that it was a historic moment when an Asian nation had defeated a European one, turning back the tide of European colonialism.[7] This appreciation of Japan by eminent Indians from the fields of philosophy, religion, literature, engineering, science and politics shaped popular regard within the Indian national movement for Asia's 'first industrial nation'.

It was therefore understandable that Prime Minister Kishi arrived at New Delhi in 1957 to a very friendly reception, which cemented an early bond between Asia's new democracies. Nehru introduced him at a public meeting in Delhi saying, 'This is the Prime Minister of Japan, a country I hold in the greatest esteem.'[8]

A Japanese businessman by the name of Toshio Yamanouchi arrived in India in the 1950s seeking to explore the promised business opportunities. He remained in India till the mid-1970s. In his fascinating autobiography, *India Through Japanese Eyes*, he writes, 'The Nehruvian age was a bright period for relations between India and Japan … Japan gave first pledge of Yen credit to India in 1957 and till Nehru's death in 1964 as much as 60 per cent of Japan's total Yen credit went to India.'[9]

A credit of up to 18 billion yen was extended to enable India to import equipment for railways, hydro and thermal power, ships and ports, along with other industrial machinery, machine tools, rayon and fertilizer.[10] The Indian Planning Commission set up the Committee for Studies on Economic Development in India and Japan under the chairmanship of C.D. Deshmukh with P.C. Mahalanobis and Bharat Ram as members and the economist Jagdish Bhagwati as member-secretary.

The committee members travelled to Japan and interacted with policymakers and analysts in Tokyo. However, even though on the Japanese side the committee's interlocutors included the influential Dr Saburo Okita, an academic who had served a brief term as foreign minister, Bhagwati recalls that very little came of it after the initial enthusiasm of the 1950s.[11] The committee remained dormant in the 1960s and was only revived in 1973 after the first oil shock.

As many analysts have noted, the enthusiasm of the 1950s was soon dissipated, with Japan and India finding themselves in different camps during the Cold War era. Apart from the Cold War, bureaucratic and diplomatic inertia in both capitals may have also played a part. Tokyo was focused on the US, East and Southeast Asia, while New Delhi looked West. Two highly regarded scholars of India–Japan relations, K.V. Kesavan and Takenori Horimoto, point to the geopolitical differences during the Cold War, accentuated by Japan's concerns with

India's proximity to the Soviet Union as creating a distance between the two Asian nations.[12]

Yamanouchi describes the post-Nehruvian period as one of 'high hopes and frustrations' and of 'uneventful tranquillity' in the bilateral relationship, blaming both the geopolitics of the Cold War and the economics of India's 'License-Permit-Control Raj' for this. Defeated and occupied by the United States, Japan remained firmly under the US umbrella, while a newly liberated India refused to join any military alliance and opted for a policy of non-alignment.[13]

India became distanced from the West and its allies on account of both Cold War geopolitics and its own inward-looking industrialization strategy and the adoption of what has been called 'bureaucratic socialism'. As Kesavan notes, Indian policymakers increasingly viewed Japan as a 'client state' of the US, while Japanese public opinion saw India as just another third-world country incapable of getting its act together.

It was not surprising, therefore, that after the 1961 visit to India by Kishi's successor, Prime Minister Hayato Ikeda, no Japanese premier visited New Delhi for over two decades. The hiatus finally ended in 1984 when India began liberalizing its foreign investment policy and Osamu Suzuki chose to enter India's automobile sector.

Courtship

India made intermittent efforts in the 1960s and 1970s to sustain the bilateral relationship with Japan. An India–Japan Consultative Committee was set up in 1966 with Okita and B.R. Bhagat as co-chairs and an intention to restore momentum to the relationship. After its first meeting in Tokyo in November 1966, the committee expressed the hope that the 'stage has been set for better relations'.[14] However, Prime Minister Indira Gandhi's visit to Tokyo in 1969 was not reciprocated through the next decade.

By 1973, eight meetings of the consultative committee had been held with little to show apart from continued Japanese aid to India. The 1973 meeting was held in the shadow of President Richard Nixon's outreach to China. This geopolitical development had unsettled both India and Japan. The focus of the meeting was on their relations with the US, the Soviet Union and China. Interestingly, the minutes recorded:

> The Japanese side made it clear that relationship with the US was Japan's primary concern. Indian side similarly gave an assessment of relations with USSR. The Japanese side was keen on knowing whether there was any thaw in Sino–Indian relations. Japan's desire to know whether there was any improvement in Sino–Indian relations is the result of its hope that New Delhi's relations with Peking and Washington would show some improvement.[15]

After Indira Gandhi's return to office in 1981, her administration's decision to liberalize foreign trade and investment policies opened the door to Suzuki's investment in the Indian automobile sector. It was only then that a Japanese premier, Prime Minister Yasuhiro Nakasone, finally visited New Delhi after a gap of twenty-three years. Touring Japan on the eve of Nakasone's visit in the summer of 1984, Indian journalist T.N. Ninan wrote, 'Each country has dropped below the horizon as far as the other is concerned. And the new attempts to forge a closer relationship now have to battle with the inertia that is the result of years of neglect and indifference.' Expressing the hope that the Nakasone visit and rising Japanese business interest in India would lead to a turning point in the relationship, Ninan concluded, 'All the signs point to India and Japan having more to do with each other in the future than in the past.'[16]

That optimism did not outlast the furious activity of the mid-1980s, a period of courtship best exemplified by a conference on India–Japan relations held at New Delhi in March 1986 that had been jointly organized by the International House of Japan and its Indian counterpart, the India International Centre.[17] The conference brought together some of the most influential policymakers and analysts of both countries. The twenty-member Japanese delegation comprised diplomats, academics and business leaders and was led by Dr Saburo

Okita. The Indian delegation—consisting of forty-six members that similarly included diplomats, academics, journalists and business leaders—was led by Dr Manmohan Singh, then deputy chairman of the Planning Commission.

The proceedings of the conference make for interesting reading. Each side presented as many as ten papers on a range of subjects including international relations, regional security, trade and investment, foreign aid, transfer of technology and cultural and media interaction. The Indian side made a persuasive case for greater Japanese engagement with India, increased aid, trade and investment and a dialogue on regional and global security. Okita told the conference, 'Japan is at a sort of turning point, with its very large economic potential; we must work out in what way, in what constructive way, to translate Japanese economic potential into political influence.'[18]

Responding to Okita, Singh said, 'For us in India, it is of great importance that we understand the Japanese mind, the working of Japanese institutions, the working of the Japanese economy ... this seminar has heightened the perception of what our two countries can gain by working together.'[19] Reading through the essays one gets the impression that most Japanese participants were cautious in their assessment of what may be called 'the India opportunity'. The record of the discussion notes that an unnamed Japanese participant considered Dr Manmohan Singh's forecast for India's development 'overoptimistic, given the stumbling blocks in the institutional framework of Indian society'.[20]

Most Indian participants, however, were enthusiastic in courting Japan. The minutes of the meeting recorded that 'the Indian side felt that Japan's greatest contribution to the developmental process was to explode the European myth that a country could modernize only if it adopted Western institutions and values' and goes on to note that 'several Indian participants asserted, and the Japanese side admitted, that Japan had to play an international role commensurate with its power, albeit economic and not military'.[21]

There was a surge of Japanese investment in India, starting with Suzuki entering both the four-wheeler and two-wheeler markets in the auto sector. Japan's share of foreign collaborations in India went up from around 7 per cent in 1981 to 12 per cent by 1986.[22] Japanese brands such as Honda, Sony, Kawasaki, Toyota, Seiko, Minolta, Hitachi and others found their way into Indian markets and homes.

Firms like Mitsui, Mitsubishi, Matsushita and Yamaha had major plans for India, which was also viewed as a base to enter East European and African markets. The president of Yamaha Corp., Hideto Eguchi, told Ninan, 'Yamaha finds it virtually impossible to sell to the USSR. But India has good relations with Russia, East Europe and some African countries, and our Indian partner, Escorts, could sell Yamaha motorcycles in these countries.'[23]

Even as Japanese participants acknowledged the emerging business opportunity in India, the attractions of China and Southeast Asia were already manifesting themselves. Indian analysts pointed to concerns about China's rising profile, but the Japanese were more concerned about the Soviet presence in the Pacific and took a more sanguine view of China. In his remarks on Japanese foreign policy, Takehiko Kamo, a professor at Waseda University, took the view that 'China would become a much more powerful nation' not only in military capability but also in economic potential.[24]

Bajpai's summing up of the 1986 conference discussion is interesting. He came to the conclusion that 'Japan was keen to have close relations with China, and did not think that either its foreign policy or its nuclear weapons posed a threat to Japan'.[25] Outside of Hong Kong, Japan became the single largest source of foreign direct investment (FDI) into China, with a share of around 14 per cent of total FDI into China in the period from 1983 to 1990.[26]

The Indian disappointment with its courting of Japan after a long gap is evidenced by the fact that Prime Minister Rajiv Gandhi did not visit Japan for four years, going to Tokyo only in 1988. In the interim, India tried to keep the focus on business and investment. Just as Japanese companies were beginning to put aside their hesitations about investing in India, the China opportunity took the wind out of the Indian sails.

By 1990, China had emerged as the top recipient of Japanese aid and became its most important trade partner after the United States.[27] Japan's focus on the China opportunity through most of the 1980s and 1990s meant that India was relegated to a secondary slot on all counts: aid, trade and investment.[28] While Japan's share of total FDI into China came down from 14 per cent in the 1980s to 8.5 per cent in the period from 1995 to 1998, it remained China's single largest source of FDI outside of Hong Kong.

Japan's low level of engagement with India in the 1990s—even as it remained heavily invested in China—reached its nadir in the summer of 1998, when Japan imposed economic sanctions on India and cut off aid for a period of three years in protest against India's decision to conduct nuclear weapons tests and become a nuclear-armed nation.

Partnership

In December 1998, six months into the diplomatic impasse between Japan and India, Prime Minister Atal Bihari Vajpayee authorized a non-official outreach. National Security Advisor Brajesh Mishra tasked the Institute of Defence Studies and Analyses (IDSA) to lead a 'track two' delegation to Tokyo with the aim of connecting with influential Japanese officials and foreign affairs analysts to explain India's decision to conduct nuclear weapons tests.

K. Subrahmanyam, the chairman of the Nuclear Security Advisory Board (NSAB), led the delegation comprising IDSA Director-general Jasjit Singh, former Defence Secretary N.N. Vohra, former Foreign Secretary J.N. Dixit and a distinguished former Indian ambassador to Japan, Arjun Asrani, as well as this writer—who was then a professor at the Indian Council for Research in International Economic Relations (ICRIER) and a member of the NSAB, and became the delegation's youngest member. Our task was to secure our Japanese interlocutors' 'appreciation' for India's decision on nuclear weapons.

Our host was the Japan Institute of International Affairs (JIIA) and the Japanese delegation was led by JIIA's eminent chairman and distinguished Japanese diplomat, Ambassador Nobuo Matsunaga. After a day's deliberation, the two sides were deadlocked on one word when attempting to draft a joint statement. We wanted Japan to 'appreciate' our decision and the reasons for it. Ambassador Matsunaga insisted that while the Japanese side 'understood' the Indian decision, it was not willing to 'appreciate' it. In the interests of resuming a relationship through dialogue, we agreed to the word the Japanese side preferred.

Diplomatic exchanges resumed after these deliberations, although it took another three years for Japan to resume bilateral aid to India. In August 2000, Japanese Prime Minister Yoshiro Mori visited New Delhi for a summit meeting with Prime Minister Vajpayee. The two leaders agreed that Japan and India would establish a 'Global Partnership in the Twenty-First Century'. The joint statement issued by the two was as follows:

> Prime Minister Mori reaffirmed Japan's commitment to working with India toward the reduction and elimination of nuclear weapons and to cooperate with India to ensure that the Comprehensive Nuclear Test Ban Treaty (CTBT) will go into force as soon as possible. Prime Minister Vajpayee said that India had conducted nuclear tests for defensive purposes but had decided of its own accord not to conduct any further tests and guaranteed that India would not be the first to use nuclear weapons in any conflict.[29]

The Mori–Vajpayee meeting was followed up by a summit meeting between Prime Minister Junichiro Koizumi and Prime Minister Manmohan Singh in April 2005. In many ways it can be said that this meeting constituted the decisive turning point in the bilateral relationship. The two leaders issued a joint statement as follows:

> As partners in the new Asian era and with this new strategic orientation of their partnership, India and Japan, as two responsible and major players in Asia, and as nations sharing common values and principles, will expand their traditional bilateral cooperation

to cooperation in Asia and beyond. With this new focus, India and Japan will be partners in peace, with a common interest in and complementary responsibility for promoting the security, stability and prosperity of Asia as well as in advancing international peace and equitable development.[30]

The two leaders agreed that the India–Japan relationship would graduate from being just a bilateral relationship to include regional and global cooperation. The wide-ranging nature of this statement reflected the maturing of the relationship and a recognition that the two Asian democracies should elevate their relationship to a wider strategic level. It is interesting, perhaps significant, that Koizumi's chief cabinet secretary at the time was none other than Shinzo Abe.

Some months later, Abe was on a visit to India and I facilitated a private meeting between him and Manmohan Singh. This was after the external affairs minister S. Jaishankar—who had served in Japan in the late 1990s—had told me that Abe was tipped to succeed Koizumi as Prime Minister. In December 2006, Prime Minister Abe hosted a summit meeting in Tokyo with Singh and the two had agreed that their strategic and global partnership would include a Special Economic Partnership Initiative (SEPI). Affirming the strength of their bilateral relationship within a regional and global context, the two leaders issued a joint statement as follows:

India and Japan are natural partners as the largest and most developed democracies of Asia, with a mutual stake in each other's progress and prosperity. Indeed, a strong, prosperous and dynamic India is in the interest of Japan, and likewise, a strong, prosperous and dynamic Japan is in the interest of India.[31]

It was clear that the regional and global context that both were alluding to was defined by the rise of China, a common neighbour. It was also clear that after half a century of maintaining a relationship comprising mainly aid and trade, the two countries were now willing to recognize the larger potential of their bilateral relationship. This harked back to the early post-WWII and post-Independence years, when Kishi and Nehru sought to build a new equation between the two nations—but whose intentions were foiled by the Cold War.

Prime Minister Abe's historic address to the Indian Parliament in August 2007 and his subsequent shaping of the bilateral relationship during his second term in office were defined both by this intrinsic bilateral basis and the evolving regional and global context. It would be limiting to view Abe's 'Confluence of the Two Seas' address as being crafted purely by the 'China threat' and considerations pertaining to regional security. Unlike most of his predecessors, and like Mori and Koizumi, Abe sought a firmer foundation for the bilateral relationship going beyond the shared concern about a rising China.

While Abe's remarks in his address on the Indo-Pacific and shared security challenges continue to attract global attention and have been commented upon by scholars and officials, his remarks on the bilateral relationship between India and Japan are equally important. In fact, the 2007 Parliament address devotes considerable space to a recount of the historical association between the two countries, including the bond between Nehru and Kishi and the significance of the post-WWII bilateral relationship. Abe summed up his thoughts by saying, 'The friendship that unites India and Japan will no doubt touch the deepest soul of the people of our two countries; of this I am convinced.'[32]

One indication of the diplomatic impact of the Koizumi–Abe initiatives on relations with India is reflected in the sharp increase in 'high level' ministerial traffic between Tokyo and Delhi. As Table 1 shows, compared to the very few ministerial visits from Japan to India in the 1980s, 1990s and even up to 2004, there was a steep jump in the period from 2004 to 2009, that has since been sustained. This period also witnessed a sharp rise in foreign direct investment from Japan into India. (Chart 1)[33]

Table 1: High Level Bilateral Visits

Period	Japan to India	India to Japan
1980s	5	10
1990s	4	14
2000–2004	4	9
2004–2009	25	32
2010–2014	20	26
2014–2020	22	21

Source: External Affairs Ministry, Government of India.

Chart 1: FDI equity inflows from Japan into India

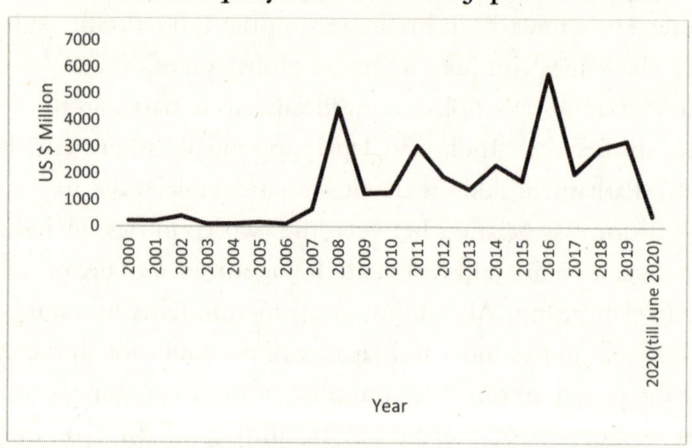

Source: JETRO, Tokyo. (Kojima, 2020)

Building on the foundation for the twenty-first century bilateral relationship laid by Koizumi, Abe and Singh, Prime Minister Narendra Modi enhanced the partnership early in his tenure to 'Special, Strategic and Global Partnership'.[34] At each step the purpose was to bring the two nations closer. Recognizing the low level of people-to-people relationship between both countries—the low population of Indians in Japan made them the smallest group of foreigners from the Indo–Pacific region, with the Chinese far outnumbering them—Abe enhanced visas for Indians and devised policies to allow more Indians to secure entry into Japan.[35]

Under Prime Minister Abe's visionary leadership, the bilateral relationship acquired a diplomatic and economic momentum that has been sustained. While both countries tend to get distracted from each other from time to time and people-to-people contacts are still minimal, there has been a substantial increase in business-to-business relations. The relationship at the government level has acquired a clear strategic dimension with growing defence ties and a shared vision of what Abe termed as 'Broader Asia': an 'arc of freedom and prosperity' across the Indo-Pacific region.

In conclusion, it can be said that Shinzo Abe's initiatives to enhance government-to-government, business-to-business and people-to-people relations between Japan and India make him the principal architect of the India–Japan relationship of the twenty-first century.

8

JAPAN–INDIA RELATIONS: MAPPING ABE'S DIPLOMACY

Takenori Horimoto

LTHOUGH IT WOULD BE too early to assess Shinzo Abe's diplomacy in terms of the Japan–India relations, it is possible to have an objective examination of it. This examination has been done without indulging in overestimation or underestimation. It is quite self-evident that any policy turned into historical fact necessitates some amount of time for all the merits and shortcomings to be tallied.

One aspect of Prime Minister Abe's diplomacy can be emphasized as particularly noteworthy: his endeavour to establish meaningful relations between Japan and India. Because attributing all positive aspects of the bilateral relations to Abe would be a disservice to him and others in the policy communities of both Japan and India, historical examinations might be necessary to have a correct understanding of the two countries. His efforts and achievements in the development of the Japan–India relationship should be mapped.

Bilateral Relations during the Cold War[1]

Japan regained self-sovereignty in 1951 by the peace treaty signed at San Francisco, where the Japan–US Security Treaty was also agreed. Prime Minister Jawaharlal Nehru refused to attend the San Francisco

Peace Conference because he objected to the stationing of US forces in Japan even after the US Occupation had ended. Later, India showed a friendly posture to Japan by abandoning all claims from Japan in the bilateral peace treaty signed in 1952. These events took place two years before Shinzo Abe was born.

The Japan–US Security Treaty was amended in 1960 because Prime Minister Nobusuke Kishi objected to a security treaty that did not obligate the US to defend Japan and which permitted the US to interfere in Japanese domestic affairs, among other issues of contention. Kishi, who had been the minister of commerce and industry before World War II, was designated a 'Class A war criminal' by the US-led occupation forces. However, he was exonerated and released by the Americans as they thought he would be a suitable candidate for future political leadership.

Bilateral relations between India and Japan between the 1950s and the 1980s were dominated by economics and trade. For Japan, Indian iron ore contributed greatly to Japan's steel industry, which was a major pillar of its high-speed economic growth that had started in the 1950s. A somewhat similar role had been played by India's raw cotton vis-à-vis Japan's industrial development during the Meiji period (1868–1912).

The Japanese image of India has been that of a peace-loving country, as epitomized by Mahatma Gandhi and then Nehru. Thus, India had been expected to play a big role in the formation of a peaceful new Asia. Nevertheless, such expectations were dashed by incidents such as India's military annexation of Goa in 1961, the India–China border conflict in 1962 and the second Indo–Pakistan war in 1965. India's severe harvest shortfalls in 1965 and 1966 further tainted India's image.

The 1960s marked the beginning of a time of change for both Japan and India. Japan showed its rapid economic growth: thereafter, its trade with India dwindled gradually. In contrast, Japan's trade with the US grew quite rapidly and continuously through the 1970s and the 1980s even as the political relations between the two nations strengthened. These relations were characterized perfectly as an alliance by Prime Minister Masayoshi Ohira of Japan on a visit to the US in 1979.

India began to direct its diplomatic efforts westward in the 1960s. Perhaps, in India's calculations, a Pakistan factor needed to be emphasized because of the wars between the neighbouring nations in 1965 and again in 1971. More apparent factors could be the Middle East being the region of oil production and the increased Indian immigration to that region.

These developments led to Japan and India diverging in their respective orientations to foreign relations. Official visits by the Prime Ministers of either of the two countries grew infrequent. Indian Prime Ministers to visit Japan between the 1950s and the 1980s were Nehru in 1957, Indira Gandhi in 1969 and 1982, and Rajiv Gandhi in 1985 and 1988. Visits from Japanese Prime Ministers to India were from Kishi in 1957, Hayato Ikeda in 1961 and Yasuhiro Nakasone in 1984.

Transition Period of the 1990s

The 1990s can be regarded as a decade of fluctuation in bilateral relations. The relationship between India and Japan has mainly been focused on economic affairs. The underlying thought on the Japanese side has rested throughout on the Yoshida Doctrine. After its wartime defeat in 1945, Japan adopted this doctrine as a strategy under Prime Minister Shigeru Yoshida, who was in office from 1948 to 1954. His main idea had focused on the reconstruction of Japan's economy, relying heavily on matters of security on the alliance with the US (the so-called 'lightly armed policy'). Japan's diplomatic autonomy was affected strongly by that mutual relationship.

Japanese Prime Minister Toshiki Kaifu's official visit to India in 1990 might be elucidated best as an extension of that doctrine, although he was fundamentally a pro-Asian advocate. At his scheduled speech in the Lok Sabha, very few Members of Parliament turned up at the assembly hall. To avoid an embarrassing situation, the secretariat staff was asked to fill the numerous vacant seats.[2]

Two years later in 1992, when Prime Minister P.V. Narasimha Rao visited Japan for the commemoration of forty years of bilateral relations, there emerged a subtle gap of interests and perceptions between the two countries. Japan was interested in India's participation in the Nuclear Non-Proliferation Treaty whereas India was looking for an increase in Japan's investment into India. By the early 1990s, India had already initiated its economic liberalization and its 'Look East' policy.

Despite gradual signs of improvements in the relationship between the two countries, a mutually irritating issue presented itself when India conducted its second round of nuclear tests in 1998. Representing victims of a nuclear attack, Japan's leadership was unable to understand India's actions particularly as it went against the international mainstream push for nuclear non-proliferation. On the other side, Indian leaders were quite dissatisfied with Japan's narrative. To them, nuclear weapons signified the country's *sine qua non* for self-defence, and could point out that Japan too benefited from a nuclear-armed defence under the US umbrella. The 1998 nuclear tests pushed Japan–India relations to estrangement. Japan suspended its official development assistance to India.

Bilateral Relations in the 2000s and Later

The Cold War period ended in the 1980s. The next decade was a transitional period into the twenty-first century. An overview of India–Japan bilateral relations since the 1990s could be compared to a triple jump: a hop, a step and a jump. The 1990s was the 'hop', with an approach run period. Its most distinguishable aspect is that the bilateral relations gradually metamorphosed from being mainly economic in nature into an economic-plus-security relationship.

In contrast, the 2000s marked a stage of step by step improvement during which the bilateral relations moved closer. Prime Minister Yoshiro Mori's visit to India in August 2000 was a landmark event. On the occasion, the two countries named their bilateral relations as 'Global Partnership between Japan and India in the Twenty-First Century'. Prime Minister Atal Bihari Vajpayee visited Japan the following year. The two premiers announced the 'Japan–India Joint Declaration', committing to high-level dialogue and cooperation in the economic, defence and anti-terrorism spheres. This was followed in 2005 by

Prime Minister Junichiro Koizumi visiting India and signing a strategic partnership with his Indian counterpart, Manmohan Singh. Since Prime Minister Singh's visit to Japan in 2006, the two countries have had their premier visit every other year. The change of mood is noticeable in the mutual traffic spike of VIP visits during the 2000s. (*See Chart on p. 106*)

This increase in high-level visits on both sides occurred for reasons of mutual necessity. From Japan's point of view, India was—and remains today—a country with attractive conditions, such as a democratic political system, huge economic potential and a gigantic domestic market. Viewed geo-strategically, Japan's strengthened relations with India carry strategic importance for its aspirations to progress from an Asian power to a global power. From India's viewpoint, its economic relations with Japan were expected to carry two points of significance: encouraging investment, trade and technology transfer necessary for India's economic development and serving as India's bridgehead in the Asia-Pacific, which had been rather neglected in past decades.

There is another common and important factor that has linked the two countries in their strategic interests. Simply put, it is China. Since the end of the Cold War, China has emerged rapidly and Japan's economic relations with China have deepened. During the 2006 financial year, China became Japan's largest trading partner, supplanting the US. Naturally, increasing concern vis-à-vis the one-sided focus on China gained momentum in Japan. As if endorsing the concern, largescale anti-Japan demonstrations took place in China. As a natural corollary, Japan showed a clear posture to emphasize Indian relations from around 2005 onwards.

Similarly, India has also been affected by changes in China. Its relations with the US gained momentum. To avoid overemphasis on that turn to the West, India was able to deepen its relations with China through eased policy. Nevertheless, because of a persistent distrust of China, Japan was important in India's diplomatic calculations. The 'jump' in the relations was a consequence. The rapid economic and military emergence of China has nudged India and China closer. They are engaging in policies of hedging and engagement. Simply put, in policy orientation, the hedging is being done for defence and security, whereas engagement is for economy and associated fields. The US is well known to have maintained its strategic engagement and hedging policy towards China after the Cold War.

Such a policy orientation was discarded during the Trump administration. Gina Haspel, the director of the CIA—in a testimony during her Senate nomination hearing in May 2018[3]—said, 'For decades, American foreign policy towards China has been rooted in the belief that as they prospered economically they would embrace democracy— they would embrace the global rule of law. That consensus I think by all accounts has been catastrophically wrong.' The US vice-president, Mike Pence, announced the end of strategic engagement with China in October 2018 and officially proclaimed a new era of strategic competition.

Abe's Rapid Emergence and Foreign Policies[4]

Abe remained a backbencher in the 1990s. However, in the 2000s, he achieved an unprecedented rise in a kaleidoscopic manner. In 2000, he was appointed as deputy cabinet secretary. Unlike in India, cabinet secretaries are appointed from among the Members of Parliament. They carry considerable political clout. Abe was again appointed as the deputy when Junichiro Koizumi became Prime Minister in 2002.

Thereafter, he was elected as the general secretary (GS) of the Liberal Democratic Party (LDP). In the LDP, only one person holds the post of the GS. Abe's appointment as the GS was an exceptional promotion. In fact, the media reported it as a 'surprising appointment'. Typically, those appointed to the post had previously been cabinet ministers or other key party functionaries. After becoming the GS, Abe went on to become Prime Minister twice: holding the post from 2006 to 2007 and again from 2012 to 2020.

In September 2006, when Shinzo Abe took office as Prime Minister for the first time, he was fifty-two years old—making him the youngest premier in Japan's post-war history. One of the main factors that contributed to his rapid emergence was that he belonged to a great political dynasty. Among his relatives are former Prime Ministers

Nobusuke Kishi (Shinzo's grandfather) and Eisaku Sato (his great uncle), and his father, Shintaro, served as foreign minister. Another factor was that he was a leader of a powerful faction of the LDP—the Seiwa Political Research Council, which is now the largest faction within the LDP. The faction has a distinctive tendency in its policy orientation: in essence, it is right-leaning, hawkish, and in favour of constitutional revision (particularly Article 9).

Historically speaking, the LDP has two main liberal and conservative clusters. From the 2000s onward, the latter has shown its ascendancy. Most of the LDP MPs share such an orientation. Very roughly speaking, Abe belongs to the conservative cluster, similar to his grandfather Kishi, whereas his father might be classified as closest to the liberal cluster. During Abe's first term in office, he initiated the Quadrilateral Security Dialogue (Quad) to counter China's growth as a superpower. He also advocated revision of the Japanese constitution—in particular Article 9, which forbids the sovereign right of armed action and armed forces with war potential.

Then during his second term as Prime Minister, Abe enforced military reform in 2015, which allowed Japan to exercise the right to collective self-defence and led to the removal of restraints imposed on Tokyo prohibiting the use of its military forces overseas in the wake of its defeat in World War II. This allowed the SDF to be deployed overseas, but making such an allowance caused a huge controversy in Japan.

Collective self-defence is the basic component of the Quad and the FOIP, which has been formalized in cooperation with the US. In the 2017 US National Security Strategy, the term 'Asia-Pacific' was replaced by 'Indo-Pacific'. It would be necessary for India to share the idea of the FOIP concept. Efforts to create a Regional Comprehensive Economic Partnership (RCEP) had been a major agenda item for Abe. These actions have all indicated clearly that Abe was a Prime Minister of the post-Cold War period of 'economy plus security', which formed the main components of Japan's foreign policy in the twenty-first century.

In terms of foreign policy, Japan had successful summit diplomacy unfold under Abe's leadership. He built close personal relationships with former US President Donald Trump and Russian President Vladimir Putin. Moreover, he made his presence felt on the international stage. Nevertheless, the issue of abductions of Japanese citizens by North Korea[5] and the dispute with Russia over the Kuril Islands[6]—which he regarded as important difficulties to be addressed by his government—showed no progress.

Development of Japan–India Relations

Relations between India and Japan have shown great promise moving forward.[7] In terms of foreign policy, the improvement of Japan–India relations could be called Abe's greatest contribution. In 2006, Abe published his first self-authored book, *Towards a Beautiful Country*, just two months before he became Prime Minister. In the book, he states his high expectations for relations with India. Although admitting that Japan–India relations were at a low ebb and foreseeing Japan–China trade as surpassing that of Japan with the US, he wrote, 'It would be no wonder if Japan–India relations were to outperform Japan–US and Japan–China ten years hence.'[8]

The first Abe administration showed eagerness for furthering bilateral relations with India. His speech to the Indian Parliament in 2007—titled 'Confluence of the Two Seas'—has played an important role in creating the 'Indo-Pacific': a strategic concept designed to encourage India to get involved in the Pacific maritime domain as a counter to China. Abe's strategic thinking was perhaps to involve India in the Pacific sphere so that Japan can add its countervailing power vis-à-vis emerging China. For Abe, the geographical concept of Asia-Pacific was insufficient to meet Chinese power by US forces alone.

In India, the Congress-led United Progressive Alliance (UPA) under Prime Minister Manmohan Singh presented a similar posture. According to Sanjaya Baru, Abe's return to power in 2012 revived the agenda of a new strategic engagement with Japan. He opines that the building of closer economic and defence ties with Japan was the only significant foreign policy achievement of the UPA government.[9] For India, policies such as the Look East policy and its extension, the Act

East policy, underscored the necessity of a wider geostrategic scope to cope with China. As Abe said in his speech to the Indian Parliament in 2007: 'We are also in perfect agreement that a strong India is in the best interest of Japan, and a strong Japan is in the best interest of India.'[10]

Abe's relationships with Prime Ministers Manmohan Singh and Narendra Modi were close. Even though these premiers were on the same page in terms of their China policy, at the same time a subtle divergence was apparent in Japanese and Indian attitudes. Essentially, Singh and Modi differed to Abe in policy orientations vis-à-vis the US and Russia: these differences are now readily apparent in India's approach to the Ukraine conflict.[11]

Conclusion: How to Proceed with Bilateral Relations

S. Jaishankar, the foreign minister of India, assigns emphasis on India–Japan relations in his recent book, *The India Way*, in which he allots a full chapter to Japan titled 'A Delayed Destiny'. To quote from this chapter: '… a Japan that was firmly placed in an Alliance was not easy to engage in the past … Much closer Indian relations with the US have made it a facilitator, rather than obstacle to India–Japan ties.'[12]

Abe promoted Indian foreign policy in the Indo-Pacific by formulating the twin policies of the Quad and the RCEP in his second term as Prime Minister. The Quad has progressed in the way Abe imagined. However, such is not the case with the RCEP, which one might understand as the economic version of the FOIP. Originally, he sought to maintain checks and balances on China through cooperation between Japan and India.

However, India opted out of the RCEP in 2019. The reason for this was reportedly its potential adverse effects on India. Perhaps India's excess of imports over exports in its trade with China might be an important factor, as the amount was estimated at around USD 60 billion. This has led to a huge objection raised in India to its joining the RCEP.

The US too quit the RCEP in 2017 under the Trump administration. Later, it proposed the Indo-Pacific Economic Framework for Prosperity (IPEF) under Trump's successor, President Joe Biden. Japan and India have joined the IPEF, but China has been excluded. However, the IPEF is a kind of administrative agreement without involvement of legislatures. Therefore, compared to the RCEP, it remains rather weak in terms of its binding nature.[13]

The Quad carries importance, but with several important challenges. Although China often criticizes it as the Asian NATO, the criticism is farfetched. Presently, the Quad remains a talk shop, although the four countries have long signed their respective bilateral defence and security agreements.

Xi Jinping began an unprecedented third term as the head of the Chinese Communist Party in October 2022. He is looking to be successful in the unification of Taiwan with mainland China. The policy paper issued in August 2022 declared that unification with Taiwan is 'indispensable' to China's 'rejuvenation', which is Xi's main political platform.[14] To retain his post after the third term, the unification of Taiwan is a *sine qua non*.

Globally, China ranks second in terms of GDP and defence expenditure. However, it might face several important challenges—one of the biggest of which is its declining population. In fact, India is expected to have the largest population among nations in 2023. In other words, China faces a decreasing 'population bonus' that can support its economy. This might deal a severe blow to the legitimacy of Chinese governance. In the past, China has legitimized governance among its populace through continually increasing incomes without real voting rights.

Presumably, China is among the most attentive observers of the processes and outcomes of the conflict in Ukraine. China's moves to act militarily against its neighbours cause gigantic difficulties for India and Japan. China's military operations would affect Japanese territory such as the Okinawa Islands. India has perennial territorial issues with China. Today, Japan and India are facing crucial boundary issues. China has let boundary issues with India simmer, to be played eventually as a political card against India.

The present Japan–US security relationship has been compared to the pike and shield[15] of the Cold War period. In that strategy, the US played the role of a pike, whereas Japan was a shield against the Soviet Union. Now, the antagonist has changed from the USSR to China.

John Mearsheimer, an American international political scientist, has pointed out that for the US—which has a rich history of acting as an 'offshore balancer'—the ideal strategy for dealing with China is to leave the task of its containment almost entirely up to the countries of the region, remaining in the background to the greatest extent possible.[16] The US has therefore remained as a supporter of FOIP and the Quad rather than a promoter. Mearsheimer suggests that instead of the US, concerned countries should make their own defence expenditure to deal with China.

So long as the US adopts and maintains the strategic posture presented during the Trump and Biden administrations, Japan and India are facing knotty situations. Prime Minister Abe's advocacy for the expansion of Japan's military strength reflects the US posture. Japan must find the financial resources to do so. Together, Japan and India are heading into unknown waters with no nautical chart.

Ministerial Visits from Japan and India

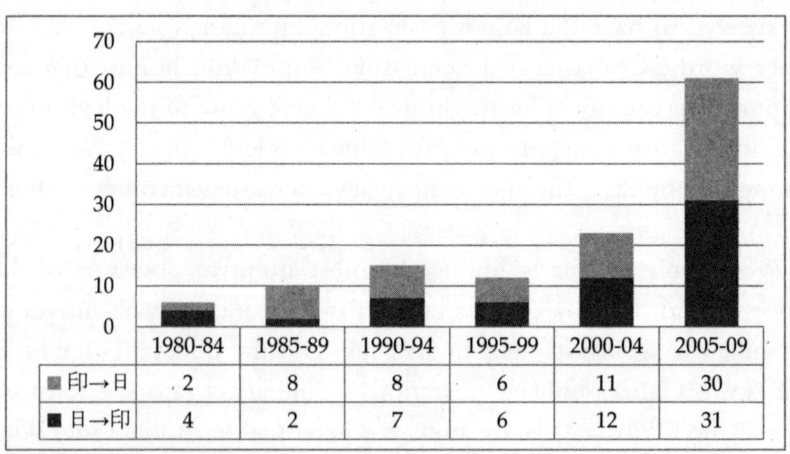

	1980-84	1985-89	1990-94	1995-99	2000-04	2005-09
■ 印→日	2	8	8	6	11	30
■ 日→印	4	2	7	6	12	31

Note: Light grey indicates Indian leaders' visits to Japan; dark grey shows Japanese leaders' visits to India.

Source: The Ministry of Foreign Affairs website http://www.mofa.go.jp/mofaj/area/india/data.html

9

INDIA AND ABE—A SPECIAL CONNECT

Deepa Gopalan Wadhwa

IN TIMES MARKED BY disruption, unpredictability and impermanence in a strictly transactional international order with shrinking space for finer sentiments, India's emotional reaction to former Japanese Prime Minister Shinzo Abe's tragic and senseless assassination on 7 July 2022 was the expression of a widespread perception of his having been a very special friend of India: 'a champion of India–Japan friendship'.[1] One cannot recall such adulatory tributes paid by Indian national leaders to a foreign dignitary upon his demise.

The homage was led by Prime Minister Narendra Modi, who was perceptibly shocked and saddened at the news. In a blog entry titled 'My friend, Abe-san', Modi writes, 'We in India mourn his passing as one of our own, just as he embraced us with an open heart.'[2] India declared a day of national mourning for Abe on 9 July 2022 despite his not holding any formal office at the time of his death—elevating him to the status of global statesmen like the former Prime Minister of Singapore, Lee Kuan Yew, and Nelson Mandela, Nobel laureate, crusader against apartheid and former President of South Africa, who had been similarly honoured on their passing.

Prime Minister Modi was also one of a small clutch of serving heads of state who made it a point to travel to Tokyo to attend Abe's state

107

funeral on 27 September 2022 and bid a personal farewell to one with whom he had established a close friendship. The chemistry between the two was much in evidence from the time of his first visits to Japan as chief minister of Gujarat in 2007 and 2012. The easy camaraderie resumed with greater effect as both met as Prime Ministers after the victory of Modi's National Democratic Alliance in May 2014.

In his blog tribute, Modi describes their relationship as a friendship which 'went beyond the trappings of office and shackles of official protocol'. Examples of the personal rapport between the two were seen in Abe's donning of the iconic Modi jacket when he visited Varanasi to perform ceremonial prayers on the banks of the Ganga together with the Indian Prime Minister, and when he invited Modi to his personal residence in Yamanashi during the annual summit of 2018.

When Narendra Modi became Prime Minister in May 2014, he let it be known to his Japanese interlocutors that his first official visit abroad would be to Japan. This was, of course, received very well in Tokyo, where I was serving as India's ambassador at the time. This decision stemmed from Modi's earlier visits to Japan during which he had succeeded in persuading the country to be a lead partner in the Vibrant Gujarat Summit initiative. This initiative had been launched by him in 2003 to attract foreign investors to his state. The reception accorded to him during his visits to Japan as a chief minister by both the political leadership and leaders of Japanese industry had clearly made a deep impact on him. This was in contrast to the travel bans imposed on Modi at the time by some Western countries on the basis of allegations of human rights violations related to events in Gujarat in 2002.

The Japanese establishment had followed the 2014 elections in India closely, but without much apprehension on the likely effect on India–Japan relations. This was because the reset in relations in 2000 had bipartisan support on both sides, and relations had segued smoothly without being affected by past changes of governments in both countries. India–Japan relations were also at a high following the state visit to India in November 2013 of Their Majesties, Emperor Akihito and Empress Michiko, followed by Prime Minister Abe becoming the first Japanese Prime Minister to be invited as chief guest at the Republic Day celebrations in January 2014.

Following these visits, in November 2014 the Japanese government made a telling tribute to the high esteem and regard for former Prime Minister Dr Manmohan Singh for his role in the consolidation of India–Japan ties by conferring on him Japan's highest civilian honour: the Grand Cordon of the Order of the Paulownia Flowers. This was on the heels of Prime Minister Modi's symbolic visit to Japan. This was quite clearly Prime Minister Abe's decision and showed that while personal affinities had a role to play, his belief in the importance of the role of India in his ambitions for a resurgent Japan transcended politics.

Despite his desire to make Japan his first official foreign visit, Prime Minister Modi had to first visit Thimphu in Bhutan and Kathmandu in Nepal, as suitable dates for a Japan visit could only be found in August 2014, three months after he assumed office. When he did eventually visit Japan, Modi emphasized the significance of his visit by saying that he was coming at the invitation of 'his good friend, Prime Minister Shinzo Abe' for his 'first bilateral visit outside India's immediate neighbourhood as Prime Minister of India, which underlines the high priority that Japan receives in our foreign and economic policies'. He also viewed his trip as 'reflective of Japan's paramount importance in my vision for development and prosperity in India and peace and prosperity in Asia at large'.[3] With this statement, Prime Minister Modi had made clear the continuing importance of Japan to India, both a bilateral partner and a collaborator in the Indo-Pacific.

From his first term as Prime Minister in 2006, Abe had institutionalized annual premier-level summits with India. Japan does not hold summits at this level and frequency with any other country. This practice gave Abe many occasions to visit India. From 2014 to 2019, Prime Ministers Modi and Abe met at five annual prime ministerial summits and at the margins of several multilateral fora, such as the East Asia Summit and UN General Assembly. These meetings provided opportunities to advance the bilateral relationship—which had already been secured in a firm framework of comprehensive exchanges—to new areas of cooperation. They also allowed the two leaders to explore uncharted waters of plurilateral collaboration, bound by matched and convergent visions for their countries that were positioned as bookends of a dynamic Indo-Pacific region—a concept ideated and realized by Abe.

Abe had wanted to visit the Northeast of India for a summit in 2019 because he had accorded priority to the development of the region—which was seen as a meeting point of Japan's Free and Open Indo-Pacific (FOIP) vision and India's Act East policy. He was responsible for the setting up of the Act East Forum to promote cooperation in the area. One of the pillars of FOIP was promoting connectivity, and the Northeast was a bridgehead for linking the Bay of Bengal through Bangladesh and to the ASEAN countries through Myanmar. Japan also has a sentimental attachment to Kohima and Imphal, as they were the locations of intense battles during the Second World War between the Japanese army and British soldiers—battles in which casualties were heavy and the dead left behind. Abe had wanted to visit a peace museum set up in Imphal by the Nippon Foundation to commemorate the battles. However, the summit planned for 2019 had to be postponed twice, first due to local unrest and then the Covid pandemic.

In India, Abe is most remembered for his address to a joint session of the Indian Parliament on 22 August 2007 during his first brief term as Prime Minister. The speech—titled 'Confluence of the Two Seas'—was where he first mooted his idea of the continuum of the Indian and Pacific Oceans. The speech is credited as having defined the contours of India–Japan relations in the current century. He used eloquence to demonstrate his personal connection with India, quoting from Swami Vivekananda and Dara Shikoh and referencing interactions between Japan and India's leading luminaries of the early twentieth century who influenced each other. Highlighting the symmetries of the value systems of the two countries fostered as practicing democracies, Abe said that the Japanese people had rediscovered India as a partner and that the two countries should work together to 'enrich the seas of freedom and prosperity', thus setting the stage for the rapid deepening of both economic and strategic ties.

The speech was also a masterly exposition of Prime Minister Abe's foresight in anticipating the emerging trends in Asia as a consequence of a resurgent and assertive China. It was the first articulation by a political leader of the compelling arguments for a geopolitical construct to be named the 'Indo-Pacific'. What made the speech a landmark in India–Japan relations was his vision of the dynamic coupling of the Indian and Pacific Oceans to advance freedom and prosperity of a broader Asia with both India and Japan as key players. The change in nomenclature from 'Asia-Pacific' was especially significant for India, because the Asia-Pacific had been focused on East Asia and the ASEAN with a remit that deliberately excluded India—as we discovered when the APEC group was established in 1992.

Prime Minister Abe's coinage was therefore clearly done with forethought to highlight not only the potential of an India–Japan strategic partnership but also India's growing economic and political heft. He also prepared the ground for the future Quad when he said, 'Japan and India coming together would evolve into a network spanning the entirety of the Pacific Ocean, incorporating the US and Australia … where people, goods, capital and knowledge would flow freely'.[4] Abe has been rightly acclaimed on his passing as a visionary. In his blog post on 9 July 2022, Prime Minister Modi described Abe as being ahead of his time and having deep insight into the complex and multiple transitions taking place in the world. He wrote that Abe had 'the foresight on the changing tides and gathering storm in the Indo-Pacific'.

The first mention of the Indo-Pacific in a formal document is in the joint statement issued in Delhi in 2015 after the Prime Ministers of India and Japan met at a summit called 'India–Japan Vision 2025'. A year later, Prime Minister Abe elaborated his FOIP strategy at the Tokyo International Conference on African Development (TICAD) in Kenya in 2016. TICAD was hosted every five years by Japan and other development agencies. He explained his vision of the Indo-Pacific as two free and open oceans that would bring together Africa and Asia—thereby expanding the geographical remit of the concept to the eastern shores of the African continent. He defined the construct as an area that would value freedom, the rule of law and market economy, free from force or coercion. He specifically mentioned that he hoped the new Indo-Pacific construct would replace the outdated Asia-Pacific one.[5]

The concept was quickly accepted by the US government under President Trump as well as by Australia, where it was used in a defence white paper in 2013. Other countries followed suit, including those in the ASEAN—despite early reservations adopting an 'ASEAN outlook to the Indo-Pacific' that avoids any strategic language in walking a fine line between competing regional powers but emphasizes the criticality of the ASEAN centrality. In the past couple of years, several European states with economic and security interests in the Indo-Pacific—such as France, the UK, Germany and the Netherlands—have issued their respective Indo-Pacific strategies. Prime Minister Abe's formulations permitted an elastic interpretation of the Indo-Pacific construct by foreign and security policy establishments depending on their geography, strategic objectives and economic interests.

India's own Indo-Pacific policy was based on its geographical location at the crossroads of the northern Indian Ocean—which harbours the principal sea lanes of the world—and the Andaman Sea, which was the bridgehead of the Malacca Straits. It was spelt out in June 2018 by Prime Minister Modi in his speech at the Shangri-La Dialogue in Singapore.[6] While adding the imperative of inclusiveness in the definition of FOIP, the principles were in keeping with Abe's vision. India joined its voice in the call for cooperation and collaboration, emphasizing the need for shared responses to shared challenges in the region. At the East Asia Summit in Bangkok, India also announced the Indo-Pacific Oceans Initiative (IPOI) with seven identified pillars of collaboration.

The Indo-Pacific has become common currency in international discourse and mechanisms and groupings such as Quad have been established to realize its principles. Abe's advocacy for India and Japan to work together in the Indo-Pacific finds mention in all important documents issued after bilateral meetings. Prime Minister Abe and his successors have maintained that India is indispensable to Japan's endeavours to achieve the objectives of FOIP and that a strong partnership with India is an important part of Japan's strategic calculus in the Indo-Pacific. A tangible outcome has been Japan's inclusion in the Malabar naval exercises as a permanent member, something which Abe had insisted on.

India loomed larger in Shinzo Abe's worldview than it had for any Japanese leader of the past several decades. This was evident in his statements, writings and actions. During the prime ministerial summit of 2018, Abe hosted Modi at his holiday home in Yamanashi prefecture, which is located in picturesque environs at the foot of Mount Fuji. At the time, he recalled the visit by his grandfather Prime Minister Nobusuke Kishi to India in 1957. It was an oft-repeated tale of how he had heard accounts of the visit seated on the knee of his grandfather as a young boy and it had left a deep impression on him. In an article published in several Indian newspapers during the summit, Abe wrote, 'At the time when Japan was not so wealthy, Prime Minister Nehru introduced Prime Minister Kishi in front of thousands of people as the Japanese Prime Minister whom he respects.' In his speech to the Indian Parliament, Abe said that Nehru had introduced Kishi as the Prime Minister of 'a country I hold in the greatest esteem' to 'the biggest audience he had ever seen in his lifetime: that of a hundred thousand people'.

Both versions of the story showed how the reception he received had made a deep impact on Kishi, who at the time was the leader of a defeated nation and seen as a controversial figure himself. Having served in the wartime government of General Hideki Tojo, Kishi had been imprisoned for three years after World War II as a suspected Class A war criminal—though he was never charged, tried or convicted. Shinzo Abe's political views and personal regard for India were influenced by his grandfather. This was in evidence in 2007, when on his first visit to India he travelled to Kolkata to meet Prasanta Pal, the grandson of Justice Radha Binod Pal.

Justice Pal is revered in Japan as an icon because he had delivered a dissenting opinion at the international military tribunal to try Japanese leaders for war crimes, which meant that they could not be found guilty.

Abe had extolled Justice Pal in his 2007 speech to the Indian Parliament, saying that he was highly respected even today by many Japanese 'for the noble spirit of courage he exhibited' during the military tribunal.

India–Japan relations in the first two decades after the end of World War II was marked by special gestures of friendship high in symbolism. These were driven to a large extent by Prime Minister Jawaharlal Nehru's sentiments towards Japan. In 1947, Nehru had welcomed Japan to the Asian Relations Conference as an independent country, despite it being under occupation of the Allied powers. In 1951, he had decided against India's participation in the San Francisco Peace Conference because he did not agree with the US proposal that placed limits on the sovereignty of Japan. Instead, he chose to negotiate a separate peace treaty with Japan in 1952 that waived all reparations.

This was followed by a succession of high-level visits by both sides, including exchange visits by both Prime Ministers in 1957. Prime Minister Nobusuke Kishi's visit, mentioned so often by Abe, had resulted in India coming forward before any other country to accept the overseas development assistance ODA that Japan wanted to extend as a proud member of the international community. For that, Abe recalled while addressing the Indian Council of World Affairs (ICWA) in 2011, his grandfather remained 'deeply thankful to India throughout his life'.

The ODA begun by Kishi in 1958 was to be the ballast of the India–Japan relationship as it plateaued into a period of benign stasis after the onset of the Cold War, which had placed the two countries in different camps. This remained until the reset in relations in 2000 by Prime Minister Mori, who is often considered to be Abe's political mentor. ODA disbursements to India began to grow as project aid to China started to be phased out. By 2003, India was the leading recipient of ODA from Japan, and Japan had become India's largest ODA partner.[7]

The logic of economic convergences was an important part of this reset with India. The lure of India's growing market and economic performance was seen as complementing Japan's financial and technological strengths. Its own shrinking domestic market had prompted Japan to search for investment destinations beyond China, diversifying its economic engagement. After a decision taken at the

2005 summit meeting between Prime Ministers Manmohan Singh and Junichiro Koizumi, a joint study group was set up to undertake a comprehensive review of economic relations between the two countries. However, it was only during Shinzo Abe's first term as Prime Minister—from 2006 to 2007—that negotiations on a Comprehensive Economic Partnership Agreement (CEPA) was launched. The agreement entered into force in 2012, the year Abe returned to office. This was the first such free trade agreement between India and an OECD country.

Abe's focus on deepening the economic engagement with India meant that several decisions of consequence were taken even during his brief first term as Prime Minister. These included the decision to promote a Delhi–Mumbai Industrial Corridor, which would be supported by a dedicated freight corridor that would reduce the time taken for transportation of goods between Delhi and Mumbai from weeks to days. This envisaged the setting up of special economic zones, smart cities and industrial townships across seven states that would receive investments from Japan. This mega project—valued at USD 100 billion—was projected to have a transformative impact on India's logistics and investment landscape.

Other decisions saw the setting up of forum for business leaders to boost the involvement of the private sector in the economic engagement, and the institution of an India–Japan energy dialogue—co-chaired by the deputy chairman of the Planning Commission on the Indian side and a METI minister on the Japanese side—to promote cooperation in areas such as power generation, clean coal technologies and renewable energy.

Importantly, a consultative mechanism was set up to address issues related to the export control systems in place. This took some time to resolve due to the entrenched bureaucracy in Japan. The removal of Indian space and defence entities from the Foreign End Users List was only completed in 2014 under Abe, marking a new phase of trust and maturity in strategic relations.

Efforts to catalyse the economic engagement between the two countries received a boost during the summit of 2014—the first one attended by Prime Minister Modi—when Prime Minister Abe announced an India–Japan investment promotion partnership with the promise of 3.5 trillion yen of private and public investment into India over five years and a doubling of the number of Japanese companies in India. Despite this, trade and investment has been consistently below par, with Japanese corporations still choosing China and ASEAN countries as preferred destinations for investment. However, Japanese ODA has been welcomed because it is earmarked for projects of priority to India, and the generous terms of loans cannot be matched by other lending institutions. An example is the USD 12 billion loan for the Mumbai–Ahmedabad High Speed Rail, which comes with an interest rate of 0.1 per cent and a fifty-year repayment schedule. Most importantly, Japan has emerged as the only country India trusts to carry out projects in the sensitive peripheries of the Northeast and the Andaman and Nicobar archipelago, which is strategically located near the Malacca Straits.

Shinzo Abe introduced strategic thinking into Japan's foreign, security and economic policies. On the foreign policy and security front, he wanted Japan to be a 'normal nation'. He reinterpreted his nation's constitution to permit for collective self-defence and made efforts to amend its pacifist provisions. Abe's enduring legacy included the setting up of the National Security Council and the adoption of a National Security Strategy in 2014. The new national defence guidelines called for Japan to be a 'proactive contributor to peace through international cooperation'. India was identified in these strategic documents as a partner with which Japan could 'strengthen its relationship in a broad range of activities, including maritime security, through joint training and exercises as well as joint implementation of international peace cooperation operations'.[8]

The convergence of strategic outlooks was reflected in a steady accretion in defence and security ties between India and Japan under Prime Minister Abe. The navies of the two countries participated in the bilateral Japan India Bilateral Maritime Exercises (JIMEX) as well as the Malabar naval exercises, the latter of which had been conducted only with the US until then. There was also initiation of joint exercises by the land and air wings of the military, signing of three key defence agreements—including on transfer of defence equipment and technology as Japan loosened self-imposed restraints—cooperation in maritime domain awareness and agreement on reciprocal supply and services. The latter—signed in September 2020—is commonly referred to as ACSA (Acquisition and Goods Sharing Arrangement) and facilitates mutual logistics support and some degree of interoperability between the navies.

The consultations on the expanded strategic and defence relations is done within a multi-layered framework of exchanges with the '2+2' ministerial dialogue between the foreign and defence ministers of the two nations and regular contact between the service chiefs. The strategic convergence has also been manifest in the agreements signed, including on cooperation in peaceful uses of nuclear energy—which could not have been concluded without the commitment of Prime Minister Abe, who had faced a strong phalanx of opposition from within his own government. Under Abe, Japan also supported India's full accession to all the major international export control regimes, including the Nuclear Suppliers Group. Agreements were also signed for cooperation in areas which will define future world conflicts, such as cybersecurity and outer space. The message to the region—and the world—was unambiguous: Japan and India believed that working together in the strategic space was necessary for their respective national security and of consequence to the maintenance of peace and stability in the region.

Shinzo Abe nudged Japan out of its diffidence and complacence to engage proactively with the world. He lead his nation in strategic innovations for building a new security architecture to confront the rapidly evolving geopolitical challenges in the region. The recalibrated relationship with India in the twenty-first century had begun with his predecessors Prime Ministers Mori and Koizumi, but it was Prime Minister Abe who widened the remit and accelerated the pace of cooperation. There was no doubt that India was a very important part of his vision of the Indo-Pacific and beyond.

Abe's outreach to India was two-pronged. The first was to ensure that India was co-opted into his plans for a restructured regional order. This he did by first positioning India as a key pillar of the refashioned

Indo-Pacific space. Then, through persistence and persuasion, he made India a part of platforms and groupings such as the Quad, through which he sought to operationalize his vision of a stable and prosperous region that could challenge the projection of military and economic power by a rogue China. Bilaterally, he needed to bind India through deepened defence ties to safeguard the sea lanes of connectivity in the Indian Ocean, which were critical for the economic security of Japan.

Abe also recognized the potential of the Indian market for Japanese economic interests, including through the export of large infrastructure projects using a combination of diplomacy and ODA. As he sought to revive the Japanese economy and realize his ambition to make it a global player, he crisscrossed continents accompanied by large business delegations that had been encouraged to make forays into new markets in Asia and Africa. He saw India as a partner in the outreach to African and other nations. At the prime ministerial summit of 2018, projects were identified in Myanmar, Sri Lanka and Kenya for joint development and an India–Japan business platform envisaged to promote joint efforts for the industrial development of Africa. However, most of these initiatives have not really taken off and remain mainly as an aspiration to be realized in the future.

The other dimension of Shinzo Abe's outreach to India—borne out of his personal belief that it was 'one of the most consequential relationships' for the two countries—was his empathetic responses to India's priorities and needs. This was evident in growing ODA commitments to promote capacity building and industrial competitiveness as India embarked on nationwide training and 'Make in India' drives. At the 2015 bilateral summit, Abe announced a Japan–India 'Make in India' Special Finance Facility of USD 12 billion to promote investments from Japan. Other examples of him being cognizant of India's priorities were seen in tweaking of policy for enhanced mobility of Indian workers and professionals, visas for Indian tourists and keeping the doors to RCEP open for India for whenever it was ready to join.

Even after stepping down as Prime Minister in 2020 on health grounds, Abe lost neither his zeal for politics nor his regard for India. In April 2022, three months before his death, he took over from Mori as the chairman of the 120-year-old Japan–India Association—the oldest friendship association in Japan. He had hoped to travel to India to receive the Padma Vibhushan conferred on him by the Indian government as a mark of genuine gratitude for his contribution as the architect of India–Japan ties in contemporary times.

In his 2007 book, *Towards a Beautiful Country,* he wrote, 'It would not be a surprise if in another decade, Japan–India relations overtake Japan–US or Japan–China ties.' While his prophetic words about India and Japan are still to be realized, he did set the partnership on an irreversible course of symbiotic closeness. As External Affairs Minister Dr S. Jaishankar said at his memorial meeting, 'He had a unique role in defining and developing our contemporary relationship, taking it to a place which normally would have taken several years.' For this generation, Shinzo Abe symbolized the special nature of India–Japan ties.

10

ABE AND INDIA: A BOND BRED IN THE BONE

Suhasini Haidar

SHINZO ABE'S INTEREST IN politics was like his interest in India: it was bred in the bone. During his first official visit to India in 2007, and on every subsequent visit, he recounted a memory of hearing about India from his grandfather, former Japanese Prime Minister Nobusuke Kishi, after Kishi had travelled to India in May 1957. During a visit to Japan in 2018 by Indian Prime Minister Narendra Modi, Abe wrote an article that was published in Indian newspapers, in which he said that the warmth of India's hospitality had been shared across generations of his family from the time when the two countries were emerging from their respective occupations by the Allied forces and Britain. 'At the time when Japan was not so wealthy, Prime Minister Nehru introduced Prime Minister Kishi in front of thousands of people as the Japanese Prime Minister whom he respects,' wrote Abe. 'Engraving the history in my heart, I have devoted myself to nurturing this friendship with India.' It was a history that appeared to influence much of Abe's other policies too: from his drive to reach and stay at the top of his country's politics as Japan's longest–serving Prime Minister, his own 'conservative' political agenda and his foreign policy. His untimely death came at the hands of an assassin who blamed the Abe family's links with a religious cult for his own misfortunes.

Abe's Political Bloodlines

Throughout his career, Abe's desire to revisit and revise history, to rebuild Japanese industry, to amend his country's pacifist constitution and review its defensive strategic stance have all been put down to 'unfinished family business'. He belongs to a family steeped in Japanese political history, and counts among his relatives two former premiers: his maternal grandfather, Nobusuke Kishi—who was Prime Minister from 1957 to 1960—and his grandfather's brother, Eisaku Sato—who led the country from 1964 to 1972. His father, Shintaro Abe, was foreign minister from 1982 to 1986. Abe's paternal grandfather was also a Member of Parliament from 1937 to 1946, but was anti-war and on the opposite side of the political divide to Kishi.

The Importance of Kishi

Abe's view of relations with three key countries—China, the US and India, today the world's largest economies—were intertwined with his memory of his most famous ancestor. It is impossible, therefore, to discuss Abe's personal connection to India without going back to the past to Kishi, the controversial figure who left an indelible mark on a young Abe—who was thirty-three years old when his grandfather died in 1987.

Aftab Seth is a scholar who served as Indian ambassador to Japan from 2000 to 2003. In his book on India–Japan ties, titled *Half a Century: My Connections with Japan*, he writes: 'Kishi's time in Manchuria as an imperial official may have influenced Abe's suspicion of the Chinese. After Japan defeated China, a much bigger country, in 1895, its elite had a sense of military superiority, but also a visceral fear of what the Chinese were planning in return, and that was probably passed down to him.'[1] Shinzo Abe's close affinity with the United States and the work he put in to get to know each US President personally was also borne from his family's political leanings and was nurtured during his time studying at the University of Southern California from 1978 to 1979.[2]

Kishi's Visit to India in 1957

Abe conceptualized the 'Indo-Pacific', which involved the US in the security of Japan's neighbourhood along with fellow democracies as a counter to China. The concept was crystallized in his 'Confluence of the Two Seas'[3] speech to the Indian Parliament in 2007. In that speech, he pointed out that his address to the Indian Parliament comes exactly fifty years after Kishi's visit to India.

'Then Prime Minister Jawaharlal Nehru brought my grandfather to an outdoor "civic reception" at which tens of thousands of people had gathered, introducing him to a crowd energetically saying, "This is the Prime Minister of Japan, a country I hold in the greatest esteem." This is a story I heard as a little boy from my grandfather,' Abe told the gathered Indian MPs, adding on a poignant note, 'As the leader of a defeated nation in a war, he (Kishi) must have been very much delighted.'

Nehru went much further to welcome his guest from Tokyo, according to a report in *The Hindu* from that day:[4]

The Japanese PM was greeted by Mr. Nehru as he alighted from a special Japan Airways Skymaster at 3.10 p.m. A crowd, which had gathered at Palam (airport) to greet the visiting PM burst into shouts of 'Kishi–Nehru Zindabad' and 'Long Live Indo-Japanese Friendship'… The Japanese PM walked along the railings to acknowledge the greetings of the crowd which was singing songs of welcome. Several placards held aloft by the crowd demanded that nuclear tests must be ended. Mr. Kishi was profusely garlanded before he drove off to Rashtrapati Bhawan accompanied by PM Nehru.

Nehru and Kishi found a common purpose as leaders of countries shedding their colonial baggage. Kishi's desire to rebuild Japan as an Asian leader was imbibed by a young Abe while sitting on his grandfather's knees.

'Kishi was also the Prime Minister who launched Japan's first post-war ODA (Official Development Assistance). Japan was then still a poor country herself, but as a matter of honour we wanted to provide ODA. At that time, the country that had accepted Japan's ODA was none other than India. My grandfather never forgot that fact either,' recounted Abe of the agreements forged between India and Japan during Kishi's visit to India and Nehru's subsequent visit to Japan the same year.

According to the ODA document, Japan agreed to make available to India a credit of 18 million yen (about Rs 240 million at the time) for 'purchase of capital goods from Japan'.[5] Kishi's plan for the ODA was actually part of a wider plan he had presented for a Japan-dominated Asian Development Fund (ADF), which was to operate under the slogan 'Economic Development for Asia by Asia'. It was a precursor to the Asian Development Bank (ADB), and helped Abe's push for infrastructure finance with the Quad and the US-led Indo-Pacific Economic Forum (IPEF).

What India gave Japan in return, Abe suggested in his speech, was a sense of mutual respect and much-needed empathy for a country still nursing its wartime losses and the catastrophic atomic bombings of Hiroshima and Nagasaki. For Abe, the Indian Parliament observing a moment of silence annually on August 6—the day Hiroshima was bombed—was an important sign of a shared ethos for disarmament. In 1957, the Nehru–Kishi joint statement had also expressed the hope that 'the Big Powers concerned will reach an agreement on the eventual abandonment of tests and the prohibition of all kinds of nuclear and thermo-nuclear weapons'. Fifty years later, when Shinzo Abe decided to make a massive exception to allow a civil nuclear agreement with India—the first non-signatory to the Non-Proliferation Treaty (NPT) that Japan had chosen to do this with—it was the culmination of decades of this shared understanding.

Reviving Ties

Although India–Japan relations slumped for decades after the Kishi visit—Japan strongly condemning India's nuclear testing in 1974 and 1998—they recovered in the early 2000s, when Prime Minister

Junichiro Koizumi decided to establish closer ties with India. By then, Shinzo Abe had worked under his father in the foreign ministry and was primed for the top post. It is a little-known fact that Shintaro Abe had also visited India as foreign minister in 1984.

In December 2006, newly appointed Prime Minister Shinzo Abe received Prime Minister Manmohan Singh—a man he later referred to as his 'mentor'[6] for his insights on development economics—at the summit held in Tokyo that year. During that conference, India and Japan agreed to hold annual summits, alternating between the two countries. Apart from his successful push to revive the Quad in 2017, Abe also took forward his grandfather's ideas on development aid. When he returned to power in 2012 after battling an illness, Abe ensured that every annual India–Japan summit included a substantial number of loans and credit arrangements, beginning with the big-ticket Delhi-Mumbai Industrial Corridor (DMIC).

In 2014, when Prime Minister Singh invited Abe to be the chief guest at the Republic Day parade, he became the first Japanese Prime Minister to receive the honour. On that occasion, both sides agreed to establish the 'India–Japan Investment Promotion Partnership', and Abe pledged to realize public and private investments worth JPY 3.5 trillion and double of the number of Japanese companies in India over the next five years. In fact, Abe's acceptance of the Indian invitation to attend the Republic Day ceremonies denoted the internal shift in Japan's military posture that he wanted to demonstrate. Seth elaborates on this decision: 'After all, the Republic Day parade is India's display of its military prowess and might. Given where Japan was at the time, it would have been not quite kosher for a Japanese Prime Minister to be witness to this display. But Abe overcame that opposition and came to India, making it clear it was very important for Japan to attend.'[7]

In 2015, Prime Ministers Abe and Modi established the Japan–India 'Make in India' Special Finance Facility of JPY 1.3 trillion. Two years later, Abe visited Modi's home state of Gujarat, and the two leaders participated in the ground-breaking ceremony for the

Mumbai–Ahmedabad High Speed Rail Project that was being funded by the Japanese International Cooperation Agency (JICA).[8]

Hard-nosed Nationalism

Sujan Chinoy was India's ambassador to Japan from 2015 to 2018. He thinks that Abe's vision for India–Japan ties was driven less by 'nostalgia' by that time, and more by his worries about the imminent future as well as his 'hard-nosed nationalism'. Chinoy points out that Abe's imprint on Japan's strategic path remains strong even after his demise. The new National Security Strategy (NSS) unveiled by Abe's successor, Fumio Kishida, envisages an increase in the defence budget to 2 per cent of GDP by 2027 while improving counterstrike capabilities, cyberwarfare and air-defence capabilities and broadening the principles for the transfer of defence equipment and technology. 'What Japan is doing with its NSS today, what it is saying explicitly, is what Abe understood and said implicitly more than a decade ago,' says Chinoy.

'Economically, he could not cut his canoe from China and simply sail away, but he realized that he needed a risk-mitigation strategy and that's why he decided to include a country like India in his plans,' says Chinoy. 'In addition, while ties with the US had many pluses, it was a relationship driven totally by Washington. The special relationship with India gave Japan a certain kind of strategic autonomy, both multilaterally, as also in the Quad.'[9] Chinoy discounts the theory that Abe was guided purely by his bloodlines and his devotion to his grandfather.

Abe's Indo-Pacific dream was his 'most enduring legacy', wrote Prime Minister Modi after the Japanese leader's assassination. In a blog post tribute to his 'Dear friend Abe-San', Modi wrote about Abe's 'foresight in recognizing the changing tides and gathering storm of our time and his leadership in responding to it'. He added, 'Long before others, he, in his seminal speech to the Indian Parliament in 2007, laid the ground for the emergence of the Indo-Pacific region as a contemporary political, strategic and economic reality—a region that will also shape the world in this century.'

Kishi's Role in Manchuria

Nobusuke Kishi could not have imagined the geopolitical architecture of the world that his grandson would deal with. However, it is clear that so many of Abe's ideas and his worldview came from what he had learnt from his grandfather. Born Nobusuke Sato, he took the name Kishi from his uncle who adopted him. Kishi served as the vice-director of the industrial department in Japan's regime that ruled over the Chinese territory of Manchuria (Manchukuo) in the late 1930s.

He was known for his work on developing Manchukuo for the purposes of servicing Japan's economic and military campaigns. Apart from the Southern Manchuria Railway Line and the Showa Steel Company, Kishi pioneered the Manchurian Industrial Development Corridor (MIDC) along with the founder of Nissan, Yoshisuke Ayukawa, who was a relative as well as a friend from school.

Kishi was part of a group called 'reform bureaucrats'[10] (*kakushin kanryou*), who were tasked with building Japan's power through rapacious commerce and manufacturing regardless of the harm inflicted on the colonized populations that were employed to carry out their plans. A biography[11] of Kishi published in 1960 quotes him as saying: 'In order for resource-poor Japan to maintain itself, it must establish itself through trade. In order to establish itself through trade, industrial technology needs to be developed, and through technological superiority, industry must be developed.'

Kishi's development plans were an amalgamation of what he had learnt during stints in the US, Germany and the USSR. They involved certain chosen companies such as Nissan investing in state-directed projects and being helped with funding by the government. Nissan, which agreed to move its entire manufacturing base to Manchukuo, was provided massive loans from Japanese state banks. Years later, economists compared 'Abenomics' to Kishi's ideas, given the emphasis Abe placed on 'state-directed growth' and strengthening defences. But it was also clear that Abe didn't just want to emulate his grandfather's ideas, but to defend his record.

Kishi's time in Manchuria, and subsequently his support as a cabinet colleague to Prime Minister Hideki Tojo when he ordered the bombing of Pearl Harbour in 1941, led to Kishi being arrested as a Class A war criminal after the US defeated Japan. However, unlike Tojo—who was hanged—Kishi was cleared and freed, ostensibly by American officials keen to develop him as an ally.

Years later as Prime Minister, Kishi signed an upgraded Japan–US Security Treaty that included US guarantees to defend Japan in case it was invaded. While the treaty brought the two countries closer than ever, Kishi faced severe opposition domestically for going ahead with it—including the famous 'Anpo protests' that eventually cost him his job. This event was something his grandson often referred to with pride. During his election comeback in 2014, Abe's campaign slogan 'This is the only path' was inspired by his grandfather's words from a 2007 essay, in which Kishi wrote that he had pressed ahead with his convictions no matter how many people were opposed, because his was the only path.[12]

Mission to Exonerate the Past

In his 2006 book, *Towards a Beautiful Country*, Abe recounts the time when he had clashed with a schoolteacher who had said that Japan should scrap the security treaty with the US—the one that Kishi had negotiated. Abe admitted that his 'conservatism' was an emotional reaction to criticism of his beloved grandfather. Alexis Dudden, a professor of history at the University of Connecticut, is an expert on modern Japan and Korea. In an interview to *The New Yorker* after Abe's death, Dudden said that Abe wrote in his book about being teased as a child. This was because kids his age would taunt him about his grandfather.[13] 'So he really saw it as his mission, his destiny, to exonerate the family name and, therefore, to overturn this notion of criminality— that, at the war crimes tribunal, Japan should not have been found guilty as charged,' she added.

During his 2007 visit to India, Abe showed how important this exoneration was when he made a visit to Kolkata to meet with the family of Justice Radha Binod Pal, one of the judges overseeing the military tribunal in 1948 that investigated Japanese atrocities during the war. Justice Pal had dissented from the majority verdict and voted to acquit the Japanese officials charged with war crimes. In 2013, Abe's insistence on paying respects at the Yasukuni shrine—which has the graves of Japanese war heroes as well as convicted war criminals—courted controversy and sparked protests from China and South Korea. However, Abe was undeterred.

Abe's interest in connecting India's Northeastern states to South East Asia and in developing the Andaman and Nicobar islands may have similarly been linked to Abe's sentiments for Netaji Subhash Chandra Bose and his Indian National Army, which fought alongside the Japanese 31st Division against the British Army in 1944. Abe was scheduled to visit India in December 2019, but the trip was cancelled at the last minute because of protests over the Citizenship Amendment Act. On the trip, Abe had plans to visit Manipur and go to the site of one of the bloodiest battles fought during World War II, where more than 50,000 Japanese soldiers and members of the Azad Hind Fauj had died fighting the British Army.[14]

His special advisor, Tomohiko Taniguchi, revealed that he had even prepared Abe's speech as he had wanted 'to deeply appreciate the help and support that local people around Manipur have never ceased to give to the Japanese who wished to recover bones and remnants of the fallen soldiers, and to pay homage to the fallen'.[15] Abe's visit to India's Northeast could never be rescheduled: the COVID-19 pandemic broke out in February 2020, and in August 2020, he stepped down as Prime Minister when his ulcerative colitis resurfaced. By 2021, he had recovered but was still unable to travel to India to receive the Padma Vibhushan he was conferred for his work in strengthening India–Japan ties.

Abe's assassination in July 2022 in the Japanese town of Nara brought a brutal stop to his plans and his mission to 'exonerate' his grandfather. The man arrested for killing him was an unemployed forty-two-year old by the name of Tetsuya Yamagami. He claimed that he wanted to avenge financial losses faced by his mother, who belonged to the ultra-right anti-communist Family Federation for World Peace and Unification Church that Abe was accused of having links with. The links trace back to Nobusuke Kishi, whose Liberal Democratic Party (LDP) was known to have helped the church set up in Japan in 1958, when its first 'missionary' travelled to Tokyo. Since then, the organization has built up more followers—colloquially known as the 'Moonies'—in Japan than any other country.

Even so, the motivations behind Abe's killing remain mysterious and conspiracy theories abound, much as they did when another former Japanese Prime Minister was attacked and stabbed six times by a suspected right-wing dissenter. The victim was none other than Nobusuke Kishi, and the attack happened at the height of the protests that forced him out of office in 1960.[16] However, unlike his grandson, Kishi recovered from his injuries.

Sentimental Diplomacy

Shinzo Abe took ties with India to new levels of engagement and intensiveness, in spheres that Nobusuke Kishi couldn't have imagined having common agendas between India and Japan. Beyond the bilateral, what stood out was Abe's efforts to forge personal bonds with each of the Indian leaders of his time: Manmohan Singh was a 'mentor' that he learnt from during long conversations, and Narendra Modi was a 'close friend and partner', whom he invited to his family home in Yamanashi prefecture, where they enjoyed a fireside chat wearing the same *uwabaki* (indoor slippers).

Abe made a special effort to connect with each Indian ambassador to Japan, inviting them for special receptions. Even when out of power, he kept his connections with India by becoming president of the The Japan–India Association in Tokyo. Abe's efforts at fostering ties with India and the unique form of *omotenashi* (hospitality) that he extended to those from the country was repaid by India when Prime Minister Modi travelled to Tokyo to attended his funeral while the nation marked a day of mourning for him. It was these touches that made otherwise unsentimental diplomacy between two countries feel genuinely emotional.

In his message to Indians in 2018, Shinzo Abe drew a comparison between Kishi's public reception in Delhi to the 'overwhelmingly warm welcome' his grandson received in Ahmedabad sixty years later. He wrote, 'Immersed in the strong impression, and thinking of my grandfather's visit to India, I swore I would remain a friend of India for life.'

11

ABE'S JAPAN IN INDIA: ACTING THROUGH THE NORTHEAST

Sanjoy Hazarika

IN SEPTEMBER 2015, I was part of the large audience at the Indian Council for World Affairs (ICWA) in New Delhi listening to then Japanese foreign minister, Fumio Kishida, speak about the 'Special Partnership for the Era of the Indo-Pacific'.[1] The foreign minister referred to his visit to India as a top priority. While placing the context of his visit in the larger framework of international relations—especially the role of the two countries in the Indo-Pacific and their economies—Kishida specifically referred to the Northeast of India as a core area of collaboration, economic partnership and growth that was destined to have a larger impact on Asia.

Seven years later, the two nations agreed on the Japan–India Investment Promotion Partnership in which Japan will contribute to the 'Make in India' initiative led by Prime Minister Modi that seeks to support India in becoming a base of economic growth for the Indo-Pacific region and, ultimately, for the world. 'Moreover, it is important to strengthen connectivity between South Asia and Southeast Asia from both sea and land while strengthening economic connectivity within the South Asian region, so that these regions can form a vast economic network,' said Kishida in 2015. 'In this way, it would become possible for the entire Indo-Pacific region to achieve vital economic growth.'[2]

Setting the stage and placing the issues in that larger context, Kishida turned to the Northeast: 'Furthermore, for the enhancement of connectivity between SAARC and ASEAN, Japan will strengthen its assistance by supporting development initiatives in Northeast India, which will serve as a connective node between the two regions.'[3] It is significant that in this address, the only specific reference to any part of India that Kishida made was to the Northeast. The rest of his remarks were focused on general priorities and broad approaches.

Although Japan had had a role in limited economic projects in the Northeast region earlier, the development relationship grew greatly after the Abe–Modi summits and the personal rapport between the two leaders. As a result, today Japan is the only country apart from Germany—which has low-key economic, development and environmental cooperation partnerships with Northeastern states—to have a significant and visible presence in the region with a large and diverse range of programmes and projects. This is, as Kishida underlined, as much to do with strategic and connectivity concerns as much as with economic growth.

The Tokyo Declaration for Japan–India Special Strategic and Global Partnership of September 2014—barely four months after Narendra Modi became Prime Minister and one year before Kishida's landmark address in Delhi—put it succinctly: 'The two Prime Ministers placed special emphasis on Japan's cooperation for enhanced connectivity and development in Northeast India and linking the region to other economic corridors in India and to Southeast Asia, which would catalyse economic development and increase prosperity in the region.'

Samriddhi Roy[4] lists a series of impressive projects that various Japanese development agencies are undertaking in the region—especially in Assam, which is seen at the heart of the prospective growth story. Indeed, the visits of Japanese diplomats and development, business, economic and trade officials to the region has become frequent and the visitors have become familiar with the local people, places and issues. In May 2022, the Japanese ambassador to India, Satoshi Suzuki, took part in an international conference in Guwahati, the capital of Assam.

The conference brought together the heads of the Japan International Cooperation Agency (JICA) and the Japan Foundation as well as the foreign minister of Bangladesh and the director-general of its foreign office. Also in attendance were the finance minister of India, Nirmala Sitharaman, and S. Jaishankar, the external affairs minister, who were joined by the chief minister of Assam, Himanta Biswa Sarma.

Suzuki has also visited other parts of the Northeast to give lectures and inaugurate symposia and literature festivals. At one event last year[5] where Jaishankar was present, emphasis was placed by participants—'while highlighting the importance of the strategic India–Japan partnership'— on 'the critical role in India's Northeast—and especially the state of Assam'. This included looking at the future of Asian connectivity by linking the landmass across the Arabian Sea to the South China Sea.

'Assam was identified as the "meeting point" and "fulcrum" of such connectivity ambitions,' Roy writes. The Japanese ambassador added that the Northeast is situated where India's Act East Policy and Japan's FOIP vision converge, emphasizing the points made by Kishida in 2015.

The list of proposed projects[6] includes:

❖ A new 20-kilometre Dhubri–Phulbhari Bridge across the Brahmaputra being built with Japanese official development assistance
❖ An inland waterway project connecting Assam with Bhutan and Bangladesh
❖ A power grid that transports power to and from India's neighbours to Bihar through Assam
❖ The trilateral India–Myanmar–Thailand highway that could be stretched to Laos and Vietnam.

Moreover, the alignment of Japan's FOIP vision with India's Act East Policy is a significant boost for development in the region. For example, the India–Japan Act East Forum provides a platform to identify specific projects for the economic modernization of India's Northeast region—including those pertaining to connectivity, developmental infrastructure and industrial linkages—and to expand collaboration with Myanmar and Bangladesh.

Japan has multiple ongoing projects in the region in areas such as water supply and transport projects as well as numerous projects in other parts of the country. But as Roy points out, 'The sheer number of India–Japan (primarily JICA-funded) projects in Northeast India supersede the engagement between the two in any other part of the country.'

This is indeed a far cry from the muted Look East Policy (LEP), which was launched by the Ministry of External Affairs in 1992 and which stirred initial interest, fascination and even excitement in the region. Communities believed it to be a harkening to the past, an opening of the mythical 'eastern door', retracing and reconnecting not just historical routes and relations but also reviving cultural and ethnic moorings. To New Delhi's policymakers, it went beyond that—Prime Minister P.V. Narasimha Rao articulated it as a strategic shift in India's vision of the world and its place in the evolving world economy.

There were eye-catching events such as car rallies from Kolkata to Kunming and Guwahati to Indonesia—the latter flagged off by former Prime Minister Manmohan Singh in 2004. Major projects—such as an India–Myanmar–Thailand trilateral highway and a multimodal road and shipping route on the Kaladan river—were announced. There was also the opening of an international trade centre named after the Assam tea pioneer Maniram Dewan where trade fairs were held. Incentives and tax holidays were announced for proposed investors.

However, there appeared to be limited international and even domestic interest from the big players. The pace slowed and more focus appeared to go into research, potential collaboration, seminars and workshops. Increasing frustration set in and the media became critical of the growth of 'talk shops', despite important research work being done by prominent institutions and thinktanks at this time that served as preparation for future projects.

In addition, there appeared to be a view in the region that the LEP was targeted at the Northeast. In reality, it was a national policy driven by the vision of a different India that needed to be more strategic, economically robust, politically nimble and connected in the post-Cold War era, after the collapse of the Soviet Union on which it had been economically and militarily dependent.

A popular saying at the time was 'Look East but through the Northeast' because it was believed that the area could become a bridgehead—a stepping stone to Southeast Asia—if not the bridge itself. Building the 'bridge'—ensuring good connectivity—is especially challenging now, given that it is supposed to go across the divided and conflicted plains and uplands of our neighbour, Myanmar.

Pranab Mukherjee was the external affairs minister at the time. He announced at a gathering in Shillong that the LEP was aimed at building a bridge between India and the ASEAN countries, keeping in mind the rapid growth of the 'economic tigers' of Southeast Asia. In his remarks, Mukherjee pointed out that Myanmar was the only ASEAN country with which India shared a land border, and that was with the Northeastern states of Arunachal Pradesh, Nagaland, Manipur and Mizoram.

From being a regional dialogue partner with ASEAN in the 1990s to becoming a participant in ASEAN summits, India has grown its relationship with Southeast Asia. However, the internal conflicts in Myanmar between the ruling regime and armed ethnic groups has worsened since February 2021, when the army overthrew the elected government of Daw Aung Sang Suu Kyi. This makes outreach and trade connectivity overland with Southeast Asia extremely challenging. Until political stability and peace returns to Myanmar, the potential dividends of infrastructure building there will remain just that: potential.

≈

Among the major reasons for the slow growth of the LEP in the Northeast was internal armed insurgencies, which had been ongoing from the late 1950s and were still in the process of winding down. Few industrial groups were interested in investing in the area as extortion and violence by various armed groups remained a factor until the first decade of the 2000s. However, over the past decade, peace processes and negotiations along with strong security action and growing public fatigue with conflict has seen safety and calm return to most parts of the region.

Indeed, this new confidence was seen in Prime Minister Narendra Modi's removal of the Armed Forces Special Powers Act (AFSPA)[7] from most of Assam, many areas of Manipur and, for the first time since it was invoked in 1958, from parts of Nagaland. Earlier, the act had been removed from Meghalaya and Tripura, reflecting the growth of peace and the diminution of violence—key factors for attracting investment and pushing growth.

In 2010, the noted economist Dr Jayanta Madhab had said that the land routes to Southeast Asia would become increasingly crucial as pressure on ports and sea routes increased. He believed that the 'much-awaited destiny' of the Northeast would be a land bridge between India, China and the Pacific Rim, and that it was 'just round the corner'.[8] He saw the positive spinoffs of large infrastructure projects in local employment generation and growth of smaller businesses and ancillary industries.[9]

Even during Suu Kyi's time, as projects crept along at a snail's pace, a former Myanmar diplomat publicly expressed his irritation about the LEP at a seminar in Kolkata. I was at the event—organized by the Ministry of External Affairs (Public Diplomacy Division) and the Confederation of Indian Industry—and took note of his remarks: 'You've been looking at us for twenty years—now you know what we look like! When will you do something about it?'

Thus, when Modi announced that the Look East Policy would now be known as the Act East policy, there was a palpable sense of relief albeit mixed with some cynicism. In less than a decade since, projects and connectivity have developed at an energetic pace—although much still needs to be done. The return of peace in a region marred by nagging militancy has been a major enabling factor. The way Modi and Abe were able to infuse the Northeastern focus into different levels and departments of their respective governments was a factor in this change.

The Act East Forum was established in 2017 across ten sectors (see Appendix) including an extensive range of projects and programmes in road-building, health, skill development, training and agriculture as part of a 'comprehensive initiative for sustainable development' of the Northeastern region of India (NER). This will complement existing developmental initiatives of the state governments of NER and the Government of India.[10]

While stressing the 'power of connectivity', Suzuki said, 'It is not simply because of the geopolitical reality that exists at India's western border, but because the future of Asia lies in that direction.' He believes that the link to the east—from Bangladesh through the ASEAN countries to Japan—is the source for further growth of India and its Northeast. 'Our national highway projects—be it in Assam, Meghalaya, Mizoram or Tripura—will be extended to the border of Bangladesh,' concludes Suzuki while pointing out that Japan and India have been working on road connection improvement projects in Bangladesh as well.[11] The pace of Japanese interest, involvement and investment continued—and even increased—despite the cancellation of Prime Minister Abe's visit in 2019 due to protests in Assam and other parts of the region against the Citizenship Amendment Act. This shows the priority that both sides accord to the relationship, with NER as one of its main areas of focus (see Appendix).

One of the new areas where Japan can bring much detailed knowledge as well as expertise and experience is that of climate change. Indeed, this should be an added focus to its first scope under the Act East Forum's project working on agriculture capacity enhancement for sustainable agriculture and irrigation development in Mizoram. The scope needs to be expanded from Mizoram to other states—especially Assam, where large populations are devastated by floods and suffer crop and livestock losses, which affect their income and livelihoods. Adaptation to climate change and mitigation of adverse weather conditions must be prioritized, as these will impact all manner of on-land or water-dependent projects—whether infrastructure or agriculture—as well as health.

This is especially necessary because NER is one of the world's biodiversity hotspots and home to great rivers such as the Brahmaputra, Subansiri, Kameng, Lohit and Barak. The Brahmaputra in particular is home to a unique geographical phenomenon in which over 2,500 islands, many of them inhabited, dot its riverscape. These islands are home to poor and vulnerable communities comprising about 8 per cent of Assam's total population of 34 million. Climate change resilience based on inclusive and participatory policies needs to be built into ongoing programmes and projects.

The visible impact of uncertain weather conditions is seen in sudden storm and water surges, even as rivers continue to shrink in the winters when waterflow drops. The adverse fallout is on both humans and the ecosystems on which they depend, such as fish and river life. Climate change impacts are being felt by diverse species, including the highly endangered Gangetic river dolphins—Assam's state aquatic animal and also the national aquatic animal—and many species of birds. The success of ongoing and future projects will also be determined by how they help communities adapt to current and future life-altering changes.

≈

Japanese scholars bring an interesting focus to other issues as they delve into the past, which often is an uncomfortable process. In a recent book titled *Northeast India and Japan: Engagement through Connectivity*[12], a range of researchers engage with historical issues and concerns. Mayumi Murayama, one of the book's editors, reflects on the first contact between the people of NER and Japan—during the World War II battles of Imphal and Kohima.

'Imphal was a goal never reached by the Japanese,' writes Murayama.[13]

> Nevertheless, the Japanese Imperial Army put its footsteps on many parts of Manipur—then a princely state—and then Naga Hills in the Northeastern Frontier of British India. The battles of Manipur and Kohima strongly affected the people living in

the region.[14] Imphal, pronounced as 'Inpāru' in Japanese and combined with the term '*sakusen*' (campaign), is a familiar name among the older generation. Even for them, however, it is difficult to tell the exact location of Imphal. A greater number of people would say it is in Myanmar instead of India. The long period of seventy-five years has seen the passing of almost all war veterans who survived the battles, complicating the transfer of individual memories.

Murayama mentions that documentaries about the battles—produced by the Japanese national television (NHK) network in 2017 and 2018—were received 'unexpectedly' well. It was also unexpected that people of younger generations would show a keen interest in them. In a book compiled as the summary of the three documentaries, their producer records: 'It is the "present-ness" that war documentaries produced by non-historians must adhere to. We must keep thinking about the "present-ness" and the "universality" of the theme.'

Murayama adds that several opportunities lie beyond the obvious that reflect the Japanese sensibilities about which they remain concerned even above economic issues. These revolve around themes of the past and of culture, which runs very deep in Japanese history. Murayama also writes about collecting the remains of fallen soldiers from Nagaland and Manipur so that their families can have closure and—as per Japanese beliefs and customs—the spirits of these ancestors can find a resting place.

The relations between Japan and NER has been given a new impetus under Prime Ministers Shinzo Abe and Narendra Modi. Along with cooperation in infrastructural development, person-to-person connections—such as inviting young people of NER to Japan—have been assigned importance. The Japanese government enacted new laws on the collection of skeletal remains in March 2016, which clarify the state responsibility for this task. It decided that intensive activity in this regard would be conducted from 2016 to 2024. Official collection of skeletal remains started in Manipur and Nagaland in 2017.

With these new opportunities at hand, revisiting our common history would surely contribute to taking the interpersonal relationship between NER and Japan to a level that we were unable to reach in the past.[15] Common factors in the economic and geostrategic approaches of both countries is also noted by Takenori Horimoto, who says that Japan and India have been cooperating not only in NER but in other regions too.[16] 'The Chabahar port development in Iran is concerned mainly with India's connectivity on the western side of India: The International North–South Transport Corridor,' writes Horimoto, who points out that Japan is cooperating with India in the formation of the Asia–Africa Growth Corridor (AAGC), an economic cooperation agreement among the governments of India, Japan and several African countries. On 25 May 2017, India launched a vision document for AAGC at the African Development Bank meeting in Gujarat.

It is important to note that India–Japan collaboration has picked up despite Japan sending its delegation to a forum for 'One Belt One Road', a Chinese project that India has steadfastly opposed. In 2018, Abe had put aside several reservations expressed in Japan against the Belt and Road Initiative (BRI), declaring during a visit to China that Japan would actively participate in BRI projects.[17] Some other opportunities for better people-to-people understanding lie in exchange visits by scholars, researchers and journalists from both countries. This is partly showcased in an initiative promoting tours to war memorials and the sites of World War II. More informed tourism presents another area of greater collaboration.

The pioneers[18] of this approach are Yaiphaba Meetei Kangjam and Hemant Singh Katoch, who write[19] about how Manipur has played a proactive role in a more nuanced understanding of the war as well as the impact of the war on villagers in both Manipur and Nagaland. With the support of the Manipur government, the Manipur Tourism Forum and the Second World War Imphal Campaign Foundation have held commemorations annually. These have involved the participation of representatives from the Embassy of Japan in New Delhi—including the ambassador—as well as from the business community. British officials have also participated on occasion, such as in May 2018.

Collaborations between Manipur and Japan on other WWII-related matters have intensified since 2014. This has manifested itself in Japanese funding for a peace museum and a fully funded trip to Japan for twenty-three young talents from Manipur as part of the IRIS program in 2017. The same year also saw a visit to Manipur from the Japan Association for Recovery and Repatriation of War Casualties as part of its effort to search for the remains of Japanese soldiers who perished there during the war. Also in 2017, NHK released the first volume of a three-part documentary on the Imphal battle.

Much is being done in Manipur and Nagaland to remember the battles and keep their memory alive. Katoch and Kangjam launched Battle of Imphal Tours for foreign visitors—especially from the UK but also from Japan—who regularly travel to Imphal to see the sites of World War II battles in the vicinity. One of the most moving and significant contributions to understanding the fallout of the battles has been the establishment of a peace museum near one of the major battle sites in Manipur through funds from the Nippon Foundation. 'The museum was opened on 22 June 2019 to mark the seventy-fifth anniversary of the Imphal battle,' say the founders of the tour company. A dedicated and well-supported museum that showcases the perspectives of all sides was something that Manipur had long needed, they say, adding that local organizations such as the Manipur Tourism Forum had made a big effort to make it a reality. Their tours have been expanded to include the main war-related sites of Assam—Digboi, Ledo and Lekhapani—and Arunachal Pradesh—Stillwell Road, Jairampur and Pangsau Pass.

In NER, the battles of Imphal and Kohima of 1944 are a shared historical experience. They uniquely connect this usually overlooked region with many different parts of the world—especially Japan—in a personal and emotional way. From 1942 to 1945, hundreds of thousands of people from around the world—including the Japanese— found themselves in Northeast India. Many thousands died there, in a place far away from home—a place whose own residents had little say in the devastating events they and their land were witness to. In recent years, this rich shared historical experience and the related heritage have begun to be drawn on by the people of the region to connect with Japan in a constructive and forward-looking approach.

≈

Shinzo Abe never visited the Northeast, the region that the Japanese government now describes as one of the 'fulcrums' of both its partnership with India as well as the larger economic, social and strategic architecture of Asia. However, the initiatives and perspectives that he promoted continue to be sustained—and remain a tribute to an enduring legacy and vision.

Appendix

Act East Forum

1. India and Japan established the Act East Forum in 2017 for (i) the development of NER and (ii) to promote connectivity within this region and between this region and Southeast Asia. The forum reflects the synergy between India's Act East Policy and Japan's FOIP vision. Six meetings of the Act East Forum have already been held.

2. In accordance with this vision, India and Japan have decided to launch a comprehensive initiative for sustainable development of NER. This will complement existing developmental initiatives of the state governments of NER and the Government of India.

3. The scope of activities under the initiative will be covered under the umbrella of Act East Forum and will build on the inherent strengths of NER.

The following includes both ongoing projects and potential future cooperation to be explored:

(i) Agriculture capacity enhancement for sustainable agriculture and irrigation development in Mizoram

(ii) Development of agro-industries, especially through initiatives for strengthening bamboo value chains in NER. Food processing—including tea industries—and organic farming and horticulture projects including support for women's empowerment. The initiative will look at encouraging B2B collaboration between India and Japan for achieving these objectives

(iii) Promotion of tourism through active information outreach as well as art and cultural exchanges between NER and Japan, such as Shillong Cherry Blossom Festival in Meghalaya

(iv) Promoting skill centres—such as the Japanese Endowed Course at IIT Guwahati—and promoting Japanese language education, including through JICA's Japan Overseas Cooperation Volunteers teachers and Japan Foundation (JF) schemes. Deploying trainees and workers to Japan under the Technical Intern Training Program and Specified Skilled Worker system while exploring further JICA knowledge programmes

(v) Cooperation in development of water supply and sewerage projects in Guwahati and promotion of environment-friendly mobility while exploring the possibility of a Japan Industrial Township in Nagarbera, Assam to attract investments and promote manufacturing and further cooperation on the Kohima Smart City mission for sustainable urban development

(vi) Strengthening the health system and quality of medical education in Assam and advancing consultations on cooperation for establishing a tertiary super-specialty cancer research centre in Aizawl, Mizoram while strengthening the functions of the medical college hospital in Kohima, Nagaland

(vii) Promoting sustainable use of forest resources in ongoing projects in Tripura, Nagaland, Sikkim and Meghalaya

(viii) Development of new and renewable energy through renovation and modernization of the Umiam Umtru stage-III hydroelectric power station in Meghalaya

(ix) Applying Japanese methods introduced under the JICA's technical cooperation project for future road development while pursuing resilient connectivity through the JICA's project for maintenance of mountain highways. Conducting mock drills in disaster management and training for regional emergency management at training institutes in Kohima, Nagaland

(x)   The following are ongoing NER road network connectivity improvement projects: Phases 1–5 includes National Highways [NH] 40 and 51 in Meghalaya, NH 54 in Mizoram, NH 208 in Tripura and NH 127B in Assam; Phase 6 is the Khowai–Sabroom stretch on NH 208 in Tripura; and Phase 7 is NH 127B in Meghalaya

ABE AND THE INDO-PACIFIC

12

THE MASTERMIND BEHIND INDO-PACIFIC AND QUAD INITIATIVES

Purnendra Jain

SHINZO ABE WAS JAPAN'S longest-serving Prime Minister and one of the most distinguished international statesmen of the first two decades of this century. He was a controversial figure at home because of his conservative, nationalist views, as well as in Japan's neighbouring countries for his stated mission to amend his nation's post-war 'pacifist' constitution that restricts its military.

Yet he led his Liberal Democratic Party (LDP) to win six consecutive parliamentary elections and maintained a relatively high popularity in polls, a feat which his rivals and successors could only envy. Abe served two terms as Prime Minister. The first term was a short one from 2006 to 2007. However, the second—from 2012 to 2020—was unmatched in length in the history of Japan's parliamentary system since its first Prime Minister took office in 1885. Given this epoch-making tenure as premier, books on Abe are numerous—mostly in Japanese, but also several in English, including a full-length political biography.[1]

The controversy that surrounded Abe while in power did not leave him even in death. Japan turned bitterly divisive when learning of Abe's connection to the Unification Church, a religious cult his assassin claimed had made his family bankrupt because of its requirements of donations from its followers. Prime Minister Fumio Kishida's decision to hold a state funeral for Abe—only the second post-war Prime Minister to receive the honour—further divided the nation, as many did not see Abe deserving of a lavish expenditure of taxpayers' money.

Divided domestic public opinion aside, as the Prime Minister, Abe received accolades and praise from many global leaders because of his transformational policy on Japan's diplomacy, his vision and foresight on international political issues and his contribution to the global community through new ideas, initiatives and regional frameworks. Not only did he aim to enhance Japan's global status by initiating new policies and frameworks, but he also persuasively convinced many of his counterparts abroad to embrace his ideas and constructs. He also introduced domestic reform, created new institutions such as the National Security Council, issued Japan's first National Security Strategy, and reinterpreted the constitution to enable his government to work more closely with allies and partners in defence and security matters.

Abe was the exception in a country whose premiers are not particularly known for their global leadership, and on average hold office for about two years. Given the tributes that flowed from world leaders such as UN Secretary General Antonio Guterres and England's Queen Elizabeth II after Abe's death, it is not hard to appreciate how much respect he commanded in the global community. Words of praise recounted Abe's sterling contribution to the international stage while there was also widespread condemnation of the violent attack that prematurely ended his life.[2] In a rare joint statement issued by the leaders of the four Quad nations, they declared: 'We will honour Prime Minister Abe's memory by redoubling our work towards a peaceful and prosperous region.'[3]

Even Abe's fiercest critic, Xi Jinping of China, acknowledged that Abe made efforts to 'improve China–Japan relations' and that he had reached 'important common understanding' with Abe on 'building a China–Japan relationship that meets the need of the new era'. Russian President Vladimir Putin called him 'a prominent statesman' and affirmed that Shinzo Abe 'did a lot' to enhance 'good-neighbourly' ties between Japan and Russia.

Abe kept a busy travelling schedule, cultivating personal relationships with foreign leaders far and wide. He had the unique skill of befriending both sides in foreign political circles. For example, in the US, he engaged the Democrat Obama and the Republican Trump equally well. In India, he initially worked closely with Prime Minister Manmohan Singh and then with his successor Narendra Modi, who was from the opposing political camp to Singh. One Indian newspaper highlighted this in its headline: 'Shinzo Abe considered Manmohan Singh a mentor, Narendra Modi a friend'.[4]

Abe had wide-ranging contributions to world politics. Here we focus on two: his new geostrategic construct of the 'Indo-Pacific', and his design of a new regional partnership consisting of four leading nations of the Indo-Pacific—the United States, India, Australia and Japan—known as the Quadrilateral Security Dialogue, or 'Quad'. Both the Indo-Pacific and the Quad have transformed in scope and significance over the years and are still evolving. These initiatives were born from Abe's foresight, as he could visualize the impact of China's rise on world politics and how Japan and the world should prepare for a new assertive China.

The Seeds of the Indo-Pacific and the Quad

Indo-Pacific

Before the term 'Indo-Pacific' came into vogue in the mid-2010s and was subsequently embraced by numerous nations, the most prevalent term to identify the region was 'Asia-Pacific'. Incidentally, even the notion of Asia-Pacific and the Asia Pacific Economic Cooperation (APEC) forum were also created by Japan in association with Australia.[5] The contemporary seeds of the Indo-Pacific can be traced back to three key speeches by Shinzo Abe.

The first of these was Abe's most famous and widely cited speech: 'Confluence of the Two Seas', delivered to the Indian Parliament in 2007.[6] In that speech, Abe likened the Indian and Pacific oceans to 'seas of freedom and prosperity' and introduced the term 'Broader Asia'. Under this rubric, India's centrality was highlighted in Japan's Asia vision. Until then, India was peripheral in the Asia–Pacific construct and institutions built around it. In his speech, Abe expressed confidence that both Japan and India would 'nurture and enrich these seas'.[7] Abe's speech was prescient and his formulation finally led to the Indo–Pacific concept becoming a reality.[8]

In this context, it is worth noting that while out of power,[9] Abe visited India in 2011 and gave a speech at the Indian Council of World Affairs in New Delhi. In that speech, he again highlighted the importance of the 'confluence of the two seas' and the freedom and prosperity the region could gain through such confluence. He also used the term 'Indo-Pacific region' in this speech,[10] which is not widely circulated and relatively unknown in the strategic and international relations community circles. Notably, Abe also underlined in this speech that in Japan, both sides of politics had formed a consensus to upgrade Japan's relations with India.[11]

The second key speech was the one he gave in 2013 at the Centre for Strategic and International Studies in Jakarta. This was soon after the LDP won the general election and Abe returned as Prime Minister for his second term. Southeast Asia and ASEAN, its regional body, have always occupied a special place in Japan's foreign policy and its Asia engagement vision. Takeo Fukuda, who was Prime Minister from 1976 to 1978, had made pledges that marked the beginning of a new relationship with ASEAN.

In the Jakarta speech, Abe outlined the direction of Japan's foreign policy and called ASEAN a linchpin of Japan's diplomatic strategy, assuring his audience that Japan remained fully engaged with ASEAN. He underlined the need for 'keeping Asia's seas unequivocally open, free and peaceful' and noted the importance of the United States, which, according to him, was 'shifting its focus to the confluence of the two oceans, the Indian and the Pacific'.[12]

Abe's third key speech was in 2016 at the sixth Tokyo International Conference on African Development (TICAD) in Nairobi, where he clearly articulated his 'Free and Open Indo-Pacific' (FOIP) concept. This speech was not much noted in diplomatic circles, but it is here

Abe stated that '[W]hat will give stability and prosperity to the world is none other than the enormous liveliness brought forth through the union of two free and open oceans and two continents. Japan bears the responsibility of fostering the confluence of the Pacific and Indian Oceans and of Asia and Africa into a place that values freedom, the rule of law and the market economy, free from force or coercion, and making it prosperous.'[13]

In these speeches and other writings, Abe pushed his new narrative of the Indo-Pacific beyond the extant construct of the Asia-Pacific. He identified India as a central player in his vision of the Indo-Pacific region—which, according to him, should remain open, free and peaceful, and become prosperous based on the rule of law.

The Quad

The Quad's origin is often traced to the cooperation between Australia, Japan, India and the United States in response to the Boxing Day tsunami in December 2004. These nations responded swiftly by harnessing their resources and working cooperatively towards humanitarian assistance and disaster relief.

The joint mission heralded a new-found synergy that gradually turned into a four-nation framework which was named the Quadrilateral Security Dialogue, and referred to as the Quad. It was first led by Prime Minister Shinzo Abe after he took office for his first term in September 2006. In a joint statement issued in December 2006 after their summit meeting, Prime Ministers Abe of Japan and Singh of India expressed their desire to begin a dialogue with 'other like-minded countries in the Asia-Pacific region on themes of mutual interest'. Note here the use of 'Asia-Pacific', which was still the main term in vogue. In his book *Utsukushii Kuni E (Towards a Beautiful Country)*—published before he became Prime Minister—Abe had proposed an elevation of the informal Japan–US–Australia–India taskforce to a formal leaders' summit.

Japan had also explored the concept of the 'arc of freedom and prosperity', proposed by Abe's foreign minister, Taro Aso. It was essentially a value-based concept and involved far too many nations. Although this idea has faded slowly, it has not died—as freedom, prosperity and democracy have always been featured in Abe's speeches.

Abe mentioned this 'arc' in his address to the Indian Parliament in 2007, as India was considered a valuable member of this concept. Furthermore, under his 'Broader Asia' concept—which would include India and Japan—Abe foreshadowed a 'network spanning the entirety of the Pacific Ocean, incorporating the United States of America and Australia'. India was of particular interest to Abe, and he had already outlined its importance in his 2006 book. Bringing India, Japan, Australia and the US into one strategic grouping was Abe's definite idea and mission, as he was concerned by how China was rising and asserting itself as a hegemonic power. Although Abe engaged China as well as he could, he was cautiously and astutely building a coalition of like-minded nations to deal with the China challenge. It was no coincidence that in 2007 Japan joined the Malabar naval exercise for the first time together with Australia, keeping with the proposal of a Quad grouping.

However, this iteration of the Quad did not progress, and the idea was put on ice as new leaders took charge in Canberra, Tokyo and Washington. Meanwhile, Beijing vigorously criticized the concept and called it an 'Asian NATO' directed against China. There was little political and strategic appetite among the proposed member nations to move the construct closer to realization without its champion, Abe.

Just before he took office for the second time, Abe penned an article titled 'Asia's Democratic Security Diamond', which essentially sent out a message to global leaders of his intention to relaunch the Quad. When Abe returned as Prime Minister in 2012, the Quad got a new lease of life. Through his efforts, it became fully active in 2017 and within two years had already held three meetings at the top level. It was the framework that Abe had envisaged back in 2006.

Trajectory of the Indo-Pacific and the Quad

Even after his sudden resignation from the post of Prime Minister in September 2007, Abe did not give up on his idea of the importance of the meeting of the two oceans nor on the security framework involving India, the US, Japan and Australia. During his speech in 2011 to the ICWA, Abe put both ideas before his Indian audience and asked them to 'work even more closely together, with the US, Australia and other maritime democracies' to build a 'robust, open, liberal, safe and stable' Asia.

In his essay published by *Project Syndicate* in 2012, Abe emphasized the deep connection and inseparability of the Indian and Pacific Oceans from trade and economic perspectives, which clearly also have strategic implications. He wrote:

> Peace, stability and freedom of navigation in the Pacific Ocean are inseparable from peace, stability and freedom of navigation in the Indian Ocean. Japan, as one of the oldest sea-faring democracies in Asia, should play a greater role—alongside Australia, India and the US—in preserving the common good in both regions.[14]

The Japanese government was relatively slow to promote the Indo-Pacific concept in Japan and to incorporate the narrative in its official documents. Although Japanese thinktanks and research institutes issued reports on the Indo-Pacific concept and its value, there was very little known about the term in wider circles in Japan even in 2015,[15] when India and Japan elevated their bilateral relations to that of 'Special Strategic and Global Partnership'. It was a key relationship with the largest potential for growth into a deep, broad-based and action-oriented partnership.[16]

A joint statement titled 'India and Japan Vision 2025' pointedly mentioned New Delhi and Tokyo's 'unwavering commitment to realize a peaceful, open, equitable, stable and rule-based order in the Indo-Pacific region and beyond'. It also added that India and Japan 'uphold the principles of sovereignty and territorial integrity; peaceful settlement of disputes; democracy, human rights and the rule of law; open global trade regime; and freedom of navigation and overflight'. The term 'Indo-Pacific' was used in the declaration to show that both Japan and India formally accepted this term.

Global Leaders Embrace the Indo-Pacific

In 2016, Abe added two adjectives before 'Indo-Pacific' to make it a 'free and open' Indo-Pacific. This seemed to have created a little apprehension in New Delhi. Modi's Shangri-La speech showed hesitancy in accepting the addition of the word 'free' to the Indo-Pacific concept as he talked about India's special relationship with Russia and strong and stable relations with China—neither is 'free' in their governance structure. Modi's adjectives did not include 'free' in his statement, which mentioned 'an open, stable, secure and prosperous Indo-Pacific region'.

Modi added that 'India does not see the Indo-Pacific region as a strategy or as a club of limited members' and therefore India's vision for the region is 'a positive one'. He concluded by saying, 'India's own engagement in the Indo-Pacific region—from the shores of Africa to that of the Americas—will be inclusive.' [17] In other words, Modi advocated an inclusive Indo-Pacific where each member has its role regardless of its governance style. Modi's speech was delivered just before the Doklam crisis between India and China at the Bhutan tri-junction, and much before the Galwan valley clash in mid-2020—after which India decided to change its approach towards China.

The most enthusiastic supporter of the Indo-Pacific has been Australia, the largest island nation that is surrounded by both the Pacific and the Indian Oceans.[18] As early as 2013, an Australian defence white paper had observed that 'a new Indo-Pacific strategic arc is beginning to emerge, connecting the Indian and Pacific Oceans through Southeast Asia'. The white paper further noted that the Indo-Pacific was still emerging as a system and that 'Australia's security environment will be significantly influenced by how the Indo-Pacific and its architecture evolves'.[19]

In 2017, an Australian foreign office white paper had a whole chapter on 'a stable and prosperous Indo-Pacific'. Australia was a great champion of the Asia-Pacific notion, but ditched it early on in favour of the Indo-Pacific. It could see the value of the Indo-Pacific as a geostrategic construct.

The United States under Obama was warming up to the notion of the Indo-Pacific, but Abe was even able to sell his concept to Trump—not an easy customer by any means. During the Trump administration, the US embraced the term Indo-Pacific in military terms and changed the name of the US Pacific Command to 'US Indo-Pacific Command' in 2018. The term was also accepted by Trump's successor, Joe Biden, whose administration issued its Indo-Pacific strategy document in 2022.[20]

This strategy advocated advancing a 'free and open Indo-Pacific', a phrase that Abe had used in 2016 during his speech in Kenya. While collaboration with regional allies and partners is emphasized, the background to it is the growing strategic competition between the US and China and the need for the US to create a network of allies and partners to maintain its domination, if not hegemony.

Although Abe presented a case for the Indo-Pacific to ASEAN members, they have been reluctant to endorse the concept as the member states don't want to choose sides—they prefer to stick with the Asia-Pacific construct as that brings China and other Pacific nations into the mix. The thirty-fourth ASEAN summit held at Bangkok in 2019 saw the release of the 'ASEAN Outlook on Indo-Pacific', in which member states acknowledge the Indo-Pacific but do not embrace it, instead wanting to maintain ASEAN-centred regional architecture.

Abe's construct of the Indo-Pacific has gained wider currency in many European nations. The twenty-seven members of the EU endorsed a 'strategy for cooperation in the Indo-Pacific', which was issued in April 2021. Individual European states have also issued their Indo-Pacific strategies. France was the first to publish its Indo-Pacific strategy in 2018. Germany issued its 'policy guidelines on the

Indo-Pacific' in 2020, and the Dutch government followed suit. In early 2021, the United Kingdom's integrated review of security, defence, development and foreign policy announced that the UK would 'tilt' towards the Indo-Pacific.[21]

Abe Resurrects the Quad

While Abe's Indo-Pacific developed linearly from its initial conception in 2007 to Abe's speech at Nairobi in 2016, the Quad moved in an odd fashion. Its first iteration was ditched by leaders of its member nations, with Australian Prime Minister Kevin Rudd formally announcing withdrawal from it. It was due to Abe's hard work and his deep commitment to the vision of Japan playing a lead strategic role in the Indo-Pacific that the Quad was not only resurrected but elevated from the official and ministerial levels to a premier-level summit. The most recent of these summits was held in Tokyo in April 2022.[22]

The Quad re-emerged when Abe invited officials of each member country to meet in Manila in 2017. The seniority level of the meeting was subsequently elevated in September 2019 and foreign ministers were invited to a second face-to-face meeting, which was held in Tokyo in October 2020. After Biden entered office, the Quad meeting progressed further to a premier-level summit in March 2021—although it was held as a virtual conference because of the ongoing pandemic. In September of that year, Biden convened a face-to-face meeting of the Quad leaders in Washington, D.C. However, Abe had already resigned from office by the time this first premier-level meeting was held.

US President Joe Biden, Japanese Prime Minister Yoshihide Suga, Australian Prime Minister Scott Morrison and Indian Prime Minister Narendra Modi declared in a joint statement that 'the Quad is a force for regional peace, stability, security and prosperity' and stated their commitment 'to refocus ourselves and the world on the Indo-Pacific and on our vision for what we hope to achieve'. The statement went further to state that the countries together 'recommit to promoting the free, open, rules-based order' that was 'rooted in international law and undaunted by coercion, to bolster security and prosperity in the Indo-Pacific and beyond'.

Tokyo hosted the second premier-level Quad meeting. There had been changes in leadership in Tokyo and Canberra: in Japan, Suga had been replaced by Kishida from his own party, the LDP; in Australia, Anthony Albanese from the Labour Party had replaced Scott Morrison from the Liberal-National Coalition. Not only had some leaders changed, but the meeting was also held in the shadow of Russia's invasion of Ukraine—a conflict on which India's position differed from the other three Quad members. However, neither the changes in leaders nor India's differing approach on the Ukraine conflict dampened the Quad spirit.

Future of the Indo-Pacific and the Quad

In June 2022, a month before his assassination, Abe wrote a brief commentary in Japanese. It was later translated into English and published posthumously in October 2022 on *Project Syndicate* pages and republished in *The Japan Times*.[23] In it, Abe outlines his initiatives in introducing the 'free and open Indo-Pacific' concept and his role in forming the Quad and notes that 'the concept of a free and open Indo-Pacific has become a major turning point in global security policy'. On the Quad, he observes that 'Japan, the US, Australia and India have forged an extremely important framework for countering the threat [China]' but stresses that 'it is important to deepen our ties with countries that share our values, including European countries'. He alludes to expanding membership of the Quad by working with other partners and allies that agree with the broad principles behind the Indo-Pacific and the Quad.

Unfortunately, the great strategist and visionary Abe is no more. He gave a new way of thinking and a new identity to his nation and created a grouping of key nations that has now attracted international attention. One keen observer of Japanese politics—who is also Abe's biographer—has called him an 'iconoclast' because of his unconventional thinking and ideas. His transformative domestic policies created new security institutions and drove Japan towards strategic initiatives that would serve its own interests as well as those of its allies and partners.[24]

Abe's concepts of the Indo-Pacific and the Quad are valuable strategic assets for the global community. It is now up to Abe's successors in Japan and the leaders of the Indo-Pacific region to ensure that both remain defining features of international relations for years to come. However they turn out, Shinzo Abe's imprint on these ideas and structures will remain forever on the pages of history.

13

SHINZO ABE AND THE INDO-PACIFIC: BEYOND A QUASI-ALLIANCE

Kanti Bajpai

SHINZO ABE'S CONCEPT OF the Indo-Pacific and his curating of the Quadrilateral Security Dialogue (Quad) are, along with the Belt and Road Initiative (BRI), the most important strategic initiatives in Asia of the past three decades. His two initiatives outrank the East Asia Summit (EAS) and perhaps also the Australia–UK–US (AUKUS) agreement. On the economic side, the most crucial initiatives are Japan's Comprehensive and Progressive Agreement for Trans-Pacific Partnership (CPTPP) and ASEAN's Regional Comprehensive Economic Partnership (RCEP). Tellingly, there are no Indian initiatives in the region that are of much consequence. India remains preoccupied with remaking itself and in any case is too weak militarily and economically to do much in Asia outside South Asia. Leadership in Asia resides with the US, Japan and China, and to some extent Australia and ASEAN.

In India, much of the discussion on the Indo-Pacific and Quad was preoccupied with Abe's outreach to New Delhi, as the former Japanese Prime Minister saw India as the only country big enough to be a counterbalance to China in the long run. That India was democratic made it a good fit for a quasi-alliance against China. I suggest, though, that the concepts of the Indo-Pacific and Quad were much more sophisticated than a mere balancing coalition against China—and indeed, as it developed, the Abe initiative took a far longer-term strategic view than a balance-of-power approach. India was on Abe's mind, but there was much more on his mind than India, at least in part because he had a shrewd understanding that New Delhi, under either the Congress or the BJP, was never going to be much of a player in the East Asian theatre of the Indo-Pacific. India was only symbolically important, with the potential—if it ever reached its potential—of playing a more material role at some point in the future.

To comprehend the scope of what Abe was hoping to do, we need to locate his views in Japan's strategic debates, particularly in the early 2000s, and then to trace through his various pronouncements on the Indo-Pacific. We then need to try to relate his thinking to earlier, foundational ideas and practices after World War II.

Before doing that, I should be clear that this essay is broadly about the Indo-Pacific idea, and it uses that locution to refer to both the concepts of Free and Open Indo-Pacific (FOIP) and the Quadrilateral Security Dialogue (Quad) to avoid awkward repetitions such as 'the Indo-Pacific and Quad'. I should also add here that I am not a Japan specialist nor an expert in India–Japan relations, so everything I say should be read with that caveat in mind.

The Development of an Idea

To see where Abe was coming from strategically, we must understand where he stood in the Japanese strategic debate. Tracing Japanese strategic thinking and practice is revealing when we consider what he was attempting to do. We need to begin with the Yoshida Doctrine, which guided Japanese grand strategy during the Cold War and remains a cornerstone. The doctrine rested on three pillars for Japan's post-war security: the centrality of a military alliance with the US; the constraints on the Japanese military, which could only be purposed for defensive duties but not offensive action or out-of-area operations; and the rebuilding of Japan economically. An economically strong Japan would help make it and the region more secure and contribute to the alliance with the US. With the end of the Cold War, it was the first pillar that increasingly came under question: since the Soviet Union was no longer a strategic competitor, what was Japan's reliance on the US about?

Fairly soon, the answer was evident: by the late 1990s, the rise of China suggested that the US and Japan faced a new rival. Yet, clearly, the rivalry with China was different. Both the US and Japan were heavily involved with China economically. An increasingly assertive China in Asia was a challenge, even more so for Japan than the US. By 2006, the Chinese were challenging Japanese claims to the Senkaku Islands. Tokyo now faced the issue of a live conflict with Beijing. From 2001, Prime Minister Junichiro Koizumi had begun to reassess Japanese grand strategy. With the relative decline of the US and the rise of China, the question was whether Japan could rely on the US for its security. The long-term forecasts were that China would surpass the US economically within fifteen years. Japan's own economy was in seemingly endless stagnation, and China had already steamed past it in terms of GDP.

If the US was in relative decline and Japan was stagnating, the two allies now had to combine to deal with a rapidly rising China. Koizumi saw two things clearly. First, Japan had to take on more responsibility strategically. The way to do this—given the memories in Asia and elsewhere about Japanese militarism during World War II—was for it to partner with the US not just in Asia but also globally as part of burden sharing. Second, Japan had to become a more 'normal' country militarily. At least one expression of Koizumi's views about Japan as a normal country was his controversial decision to visit the Yasukuni Shrine, which honoured Japanese soldiers who had died in the war.

Abe was Koizumi's chief cabinet secretary from 2005 to 2006 and soon replaced him as Prime Minister. He was a political conservative and a revisionist about aspects of Japan's wartime policies. Koizumi's less apologetic stance on war-related matters and his desire to chalk out a more global partnership with the US—instead of one that focused only on East Asia—were attractive to Abe. The challenge was how to achieve that aim.

Abe found an ally in Taro Aso, who was Koizumi's foreign minister at the time and who stayed on for a year in the foreign ministry under the new Prime Minister. Aso was a member of the deeply conservative and revisionist Nippon Kaigi, an organization that had Abe as its parliamentary league advisor. Together with senior advisors, Abe and Aso plotted a new grand strategic course that carefully and shrewdly built on various legacies and streams of strategic thought.[1] The climax of their efforts was the Indo-Pacific concept. Perhaps the founding moment, or opening move, was Taro Aso's speech on 30 November 2006 at the Japan Institute of International Affairs. In the speech, he stated that Japan would support an 'arc of freedom and prosperity' based on a 'value-oriented diplomacy' that endorsed the ideas of 'democracy, freedom, human rights, rule of law and the market economy'. Aso proposed that Japan would design this 'arc' along the Eurasian rim.[2]

This was a hugely ambitious statement: in Aso's conception, the rim included Japan, Southeast Asia (specifically Cambodia, Laos and Vietnam), Central Asia, the Caucasus, Ukraine, Turkey, Central and Eastern Europe and the Baltic states. Aso stated that Japan would also strengthen its ties with Australia, India, the US and the EU nations, which he referred to as 'friendly nations that share common views and interests'. In almost an afterthought, he devoted one paragraph to India to note that relations with it were underdeveloped. The invocation of the idea of the Eurasian rim signalled a geopolitical view: if there is a rimland, there must be a heartland. The heartland to Aso's rimland could only be China and Russia.

Here then was a very public statement of Japan's strategic vision: Tokyo would lead an economic and political stabilization of the rimlands. Though Aso's speech did not contain the term 'Indo-Pacific', the evocation of a 'rim' pointed to a connecting of the Indian and Pacific oceans. What is striking about his description of Japan's role in constructing the rimland arc is that it was couched in terms of economic aid from Tokyo and its assistance in capacity building in legal and judicial systems. Japan could not play a role similar to the US and aim to be a diplomatic–military leader in these regions and countries; instead, it could play to its strengths in supplementing US and European efforts with capacity building and development aid.

Aso's speech was followed by various interventions by Abe. Interestingly, Abe was allusive and succinct and never made a long statement on his idea of the Indo-Pacific.[3] Nor is there an official Japanese statement—at least not in English—that lays out the rationale for the initiative at any length. Indeed, the US, Australia, Indonesia and ASEAN have much more extensive statements on their conceptions of the Indo-Pacific. Similarly, except for Narendra Modi's speech at the Shangri-La Dialogue in 2018, there is no detailed official Indian statement on the Indo-Pacific. It could be that Japan and India are simply not in the habit of writing publicly available policy papers on issues such as this.

The grand strategy baton was passed to Abe, who first shared his idea of the Indo-Pacific in his speech—titled 'Confluence of the Two Seas'—at India's Parliament on 22 August 2007. In the speech, he explicitly connected the Indian and Pacific oceans—though again not using the term 'Indo-Pacific'—and invited India to work with Japan as they shared 'fundamental values such as freedom, democracy and the respect for basic human rights' as well as 'strategic interests'. The incipient 'Strategic Global Partnership' with India was vital—as maritime states, the two countries had convergent interests in securing the shipping routes along the rimland.

Yet, most of Abe's speech was not about a strategic partnership in a military sense. Instead, he spoke more about the historical links between the two countries and Japan's role in India's economic development. Abe was testing the waters in search of a bigger role for Japan beyond East Asia (as announced in the Aso speech), for which he hoped to get India to work with Japan, Australia and the US in what he termed 'Broader Asia'.[4] He avoided reference to a strategic-military partnership because he did not want to alarm the international community. Nor did he want to startle timid Indian decision-makers who are often trepidatious about joining any strategic-minded clubs. He eventually played his strategic and military card by trying to revive the Quad.

The idea soon collapsed because neither Australia nor India wanted to anger China, but Abe remained undeterred, even though he somewhat backed off the strategic elements of the Indo-Pacific. In time, he would make the Quad a reality.

The Indo-Pacific idea needed US acquiescence and support, but it was a challenge to convince Washington. Regardless of the government in charge, the US would have concerns about factors such as: growing Japanese strategic autonomy; any dilution of its alliance with Japan; possible hostility from China; and the reception of the idea in other Asia nations given Japan's wartime past. That said, the US was keen on greater burden sharing, and the Indo-Pacific concept offered a solution. With it, Japan and the US could develop a grand strategic division of labour in which the US would be the military security provider and Japan the economic security provider in Asia and beyond. Hilary Clinton used the term 'Indo-Pacific' in 2010, indicating that by then the Americans were already cognizant and supportive of the Japanese initiative. However, they were not yet taking it as seriously as they were to do in the years ahead.[5]

On 27 December 2012, Abe published an article that outlined his intentions to enlarge the scope of the Indo-Pacific idea. Titled 'Asia's Democratic Security Diamond', the article argued for Australia, India, Japan and the US to form a security grouping in Asia. Abe underlined the importance of India to the grouping and also urged France and the UK to return to Asia as security providers. Some years later, those two European powers—as well as Germany—would heed his call.[6] Aso's 'arc of freedom and prosperity' in 2006 had envisaged Japan cooperating with the US, Europe and NATO in stabilizing the rimlands of Eurasia. Abe's 'security diamond' returned to the theme of European involvement. Japan once again was taking a more global view of peace and security than had been the case up to that point.

The next important intervention by Abe in his construction of the free and open Indo-Pacific was not till January 2013, when he was due to deliver a speech in Jakarta. Before he could make his address, a hostage crisis in Japan forced him to return to Tokyo. However, the text of the speech was made public. In it, Abe argued that in the context of the 'confluence of the two oceans', Japan and ASEAN 'must work together side by side to make our world one of freedom and openness, ruled not by might but by law'.[7]

This was followed by arguably the pivotal statement on the Indo-Pacific concept. It was Abe's speech in Kenya, delivered on 27 August 2016 at the Tokyo International Conference on African Development (TICAD).[8] While Aso's 'arc of prosperity' speech had left out Africa and Latin America (though it had acknowledged the importance of both continents), by 2016 Abe had understood that Africa—with its growing population, surging economic growth and enormous natural resources—was a crucial region.

Chinese influence and investments in Africa were by then the talk of international politics. Beijing's massive BRI project had already begun in 2013, encompassing much of maritime and continental Asia but also key countries in Africa, where China had growing economic stakes. If Japan's larger global role was to mean anything, it could hardly ignore Africa—a place where the Asian heartland state, China, was making considerable political, strategic and economic inroads.

Since the Indian Ocean reaches the shores of East Africa all the way down to southern Africa, the African continent had to be part of the Japanese Indo-Pacific initiative. Again, it bears repeating that Tokyo's engagement would be primarily economic: ODA (particularly in health and education); encouragement of private investment; building quality infrastructure and connectivity; human resource development; and capacity building in the private sector (using kaizen practices).

Finally, Abe made a crucial visit to US President-elect Donald Trump, just days after the candidate's electoral victory. During this visit, it is likely that the Japanese Prime Minister promised that his nation would be a more active and burden-sharing partner of the US. The following year, Japanese officials were energetically selling the idea of FOIP to their US counterparts. By October 2017, US Secretary of State Rex Tillerson was already publicly referring to the 'Indo-Pacific',[9] and the very next month, Trump used the term in his remarks at the APEC

CEO Summit.[10] By 2018, the US had changed the name of its erstwhile Pacific Command to the 'Indo-Pacific Command' to align with the new strategic conception. Finally, in June 2019, the US Department of Defence unveiled its new Indo-Pacific strategy report.[11] The FOIP concept has continued to be part of the US's Asia policy under President Joe Biden, even though it has changed in focus and substance.

In sum, Abe's vision for the Indo-Pacific was a coalition of leading military powers in an expanded region spanning maritime Asia. Outside China and the two Koreas, Australia, India, Japan and the US are the biggest military players in Asia. The coalition was intended not just as a coming together militarily of these four powers; in Tokyo's view, the grouping was also a diplomatic coalition that would coordinate and combine in regional and multilateral forums.

The central objective of the grouping was to deal with China. Whatever the four powers may say to the contrary publicly, the Indo-Pacific was—and remains—a military and diplomatic coalition aimed primarily against China. However, when Japan and its three partners say that they are not attempting to contain China, they are being truthful. US containment during the Cold War foresaw the defeat and dissolution of the Soviet empire. The Indo-Pacific powers are not plotting the strategic defeat or break-up of China or even the demise of the Communist Party of China; rather, they are committed to deterring and defending against an aggressive and expansionist China. Despite Beijing's fulminations, the Indo-Pacific is defensive in intent.

The Indo-Pacific initiative was also a means of building greater trust between the four constitutive powers. The coming together of Australia, India, Japan and the US may seem 'natural' and seamless given the common threat of Chinese power, but in fact there is a history of mistrust. Australia and Japan fought each other during World War II. India and Japan were on opposing strategic sides during the Cold War and have had differences over nuclear matters as well. Australia, too, was on the opposite side to India for much of the Cold War, and in the 1980s, it was critical of India's naval expansion. While India and the US have certainly become closer since 2001, they have little experience of working together either in the Indian Ocean or the Pacific. In short, trust between the quadrilateral of powers was not a given.

While Abe's Indo-Pacific idea presented itself as a military-diplomatic strategic initiative, it was always more than that. In November 2019, a document released by the Japanese Ministry of Foreign Affairs—titled 'Towards a Free and Open Indo-Pacific'—reviewed Japan's contributions in the following areas: promotion and establishment of the rule of law, freedom of navigation and free trade; pursuit of economic prosperity; and commitment to peace and stability. The document details Japan's financial and other contributions to countries in Asia, Africa and Oceania in a broad range of areas: economic, developmental, connectivity, infrastructure, environment and disaster management, maritime security, health security, governance capacity building, legal system reforms, energy investment and public–private partnerships in sustainable infrastructure (such as the Blue Dot Network with Australia and the US).[12]

Since the Indo-Pacific does not constitute an alliance, what is the strategic rationale for the grouping? In essence, it is an exercise in what experts in international relations call 'soft balancing'—a coalition that avoids a head-on, direct confrontation and instead seeks to complicate the strategy of an opponent by promoting norms of appropriate international behaviour, by constantly creating doubts and uncertainties in the opponent's decision-making and by placing obstacles in the way of its diplomatic outreach.[13] Beyond this, the Indo-Pacific signals that Australia, India, Japan and the US could abandon their quasi-alliance and turn it into a formal alliance if China continues to be aggressive and if soft balance does not work. Soft balancing could then be replaced by 'hard balancing'—i.e., military-economic opposition.

Another rationale for the Indo-Pacific grouping is to build a looser coalition of secondary states, particularly in Asia. The aim is not to band together these other states in a united military-diplomatic front against China but instead to deny them to Beijing—to have them continue sitting on the fence and exploiting Chinese economic largesse while remaining politically and diplomatically independent. Put differently, the Indo-Pacific's value-based engagement as well as economic and capacity-building efforts are directed to help Asian nations maintain their unique identities and develop economically so that they do not fall into a Chinese sphere of influence.

The Roots of the Indo-Pacific Idea

What are the roots of Abe's FOIP idea? While credit is due to Abe and Aso for developing the concept, notions such as these arise from older and deeper roots. It is important to understand those roots because the more embedded an idea is in a larger strategic culture, the more likely it is to endure. Japan scholars will have a better sense of this, but as an interested outsider that pays some attention to Japanese affairs, I would point to three historical sources: grand strategy orientations; Japan's notion of comprehensive security going back to the 1950s; and its human security concepts and policies in the 1990s.

Richard Samuels, in his influential book *Securing Japan: Tokyo's Grand Strategy and the Future of East Asia*, argues that the Japanese strategic community has four leading grand strategic conceptions that can be depicted in relation to two axes. The first axis is the disposition towards the US alliance—for and against. The second axis is the disposition towards the use of force internationally—for and against. The result is four grand strategies: normal nationalism, middle-power internationalism, neo-autonomism and pacifism.

Normal nationalists are for the US alliance and for the gradual normalization of Japan's defence capabilities from a purely defensive force to a more all-spectrum one (but without nuclear weapons). Middle-power internationalists are for the US alliance but want to preserve Japan's defensive military posture. They envisage security not just based on the alliance but also on functional cooperation with other middle powers. They also regard economic prosperity as a bedrock of security. Neo-autonomists, by contrast, oppose the alliance with the US and want Japan to be strategically independent. They would want to build Japan into a first-rate military power prepared to use force in the service of its interests. Finally, pacifists oppose both the alliance with the

US and Japan's use of force and want to rely on economic prosperity to provide security.[14]

At any given time, Japanese grand strategic preferences are some combination of the four schools. This is the case because domestic politics encourages compromises and hybrid approaches even if there are conceptual and practical tensions as a result. It is not surprising then that the Indo-Pacific idea reflects a 'Goldilocks' position: a middle position between conservative normal nationalists and neo-autonomists, on one side, and liberal middle-power internationalists and pacifists, on the other.

Abe's Indo-Pacific concept was premised on the continuation of the alliance with the US and a normalization of Japan's military capabilities and missions. But it sought to compensate for the relative decline of the US—and to hedge against its possible retreat from Asia—by constructing a coalition that included two regional powers: Australia and India. And by embedding Japan in a larger grouping, it sought to disarm domestic opponents of Japanese normalization as a military power and to reassure nations in Japan's neighbourhood that would fear a militarily resurgent Japan. These moves were consistent with the preferences of normal nationalists and to some extent neo-autonomists.

By contrast, the features of the second element of the Indo-Pacific idea—value-based engagement, functional cooperation, economic aid and capacity building in a larger Asia around the Indian and Pacific Oceans—are closer to the preferences of middle-power internationalists and pacifists. While middle-power internationalists accept the alliance with the US, they want more functional cooperation with a range of countries (including China) as well as economic diplomacy to keep Japan safe. Pacifists would oppose the Indo-Pacific as being too alliance-like, but they would go along with the value-based engagement and economic diplomacy of Abe's initiative.

The Indo-Pacific can also be related to Japanese notions of comprehensive security (to be distinguished from 'comprehensive national power'). Comprehensive security went through several phases after World War II. In the 1950s it encompassed five elements: a reliance on the US alliance and an aversion to military instruments; the use of

Japanese business links for diplomatic purposes; the use of transnational socioeconomic activities to influence other states; recognizing the China–US–Japan strategic triangle as the defining matrix of Japanese security concerns; and the importance of Southeast Asia and Oceania for Japan's security and wellbeing.[15]

In the early 1970s, the 'triple shock'—the US–China rapprochement, relinquishing of the gold standard by the US and the oil crisis of 1973—changed Japan's comprehensive security view. Tokyo understood that to continue to anchor the US in their alliance after the change in the American relationship with China, it had to shoulder a larger military burden without alarming other Asian nations about Japanese 'militarism'. In addition, there needed to be economic engagement not just with Southeast Asia and Oceania but also with Communist China. Given its growing economic strength, Japan would also use trade and Japanese private investment along with ODA to promote the cause of peace and security worldwide.[16]

The Indo-Pacific sits comfortably with Japan's comprehensive security notions and policies. The Indo-Pacific's rationale is the rise of China since the early 2000s. It is premised on the continuing centrality of Japan's alliance with the US and a limited role for Japanese defence forces—even though Japan's military is now far more capable and has expanded its role. Comprehensive security identified China as the main strategic challenge for Japan as early as the 1950s. It placed the US alliance front and centre and saw Japan's defence forces in a limited role.

The Indo-Pacific recognizes that the relative decline of the US entails Japan enlarging its role not just in Asia but also globally and building links with key powers beyond its neighbourhood as well as smaller states in East Asia and the Pacific islands. Particularly after the three shocks of the early 1970s, Japanese comprehensive security entailed taking on a larger role. One of the key results of the reorientation was the Fukuda Doctrine, which laid emphasis on Japan's relations with neighbouring countries, particularly in Southeast Asia. The Indo-Pacific's economic and capacity-building components in the larger region find a counterpart in comprehensive security's economic diplomacy, particularly in Southeast Asia.

The Indo-Pacific also incorporated elements of Japan's human security thinking. After the Cold War, Japan had to become aware of a range of 'social hazards' that could undermine peace and stability in its region and farther afield. These hazards included threats to energy and food supplies; to financial, communication and transportation systems including sea lanes; and to social peace. After 1990, Tokyo also had to recognize that it needed to strike a better balance between the economic and military elements of security: Japan could not simply throw money at its problems.[17] Not surprisingly, given this post-Cold War line of thinking, Japan alighted upon the idea of human security. At the heart of human security is the view that the safety and well-being of individuals and communities are as vital for long-term peace and stability as is the security of the state. Thus, between 1995 and 1998, Japan articulated its concept of human security, and in 2001 it launched the Commission on Human Security (among the members was Amartya Sen). The commission recommended that Japan support human security in terms of protecting people in violent conflict and post-conflict situations as well as help migrants and refugees at risk, promote market mechanisms and 'minimum living standards' and strengthen a range of basic health and education entitlements.[18]

How was Japan to achieve this beyond providing generous funding? Tokyo recognized that it was necessary to work with governments, international organizations and non-governmental organizations to change political and economic values, norms and practices. It eventually also recognized that in situations of conflict, it might be necessary for the international community to deploy a protective military force under UN auspices. Thus, it finally authorized the Japanese Self-Defence Forces (SDF) to participate in peacekeeping missions beyond its shores.

After the events of 11 September 2001, Japan would go further and support the US militarily in Iraq. The general view is that Tokyo's foreign policy based on human security effectively petered out in the wake of 9/11, when it became clear that dealing with global terrorism needed multilateral cooperation and strategies beyond human security. Yet, one could say that Japan's continuing its economic diplomacy as well as participation in peacekeeping—and even its support of US military operations in Iraq—had a human security rationale.[19]

The Indo-Pacific idea is commensurate with many of the ideas of human security. Abe's initiative was aimed at traditional security concerns and the safety of the state but also the 'promotion and establishment of the rule of law' for the protection of individuals and communities. It emphasized liberal norms and democracy not only as a binding political glue between the four major members but also as a value that protects individuals and communities, promotes internal political stability in countries in the regions and immunizes them against Chinese influence and disruption. Human security by no means ignores the safety of the state, without which the lives and freedoms of individuals and the well-being of communities can hardly be sustained (even if sometimes it is the state that jeopardizes its own citizens). However, above all, human security is about the protection of individuals and communities from physical, political and other forms of harm—and the promotion and establishment of the rule of law is a fundamental means of protection.

Japan's funding of economic and developmental projects including connectivity and infrastructure—both bilaterally and as part of the Indo-Pacific initiative—is commensurate with its human security approach of the 1990s. It recalls the post-Cold War concern in Japan to deal with social hazards and to fund basic education and healthcare in Asia and other vulnerable countries around the world. Economic prosperity and development along with improved connectivity and infrastructure would increase social resilience and undergird political stability. In turn, internal political stability would lead to regional stability and the closing of opportunities for Chinese influence.

Conclusion

The Indo-Pacific concept evolved in Japanese thinking and policies from 2006 to 2018 and was about dealing with a rising China. Despite

Chinese hysteria, the Indo-Pacific is a defensive grouping. It was intended to be a quasi-alliance of Australia, India, Japan and the US with the aim of being a 'soft-balancing' coalition. It was also about trust-building between the four coalition members, especially with India as it had never been a strategic partner with the other three. However, the Indo-Pacific is not just a military-diplomatic coalition; it is also about economic and other forms of capacity building in the region so that smaller countries would not become susceptible to Chinese economic blandishments, particularly after the launch of the BRI.

Abe's Indo-Pacific idea is not a decisive break from the past: it has lineage that can be traced to the Yoshida Doctrine as well as Japan's comprehensive security and human security ideas and policies. Japan has been far more active in constructing a regional order—from the time of the Yoshida Doctrine to the present Indo-Pacific—than it usually gets credit for. Indeed, if we include its various economic initiatives—the Asian Development Bank; its involvement in the Chiang Mai Initiative and its rescue role during the Asian financial crisis of 1997; its cooperation with Australia in launching the Asia-Pacific Economic Community (APEC); and its salvaging of the Trans-Pacific Partnership after the US withdrawal—a very different picture emerges of Tokyo's role in Asia. It was always much more than a junior partner to the US.

This chapter is not about India and the Indo-Pacific, but it is worth saying a few words that can probably be validated more convincingly by some empirical hard work. Abe knew from the start that India would be a weak link: because India cannot project military or economic power beyond the Indian Ocean; because it is averse to alliances; and because it fears China. Narendra Modi's Shangri-La speech in 2018—with its call for a free and open and 'inclusive' Indo-Pacific—was intended as an olive branch to Beijing.[20] The fracas at Galwan in 2020 caused New Delhi to somewhat revise its Indo-Pacific hesitations, but it is clear that India is still 'hiding' strategically.

It is also clear that India is 'free riding'. AUKUS has shown that the Anglo-Americans do not think much of the Indo-Pacific idea beyond a point and can construct their own hard-balancing coalition against China beyond the US–Japan alliance; and FOIP has shown that Japan will do most of the heavy lifting—with some help from Australia and the US—in the economic domain of the Indo-Pacific because India lacks the resources to help. Anglo-American military cooperation and Japan's economic role suit India. India does not have to do much militarily in the Pacific Ocean area, and it does not have to devote economic resources to help vulnerable Southeast Asian and Oceanic countries.

To conclude, Abe's Indo-Pacific idea was an important initiative in a period marked by the rapid rise of China and the relative decline of the US. It is a sophisticated concept as it does not rely simply on a quasi-alliance but rather invests more broadly in strengthening the economic and political resilience of the larger region. While Abe and his team deserve credit, they built on the ideas and policies of earlier Japanese administrations. The continuity will help maintain Japan's support for the Indo-Pacific approach.

This review of the Indo-Pacific has also shown that Japan has helped shape regional order in Asia since 1945 and will likely continue to do so. As for India in the Indo-Pacific, little is expected of it apart from continuing to stay in the fold. Japan, along with Australia and the US, will largely carry the idea forward. The Indo-Pacific idea has evolved since Abe's time and will undoubtedly continue to do so, but his mark on it will be enduring.

14

THE ROOTS OF ABE'S INDO-PACIFIC VISION

Ravi Velloor

SHORTLY BEFORE HE WAS assassinated in July 2022, Shinzo Abe laid out his vision for the Indo-Pacific for the last time. His case was buttressed by the Russian invasion of Ukraine, in which he saw parallels with a likely future situation in Taiwan. The Russian invasion, he wrote in an article in *Project Syndicate*, 'attests to the extreme difficulty a single state can face in protecting its territory and its people's lives and property by itself'. He concludes that 'it is not unrelated to the security environment surrounding Japan'.

The security environment Abe refers to is the influence of China on Asian and global affairs. From the time he read every key government paper as chief cabinet secretary and later as Prime Minister, Abe was clear-headed on China. He saw China expanding its influence in various regions—backed by its huge economic power—and building military bases at the same time. He also saw that China increasingly tended to display exceptionalism in its behaviour and thought that it could potentially pose an existential challenge. In the month before his assassination, polls showed that 90 per cent of the Japanese public believed that Japan must prepare for a Chinese invasion of Taiwan.

In his first term as Prime Minister in 2007, Abe and Chinese premier Wen Jiabao signed an agreement to create a maritime and air communication mechanism to prevent unexpected situations in sea and air. As Abe said at the time, 'We do not welcome dangerous encounters by fighter aircraft and vessels at sea. What we must exchange are words.' However, this mechanism the two leaders agreed on failed to materialize. This led Abe to the conclusion that the relationship with China would be unpredictable. Thus, he realized that it was important to be prepared lest China's trajectory leads to situations that threaten Japan and the nations most important to it.

Abe found a kindred spirit in Australian Prime Minister John Howard, who was in office from 1997 to 2006. The Quadrilateral Security Dialogue (Quad) is the result of this concord of perceptions. The Quad nations—Japan, the US, Australia and India—have forged an extremely important framework in the still-coalescing effort to counter the threat. However, Abe felt it was important to build ties with other countries that share Japan's values, including those in Europe. He was aware that Japan must first strengthen its defence capabilities and further deepen its alliance with the US if he was to realize his vision of a free and open Indo-Pacific.

It was not as though Abe was a reflexive China sceptic as some in Beijing—and a few in Southeast Asia—have sought to see him. Neither was he a rank sentimentalist, as thought by some in New Delhi who warmed to his outreach to India and were heartened by it. He was open to cooperating with China on President Xi Jinping's signature Belt and Road Initiative, even as he went about building new alliances to keep Beijing in check.

In short, he was a man acutely attuned to the shifting sands of global geopolitics, the relative strengths of nations and what it could mean for his nation. This made him a supreme pragmatist. He weighed his own assets with the precision of a field commander while carefully also assessing enemy strength, and what it would take to level any imbalances that may exist.

Therefore, at the heart of Abe's Indo-Pacific vision was the logical conclusion that it would take the combined defence budgets and military capabilities of his own nation and those of the US, India and Australia to present China with a credible deterrence based on traditional power. In India, he saw the only Asian power with the size, the heft—and possibly, the resolve—to stand up to a rampaging China.

Even as Abe marshalled his hard power to counter the China threat, his government spent considerable resources and energy in building up people-to-people ties with their larger neighbours. The success of this move has not been fully appreciated. The Chinese, raised on history lessons that painted Japan in a bleak light, have been pleasantly surprised at the correctness and politeness of the welcome they received during visits to Japan. In 2019, Abe's last full year as Prime Minister, the number of Chinese tourists visiting Japan outnumbered the visitors from China to Thailand—which had been the top Asian destination for Chinese tourists until then.

Chinese President Xi Jinping appreciated the clarity of purpose and the sophistication of Abe's approach. Upon Abe's death, Xi sent condolences to Japanese Prime Minister Fumio Kishida saying that he 'deeply regrets' Abe's sudden passing. Xi noted that Abe and he had reached a consensus on building a China–Japan relationship that met the needs of the new era. This represented a significant mellowing of perceptions at the Chinese end. Certainly, it contrasted with the view in 2014 of Liu Xiaoming, China's ambassador to Britain at the time, who wrote an opinion piece in *The Telegraph* that year comparing Japanese militarism with the haunting presence of Lord Voldemort in the *Harry Potter* series.[1] Eight years after that comparison, Xi's condolence message was of a very different tone when it stated that 'Abe made efforts to improve China–Japan relations during his time in office and contributed positively to this endeavour'.

By 2014, Abe had settled into his long second term as premier and his vision of the Indo-Pacific had crystallized. He seemed energized by the reception it was receiving around the world. Abe quickly issued Japan's first National Security Strategy (NSS), promoting his doctrine of 'proactive pacifism'. As the security environment around him shifted, he bolstered his country's defence capabilities. He also established the National Security Council, streamlined Japan's crisis management and lifted his country's long-standing virtual ban on arms exports. Abe seemed ready to build a military–industrial complex.

Abe also steadily advanced Japan's security alliance with the United States, avoiding havoc during the Donald Trump era with some swift pre-emptive moves within days of Trump's election to office. He paid the President-elect a visit at Trump Tower long before the real-estate mogul had even drafted his inaugural speech. This move allowed Abe to forge a close personal connection with the mercurial American.

More consequentially, Abe reinterpreted Japan's post-war constitution to allow his country to participate in collective self-defence operations in support of allies and security partners. In his speech at the Shangri-La Dialogue in Singapore in 2014, he averred that 'freedom, democracy and the rule of law form the Asia-Pacific's rich basso continuo that supports the melody played in a bright and cheery key' and that he found himself 'newly gripped by that sound day after day'.

Abe's vision of the rule of law on the global commons rested on three principles—he detailed these to his audience, which included the Singapore founding Prime Minister, Lee Kuan Yew, and his son and successor, Prime Minister Lee Hsien Loong. The first principle was that states shall make and clarify their claims based on international law. The second principle was that states shall not use force or coercion in trying to drive their claims, and the third was that states shall seek to settle disputes by peaceful means.

Abe pointed to the recently settled dispute between the Philippines and Indonesia over exclusive economic zones as an example of what he meant. And he left no one in doubt as to who he was targeting when he went on to say that 'movement to consolidate changes to the status quo by aggregating one fait accompli after another can only be strongly condemned'. He highlighted such actions as contravening the spirit of these three principles. The audience knew he was taking aim at Beijing's creation of artificial features in the South China Sea.

In that speech in Singapore, Abe laid out hints of what initiatives were to come. One of these was Japan's solidifying security cooperation with Australia into a trilateral arrangement with the US—'a new special relationship'. Abe had deep admiration for the Australian spirit and its relish for a good fight in aid of a worthy cause. If Canberra saw itself as America's deputy sheriff, Abe had no quarrel with that view.

When Tony Abbott led Australia, Abe tried to convince Canberra to buy the high-quality, super-silent Soryu-class Japanese submarines despite his own defence ministry fearing it could lead to a leak of the strategic technology on board. When Australia instead chose the French Naval Group's DCNS submarines, the Japanese defence ministry was quietly relieved. The French, themselves, would be subsequently thwarted; in 2021, Australia, United Kingdom and the US announced a new security arrangement called AUKUS that would see the US or Britain transfer nuclear-powered submarines to Australia.

In October 2022, Abe's ambition for tighter security relations with Australia became a reality when Kishida visited Perth to sign an enhanced security partnership between the two nations. A joint declaration from the two stated that they agreed to work together to deter 'aggression and behaviour that undermines international rules and norms'. Separately, Australian Prime Minister Anthony Albanese said that the 'landmark' declaration 'sends a strong signal to the region of our strategic alignment'.

Abe was peculiarly sensitive to Southeast Asia, making it a point to visit each of the ten ASEAN states early in his second term. While not expecting Southeast Asian states to choose sides or name their preferences, he prodded his government to help increase the capabilities of many of these nations. In particular, Indonesia, Vietnam and the Philippines were given vessels to bolster their coast guards and training to support those efforts. In July 2020, Japan agreed to lend Vietnam 36.6 billion yen for the procurement of six patrol vessels for the Vietnam Coast Guard. Such actions are guided by Japan's Vientiane Vision, which seeks to develop practical defence cooperation with Southeast Asian countries.

Abe even envisioned a bigger, more formal role for the East Asia Summits convened by ASEAN annually. He thought the way to achieve this was to create a committee of permanent representatives to ASEAN from the member countries, who then would prepare a roadmap to bring renewed vitality to the conferences. Abe thought the East Asia Summit could function in a multi-layered fashion along with the ASEAN Regional Forum and the meetings of ASEAN defence ministers.

Yoshihide Suga was Abe's closest ally and succeeded him as Prime Minister. He continued the tradition of prioritizing Southeast Asia, and his successor, Kishi, followed suit. Both chose a Southeast Asian nation for their debut official visit after taking office as premier. These initiatives have not gone unnoticed by a region that has endured painful memories of Japanese occupation during World War II. In October 2018, the region welcomed the presence of the Japanese helicopter carrier *Kaga* as it traversed Southeast Asian waters, sailing to Colombo and back.

In many ways, the durability of an idea is in the validation of it. In that sense, Kishida, Abe's foreign minister for five years, has shown no indication that he is anything but the 'third chapter' of the Abe era. Indeed, Kishida has followed in Abe's footsteps with his realistic 'diplomacy for a new era'. While Kishida's ideas mark continuum—Japan has been enlarging its strategic space since the Miyazawa government in 1992 deployed Japanese Self-Defence Forces in a peacekeeping role in Cambodia—things have lately taken on a new urgency in Tokyo.

By 2027, the defence budget will be doubled to 2 per cent of gross domestic product. For Japan, this is a significant leap and the absence of any major opposition to the plan derives from the swiftly deteriorating situation in the East China Sea and the Taiwan Straits. Japan is also concerned about repeated nuclear testing and missile launches by North Korea, as well as the Russian invasion of Ukraine—which so chilled leaders of small states that need to coexist with large and powerful neighbours.

At its heart, the five-pillared Kishida 'Vision for Peace' is the fundamental reinforcement of Japan's defence capabilities and the tighter strategic alliance with its only ally, the United States. But it also includes building new forms of security cooperation with like-minded countries such as Australia. The next NSS could include counterstrike options, according to Kishida.

Japan today finds itself in a position where it is the outside world that is urging it to raise its defence outlays. Its successful attempt to create the Comprehensive and Progressive Agreement for Trans-Pacific Partnership (CPTPP) has shown Japan to be a sophisticated, responsible regional player. It has not given up hope of having the US join the CPTPP. Japan has made also positive contributions to Regional Comprehensive Economic Partnership (RCEP) negotiations that have enhanced its credibility in this direction.

The epoch-defining 'Indo-Pacific' concept is now very much in place and is increasingly capturing global strategic discourse—and it started with the simplest of personal gestures between a rising Japanese political figure and a veteran Indian politician widely considered to have been a reluctant Prime Minister. The concept of the 'Free and Open Indo-Pacific' goes back to an unusual meeting in 2006 between Shinzo Abe, then visiting New Delhi in the capacity of chief cabinet secretary of Japan, and Indian Prime Minister Manmohan Singh, the economist and bureaucrat who was unexpectedly thrust to the premiership in 2004.

Prime Minister Singh was surprised to receive an unusual request: a Japanese politician named Shinzo Abe was in New Delhi and had inquired whether it would be possible to get a meeting with India's leader. The rank-conscious mandarins in the East Asia division of the Indian Ministry of External Affairs declined the request. Abe, they sniffed, was too low in the official hierarchy—a mere calf in the old-boy herd of Liberal Democratic Party (LDP) elephants—to merit a meeting with the leader of the world's largest democracy.

However, the division head for the Americas, Dr S. Jaishankar—presently the foreign minister—was aware of Abe's presence in the Indian capital and sensed opportunity. A decade earlier, when Jaishankar was posted as deputy chief of mission at the Indian embassy in Tokyo, he had befriended the then backbencher, Abe. It was possibly that Jaishankar had figured that the political blue blood was capable of rising up the ranks of the LDP in the future. Besides, Abe seemed to have good feelings about India.

He told Jaishankar how, as a child, he had heard his grandfather, Prime Minister Nobusuke Kishi, speak warmly about India and a trip to see Jawaharlal Nehru. India's first Prime Minister had not only received Kishi warmly but also organized a huge public reception in New Delhi for the visitor. There, Nehru had proclaimed his admiration for Japan—much to the happiness of Kishi, a leader whose nation was emerging from defeat in war. Jaishankar approached Dr Singh's press advisor, Sanjaya Baru—who was a friend from university—and explained why it might be worth the Prime Minister's while to meet Abe.

Baru had his own reasons for endorsing the suggestion. In late 1998, he had been part of a delegation sent by then Prime Minister Atal Bihari Vajpayee to explain the series of nuclear tests India had carried out a few months earlier and seek an easing of the sanctions that Japan had consequently imposed. During that trip, the Indians were told that Abe was among the few in the LDP who seemed sympathetic to India's reasons to test and build a strategic deterrent. When Baru checked with the Prime Minister, he was quick to accept the suggestion. Abe was invited for tea and shown great courtesy by the Indian leader, who was a generation ahead of the Japanese in both age and career. The following year, when Abe was next in New Delhi, he was Japan's new Prime Minister—and keen to sign a wide-ranging strategic partnership with India.

Months before that trip, Shyam Saran had visited Tokyo as Singh's special envoy to seek Japanese support for the civilian nuclear deal with the US. He was given a long lecture by the Japanese chief cabinet secretary, Taro Aso, on Japan's objections to nuclear proliferation. However, once the formal meeting concluded and Aso walked Saran to the elevator, he assured the envoy that whatever be its public position, Tokyo would give its backing to the US–India nuclear deal. Thus enthused, the Indians rolled out the red carpet for Abe when he visited and invited him to address a joint session of Parliament. It was there that he laid out his vision in the famous speech titled 'Confluence of the Two Seas'.

'The Pacific and the Indian oceans are now bringing about a dynamic coupling as seas of freedom and of prosperity,' Abe had said in that speech in August 2007. 'A "Broader Asia" that broke away geographical boundaries is now beginning to take on a distinct form. Our two countries have the ability—and the responsibility—to ensure that it broadens yet further and to nurture and enrich these seas to become seas of clearest transparency.' Most Indians did not immediately catch the significance of Abe's speech as it was delivered in Japanese. In any case, Abe would step down as Prime Minister soon after because of bowel-related bad health. Ashwani Kumar, the Indian minister–in–attendance to Abe, filed a report about the Japanese leader's frequent toilet visits.

In subsequent years, however, Abe never forgot that early gesture by Prime Minister Singh. When Singh had stepped away from the highest office after a decade in power, Abe saw to it that the Japanese government gave him its highest imperial honour. Jaishankar was also recognized. On a visit to Tokyo as India's foreign secretary, he was surprised to be given the honour of a meeting with the emperor, unusual for someone his rank at the time. It was even more of a thrill for Jaishankar personally, because his wife is Japanese.

Of all the foreign policy accounts Abe directed personally in his second stint as Prime Minister, the US and India were of the top priority. While keeping ties with US President Donald Trump superbly well-oiled, Abe worked on his relationship with India—first with Singh and then his successor, Narendra Modi. He had met the latter for the first time when Modi was visiting Tokyo as the chief minister of Gujarat even as Abe was planning his own comeback.

It was not surprising that Abe had his plans ready when he returned to office in late 2012 after his health had improved. Within months, he choreographed the Japanese emperor's visit to India, paying attention to the minutest details. That included asking a senior Japanese diplomat and seasoned India hand then stationed in Bangladesh to lead the on-ground preparations in New Delhi for the Japanese side. When Japanese officials frequently became exasperated with India's political gridlock, ponderous bureaucracy and rigid legal system, Abe ordered them to stay the course. Once settled into office, he assiduously preached the Indo-Pacific doctrine, including at the 2014 Shangri-La Dialogue in Singapore.

Strictly speaking, though, Abe did not father the Indo-Pacific concept. Rather, he was more of an efficient midwife. The concept's roots lie in an American effort—the Proliferation Security Initiative. It was launched in 2003 to counter seaborne proliferation of weapons of mass destruction. Its beginnings can also be traced to the stirrings of worry at the Pentagon, in Tokyo and in New Delhi over China's strategic ambitions that began at the turn of the century. That led some analysts—including Indian naval expert Gurpreet Khurana—to discuss with Japanese officials ways to collaborate on putting a collar, if necessary, on the sea routes on which China depended for its energy security.

It is possible that before making his speech to the Indian Parliament in 2007, Abe had been made aware of a paper in that January's issue of *Strategic Analysis*—published by New Delhi's government-backed Institute for Defence Studies and Analyses—that discussed the Indo-Pacific concept. The paper also explored ways for Japan and India to collaborate in keeping sea lanes open. Indeed, some strategic coordination between the two had already been initiated.

Two weeks after the speech to the Indian Parliament, and shortly before he bowed out for the first time, Abe had the satisfaction of seeing the Indians move the annual Malabar naval exercise from their western seaboard to the China-facing eastern seaboard. Joined by American carrier USS *Kitty Hawk* and Indian carrier INS *Viraat*, the US, Japanese and Indian navies—as well as ships from the Australian and Singapore navies—carried out war exercises between 4 and 9 September 2007 in a vast stretch of sea from the south-eastern Indian port city of Visakhapatnam to the Andaman Islands at the mouth of the Malacca Strait.

However, that was seen as a one-off exercise. The Indians had no appetite for needling China. For this reason, the idea of the Indo-Pacific lay dormant for a while after Abe stepped down as Prime Minister. It was revived only after he returned to power and began pushing both the concept and for US–Japan–India trilateral military collaboration to be expanded to include Australia.

In parallel, the US was planning its own moves to entice India into its strategic fold. President Barack Obama sped up plans that had been set in motion by his predecessor, George W. Bush. The Obama administration had initially viewed Abe as a trouble-stirrer in East Asia but had slowly begun to come round to his point of view on the region. In 2015, after a visit to the US Pacific Command in Hawaii, I had reported in *The Straits Times* that US military strategists were increasingly talking of an 'Indo-Asia-Pacific' region, which had started to be shortened to 'Indo-Pacific'.

Trump's arrival in the White House and Abe's assiduous courting of the American leader gave fresh momentum to the idea. The Indo-Pacific Command finally became a reality in May 2018, when James 'Mad Dog' Mattis, defence secretary to President Trump, stopped in Hawaii on his way to the Shangri-La Dialogue and announced the change. Although 'Indo' in the name stands for Indian Ocean, the US probably also figured that India would be pleased by the new name. To further that effect, Mattis defined 'Indo-Pacific' as stretching 'from Hollywood to Bollywood'.

Abe had less success in drawing Australia and India into closer cooperation on defence production—another element that would have fed into his vision of a framework that pooled the defence capabilities of four powerful democracies. Kishida now must set the pace of that relationship. He began by trying to transfer top-class US-2 amphibious planes to India, but the Indians consider the US-2 planes way too expensive and are yet to bite. However, the Malabar exercise has been invigorated. The Australians joined the exercise again in 2020 and have been regulars since.

These exercises have become increasingly sophisticated and ambitious. Last year, the four navies conducted war games off the Philippines. Today, it is seen as the sword arm of the Quad, which groups the US, Japan, India and Australia. The Quad itself now regularly meets at the summit level. In addition, France–India defence cooperation has intensified and resumption of France–Australia defence contacts have resumed after a chill period following Canberra's decision to join AUKUS and ditch the French naval submarine programme.

Thus, it is not inconceivable that a European power—France or possibly Britain—as well as Canada may join future exercises. Abe's Indo-Pacific vision was expansive, and its fulfilment is a work in progress.

It is not surprising, therefore, that US President Joe Biden ordered the White House and all government buildings to fly their flags at half-mast to mourn Shinzo Abe's passing even though he was no longer the Prime Minister at the time of his death. India went even further, with Prime Minister Narendra Modi declaring a day of national mourning for the Japanese political stalwart.

15

SHINZO ABE'S GRAND STRATEGY: DRIVERS AND LEGACY

Yuka Koshino

Leader with a Global Vision

SHINZO ABE STARTED HIS second term as Prime Minister in 2012 determined to restore Japan's global prestige. He promised to the world that 'Japan is not, and will never be, a tier-two country' during his visit to Washington, D.C. in February 2013.[1] His second administration pursued a 'proactive contribution to peace' and 'diplomacy that takes a panoramic perspective of the world map'.[2]

Prime Minister Abe visited eighty countries during his second stint in office, flying an astonishing 1,581,281 km from 2012 to 2020. He even sought to establish relations with 'difficult' countries such as Russia and Iran.[3] Abe was also active multilaterally, hosting the G7 and the G20 Summits in 2016 and 2019, respectively. The attendance by representatives of 218 states, regions and organizations at his state funeral in September 2022 was evidence of his global recognition.

Abe's global foreign policy posture derived from his concern about Japan's eroding international presence, which, in his view, had been affected by the economic and political turmoil of the 1990s and the 2000s. Japan's political scene had also been unstable from 2006 to 2012,

187

with six consecutive Prime Ministers staying in office for less than a year and none able to push through tough reforms. This number includes Abe's first term from 2006 to 2007, which had ended abruptly due to his health issues. Although the opposition Democratic Party of Japan (DPJ) won the general election in 2009 with a large majority, the instability of the DPJ administrations tarnished Japan's global prestige. It even damaged Japan's relations with the US, shaking the US–Japan alliance—the fundamental underpinning of Japan's security.

At the same time, Japan's external strategic environment was also drastically changing. The economic and political power of Japan's neighbour, China, rose rapidly after it joined the World Trade Organization (WTO) in 2001. Beijing also began using the gains from its brisk economic growth to modernize its military. The resilience of China's economic system after the global financial crisis in 2008 emboldened Beijing to challenge the post-WWII US-led liberal order. This led to China becoming increasingly assertive in pressing its territorial ambitions in the East China Sea.

There was a collision between a Chinese trawler and the Japanese Coast Guard in 2010 near the Senkaku Islands—which Japan controls but China claims, calling them 'Diaoyu'—and this incident led to China halting rare earth mineral exports to Japan to protest Tokyo's decision to detain the Chinese captain. It was a wake-up call for Japan, who then understood that China was willing to weaponize trade relations to further its own strategic interests. In the same year, China's GDP overtook Japan's for the first time.

A key legacy of Prime Minister Abe's second term is Japan's diplomatic activism, which has been continued by the subsequent administrations of Prime Ministers Yoshihide Suga and Fumio Kishida. However, a closer examination of his policies reveals that it was his deep understanding of the challenges posed by the rise of China and his crafting of a grand strategy to respond to them that made his term so consequential for Japan and beyond. Indeed, Abe was perhaps the first world leader to craft a realistic and pragmatic China strategy that combined diplomatic, military and geoeconomic tools. This stood in contrast to many other countries that viewed China's rise as a largely benign phenomenon.

Abe's China Strategy: 'From a Position of Strength'

Abe began conceptualizing his approach towards China even before his first term as his nation's premier. In his de facto political manifesto—*Utsukushii Kuni E (Towards a Beautiful Country)*, published in 2006—he raised concerns about the consequences of the rise of China for the world and for Japan's security.[4] However, he also recognized that Japan's relations with China are 'inseverable' ('*kitte mo kirenai*') and believed that creating a stable relationship with China through diplomacy, economic relations and people-to-people exchanges is important for Japan.

Based on these assumptions, Abe agreed to pursue a 'mutually beneficial relationship based on common strategic interests' with China.[5] He kept this goal with China in his second term, even after Chinese assertiveness grew under the new Chinese President Xi Jinping.[6] For Abe, the key to dealing with the rise of China was managing relations from a position of strength. Three elements of his China strategy are worth highlighting as evidence of the strategic and innovative thinking in Abe's approach, which have been followed by like-minded partners to some extent.

The first was the internal and external balancing strategy designed to restore Japan's strength as a proactive actor in regional and global affairs. There were two dimensions to the internal balancing strategy. One was the revamping of Japan's policymaking architecture for foreign policy to increase the effectiveness of government administration.[7] At the core was the setting up of the National Security Council (NSC) and the crafting of Japan's first National Security Strategy, both in 2013, which integrated Japan's military, diplomatic and intelligence goals and tools.

In the same year, the Abe administration passed a state secrecy law to improve information security. Abe believed that this was critical for enhancing relations with allies and like-minded partners. The other dimension was his signature 'Abenomics' economic policy. Through the three 'arrows' of Abenomics—quantitative monetary policy easing, fiscal stimulus and structural reform—he sought to revitalize Japan's economy, thereby satisfying voters' needs but also boosting Japan's international presence and influence.

Abe also moved quickly on external balancing on his return to power in 2012. The most important piece of this strategy was to rebuild trust in the US–Japan alliance. He visited Washington, D.C. in February 2013 and consistently pressed to strengthen security cooperation with the US to deal with the deteriorating security environment in Northeast Asia. Major efforts here included the reinterpretation of Japan's constitution in 2014 to allow collective self-defence and the passage of the controversial security legislation in 2015 that allowed the Japanese Self-Defence Forces (SDF) to provide support for US military operations closely linked to Japan's security. The legislation also allowed Japan to send the SDF overseas to take part in UN peacekeeping missions. In 2015, the two governments also updated the guidelines for US–Japan defence cooperation for the first time since 1997 to pursue a 'seamless, robust, flexible and effective bilateral response' from peacetime to contingency and in the new domains of cyber and space.[8]

Abe's focus on the strength of the US–Japan alliance was further evident in his surprise visit to Trump Tower in New York in December 2016 to meet the then President-elect Donald Trump and explain the value of the alliance to him. Abe later became known as the most influential foreign leader when it came to dealing with President Trump, largely through many rounds of 'golf diplomacy'. His persistent courting of Trump and his efforts to increase Japan's role in the alliance stabilized bilateral relations between their nations. An example of a successful negotiation with Trump by Abe was his securing US commitment to defend the Senkaku Islands under Article 5 of the Japan–US Security Treaty even in the face of Trump's push to reduce the financial burden to the US from the alliance.[9]

Beyond strengthening the Japan–US alliance, Abe sought to build stronger ties with India. He saw the world's largest and fastest-growing democratic country as a strategic partner that could serve as a counterweight to China.[10] His strategic view on India was already evident in *Utsukushii Kuni E*, but his vision became clear in his important 'Confluence of the Two Seas' speech to the Indian Parliament in August 2007.[11] In that speech, he called for Indo–Japanese cooperation 'for the future of this new "Broader Asia"' to 'enrich the seas of freedom and prosperity', outlining Abe's early thinking of the 'Indo-Pacific' as a strategic concept.

In May 2007, shortly before this speech, Abe had launched the Quadrilateral Security Dialogue, known as the 'Quad', with the US, Japan, Australia and India as members. The aim was to enhance maritime security cooperation in the region, but the mechanism withered after changes in leadership in member countries and their ambivalent positions towards China. As soon as Abe returned to office in 2012, he launched the idea of 'Asia's democratic security diamond' and set about reinvigorating the Quad to ensure the rule of law in the maritime space of the Indo-Pacific.[12] Abe also established close personal relations with Indian Prime Minister Narendra Modi and deepened economic and security relations with India through the setting up of meetings between the foreign and defence ministers of the two nations in 2019.

The second element of Abe's China strategy was a geoeconomic one. Abe understood the strategic implications of China's use of geoeconomic power, its use of economic endowments and tools to pursue its strategic interests and its growing impact on the post-war rules-based liberal economic order from which Japan has benefited. China's use of economic coercion after the earlier-mentioned Senkaku Islands incident in 2010, its launch of the global investment and development project Belt and Road Initiative (BRI) in 2013 and its proposal to set up the multilateral Asian Infrastructure Investment Bank (AIIB, formally launched in 2016) all demonstrated Chinese competitiveness and its ambitions to set new rules, standards and norms for the region's economies.

Tokyo's concerns about the strategic implications for Japan of Chinese economic development grew further with the launch in 2015 of China's 'Made in China 2025' industry strategy as well as its military-civil fusion (MCF) strategy, which incorporates civilian technologies for military technology development and vice-versa. Japan also viewed with concern Chinese dominance of 5th generation (5G) wireless networks in global markets and the spread of Chinese digital technologies through China's 'Digital Silk Road'—the digital dimension of the BRI—which gave the Chinese government and the country's technology companies further strategic advantages.

Abe's response to these geoeconomic challenges had three main parts. Firstly, he actively sought to shape rules and norms of economic activities that are critical for sustainable development under the rules-based order. In the realm of trade, Abe retracted his initial position against joining the US-led Trans-Pacific Partnership (TPP) mega trade bloc after recognizing the strategic role of the agreement in setting high standards for future regional trade. The US's withdrawal from the TPP in 2017 was a major blow for Japan and like-minded partners given the importance and size of the US market.

Still, Abe filled the leadership vacuum to conclude the successor to the TPP—the Comprehensive Progressive Trans-Pacific Partnership (CPTPP)—with the eleven remaining countries and championed free trade in the region. The CPTPP set high standards on labour and restrictions on data localization requirements in e-commerce. The CPTPP ranks as one of the most important foreign-policy achievements of Abe's second term as Prime Minister.

As the chair of G20 in 2019, Japan also made landmark achievements to push forward principles and standards it proposed in the realm of infrastructure and cross-border data transfers. One was the principle for 'quality infrastructure' financing that Tokyo had been seeking to advance since 2015 to ensure the financial sustainability of countries borrowing to fund infrastructure projects. With this, Tokyo was trying to provide an alternative to the perceived 'debt-trap' diplomacy of China's BRI.

An example of the latter was seen in the case of the Hambantota port redevelopment in Sri Lanka with the help of Chinese funding. Colombo's subsequent difficulties with the repayment of loans from China to fund the project allowed Beijing to manipulate the situation to its advantage. In 2017, Sri Lanka was compelled to sign an agreement under which China would write off the debt in return for 80 per cent control of the port on a ninety-nine-year lease.

Tokyo also promoted 'Data-Free Flow with Trust (DFFT)', a concept that attempts to prevent data protectionism. DFFT also seeks to bridge differences between the US and the EU's approach to data governance by agreeing to encourage cross-border data after ensuring security. DFFT has now been used in subsequent G7 and G20 meetings as well as the negotiations for the e-commerce ruling under the WTO.

The second part of Abe's response to the Chinese geoeconomic challenge was the development of defensive and active measures to deal with geoeconomic issues concerning national security under the concept of 'economic security'. After the Senkaku Islands incident in 2010, Japan began its first efforts to diversify supply chains of critical materials and strategic goods away from China via its 'China Plus One' strategy. Building on these early efforts, the new economic security concept focused on identifying, protecting and promoting dual-use technologies to maintain Japan's competitiveness. This included banning Chinese digital communications infrastructure from government networks, excluding Chinese 5G from civilian and government networks and tightening investment screening processes to prevent technology outflow to China. It also sought to invest in dual-use technologies to maintain Japan's competitiveness in setting standards for future critical technologies.

The focus on high-technology and the drive to upgrade the policymaking apparatus to take an integrated approach to dealing with this challenge attracted attention from other countries trying to approach similar challenges. A notable example of the attempt to improve policymaking efficiency was the setting up of an economic division in the National Security Council's administrative body as its second largest division in 2020.

The third element of Abe's China strategy was the 'Free and Open Indo-Pacific' (FOIP) concept, which was later rephrased as the FOIP 'vision'. FOIP was launched in 2016 at the Sixth Tokyo International

Conference on African Development (TICAD VI) in Kenya as a vision based on principles and values to uphold the rules-based order across the Pacific and Indian oceans. No strategy document has been published since the launch of the vision to clarify the means and ways to make the FOIP vision a reality. However, according to a document published by Japan's Ministry of Foreign Affairs, the primary activities under FOIP are supporting the economic and maritime order, enhancing physical and digital connectivity and enhancing peace and stability through capacity building.[13]

FOIP was not merely an ambiguous vision but served as a useful framework for achieving Japan's strategic interest. It allowed Japan to build a coalition among like-minded partners that could counter the growing Chinese strategic and economic influence in the region. It also brought in India as the democratic counterweight against China and helped to keep the US embedded in the region by promoting joint economic initiatives under its shared goals. This came at a time when American economic and political presence in the region was declining after the nation withdrew from the TPP in 2017 and Trump pursued his 'America First' trade policies.[14] In fact, the Trump administration went on to 'borrow' the idea of FOIP and began using it in its 2017 National Security Strategy as well as other foreign policies and economic initiatives.[15]

FOIP's early milestones—such as the conclusion of the CPTPP and strengthening of infrastructure financing between the US, Japan and Australia to enhance regional connectivity—also suggested that the concept was both a goal and a tool for Japan's geoeconomic strategy. The open and inclusive nature of FOIP resonated well with many regions and other countries that sought to uphold rules-based order but wanted to avoid picking sides in the US–China strategic competition. The principles of 'openness' and 'inclusiveness' of FOIP were echoed by Australia, India and the Association of Southeast Asian Nations (ASEAN).[16] Like-minded countries in Europe—such as France, Germany, Netherlands and the UK—also followed the path. In principle, FOIP also remains open to China if it conformed to the rules and norms shared under the vision.[17]

Abe's Legacy amid US–China Great Power Competition

These three interlinked elements of Abe's grand strategy for dealing with the rise of China constitute an important part of his legacy in the realm of foreign and security policy. Abe successfully transformed Japan's grand strategy from the Yoshida Doctrine, which was the strategy set by Japan's first post-WWII Prime Minister, Shigeru Yoshida—who was in office from 1946 to 1947 and again from 1948 to 1954. Yoshida's strategy was to rely on the US for Japan's security and to focus his nation's efforts purely on economic growth. The various security reforms conducted in Abe's second administration enhanced Japan's domestic capabilities, expanded its role in US–Japan defence cooperation and saw the dispatch of SDF troops for intelligence, surveillance and reconnaissance (ISR) missions in Oman and peacekeeping missions in South Sudan and the Sinai Peninsula. These were seen as a structural break for Japan's security posture. The continuation of his policies by the subsequent Suga and Kishida governments suggests that Abe may have effected a permanent shift away from the Yoshida Doctrine.

In the security realm, the administrations of both Suga and Kishida had stated security interests in the Taiwan Strait and Ukraine that showed Japan as being much more willing to contribute to security challenges beyond Japanese territories. This is a stark difference from Japan's decades-long position to focus only on limited areas surrounding its territory. The summit between Suga and Biden in April 2021 led to a joint statement that underscored 'the importance of peace and stability across the Taiwan Strait'.[18] It was the first time for the alliance to mention Taiwan since the Nixon–Sato statement in 1969, and implied that Japan could play a role in a case of contingency.

These statements were further backed by the Kishida administration's commitment to 'fundamentally reinforce Japan's defence capabilities within the next five years and secure substantial increase of Japan's defence budget needed to effect it' and the public support he gained to pursue this after winning the upper-house election in July 2022.[19] The signing of a reciprocal access agreement with Australia in January 2022 was followed by the Japan–Australia joint declaration on security cooperation in October 2022 that mentioned consultation on responses to regional contingencies for the first time. Such enhanced cooperation with like-minded partners is further indication that a reversal of Japan's outward posture is unlikely.[20]

In the economic realm, Abe's geoeconomic strategy also deviates from the Yoshida Doctrine, as it actively seeks to use Japan's economic strength for strategic purposes. For instance, Tokyo is promoting research and development in dual-use technologies not just for economic growth but also for maintaining competitiveness of advanced military technologies. Kishida's economic security policy features a concept of 'strategic indispensability' which also has an active approach to creating Japan's leverage in the chokepoints of supply chain for strategic purposes. This is not merely about focusing on domestic economic growth or provision of ODA.

Japan's agency in maintaining and reinforcing the regional security and economic architecture in the Indo-Pacific allows Japan to act as a bridging actor between Southeast Asia, Europe and India. Each of these regions has perspectives and priorities divergent from the US when it comes to navigating the US–China 'great power competition'. For example, Biden's focus on the Quad and the binary approaches to US–China competition though the narrative of 'democracies versus autocracies' are fuelling concerns in Southeast Asia about threats to 'ASEAN centrality' and even the unity of ASEAN. As a country that built a high level of trust with ASEAN through long-time pragmatic and consistent effort to support the bloc's political and economic development—even at difficult times after the military coup in Myanmar—Japan continues to play an important role as 'the most-trusted major power' to reconcile diverging interests and priorities between the US and Southeast Asia.[21] Although it would prefer the US to return to the CPTPP, Japan supported the Biden administration's Indo-Pacific Economic Framework (IPEF)—a US-led economic initiative to set regional rules and standards. This added weight to American efforts to improve its economic engagement with the region and thereby to the role of the US as a counterweight to growing Chinese economic influence.

Since Russia's invasion of Ukraine in February 2022, Japan has also been playing a key role as a bridge between the West and the Indo-Pacific, building on Abe's legacy of strengthened relations with multilateral groupings such as the G7, the EU and NATO. The Kishida administration's tough and swift response against Russia's invasion of Ukraine came as a surprise to many European countries given Japan's dovish response to Russia's annexation of Crimea in 2014. For Kishida, however, growing Sino–Russia cooperation and Russia's violation of international law were unacceptable given Japan's concerns about the security threat in the Indo-Pacific from China.

As the G7's only Asian country, the Kishida administration has sought to serve as a link between the West and Asia to defend the status quo by repeatedly stating that 'Ukraine today could be East Asia tomorrow'. Kishida's aim is to raise awareness of the links between Russian and Chinese revisionist aims in Asia and Europe, especially given the risk of a decline in European focus on the Indo-Pacific after the invasion. Kishida also visited India in March 2022 as part of his design to keep India committed to the Quad, after New Delhi's initial ambivalent reaction to the Russian invasion.

The Outlook for Abe's Legacy in Foreign and Security Policy

Abe's legacy of making Japan a proactive player with an outward diplomatic and security posture in responding to the rise of China has given Japan's diplomatic, geoeconomic and security posture a framework for years to come. The strategic concept of the Indo-Pacific and the linking to this of a geoeconomics element to deal with the rise of China has had a far-reaching impact on the China strategies of other like-minded partners such as the US. Despite the growing momentum with Japanese policymakers and support for this concept in Japanese society, it is also important to note that Tokyo's capability and capacity to allocated resources and to afford such proactive posture could face several challenges.

One such challenge is the drastic change in Tokyo's external environment after Russia's invasion of Ukraine. On top of the ever-deteriorating security environment in East Asia—which is being driven by Chinese assertiveness around Taiwan and North Korea's growing nuclear and ballistic missile capabilities—the war in Ukraine and growing Sino–Russia military collaboration are adding further pressure on Tokyo's response capabilities. Here, Abe's two missed opportunities in his external balancing strategy—strengthening diplomatic and security ties with South Korea and normalizing relations with Russia to prevent closer Sino–Russia ties—constrains Tokyo's options and resources for maintaining peace and stability in East Asia.

Japan's leadership capacity as the global defender of the status quo is also constrained. Kishida's solidarity with the West strengthens the unity of the G7 but raises questions on whether Abe's panoramic diplomacy beyond the Indo-Pacific region will remain active. Abe's all-encompassing diplomacy—including engagement with the Middle East, Africa and Latin America—was strategic as it aimed to support the capacity and resiliency of the 'Global South' against Chinese political and economic encroachment. However, the division between the West and the Global South has widened since Russia's invasion of Ukraine, as the subsequent voting behaviour in the United Nations General Assembly shows. Moreover, China has begun to exploit such differences between the Western democracies and the Global South by creating a narrative that resonates with the latter under the Global Security Initiative (GSI)—although its effects remain ambiguous.

Another challenge is the enduring domestic constitutional, fiscal and normative constraints that restrict Japan's capacity to fulfil its ambitions. Article 9 of the Japanese constitution still limits SDF activities to deal with high-tempo operations under contingencies and the possession of offensive capabilities to enhance deterrence. Anti-military norms and a hesitancy to take part in military-relevant R&D remains strong in Japanese academic institutions and the private sector, and limits Japan's competitiveness in dual-use technologies that have become important both for its security and its economic growth. Japan's economic health is at question as public debt continues to mount and structural reforms fall short despite Abenomics. This makes it difficult for Tokyo to continue financing Japan's outward defence posture, diplomatic activism and geoeconomic initiatives.

Abe's grand strategy was thus not always successful, but he had a clear vision to bring Japan back to a leading role on the international stage. Whether future Japanese leaders can implement its outward foreign and security policy posture will largely depend on their ability to create a robust political and economic base to deal with these enduring agendas.

16

ABE'S FOREIGN POLICY: THE STRATEGIC AND THE NORMATIVE

Rohan Mukherjee

IT IS OFTEN CHALLENGING to unearth the role of the individual in the conduct of international affairs. States and their governments are large, complex entities with a multitude of organizational procedures and decision-making junctures. The business of government is conducted by not one but thousands of individuals. Yet, it is possible to identify the role and impact of prominent leaders, who can exert influence over policy by virtue of their institutional position.

This is more evident in the case of a politically successful and nationally popular leader such as Shinzo Abe. It is hard to deny that he played an outsized role in Japanese politics and foreign policy over the last two decades. Yet, Abe himself was a manifestation of deeper changes in Japanese society and politics. The widespread support he enjoyed was a sign of longer-term shifts in the attitudes of Japanese elites and the public, which arguably were at least in part occasioned by shifts in Japan's geopolitical environment. In taking stock of Abe's legacy, therefore, one has to understand both the roots of his approach to the world as well as the extent to which he reshaped the world as he found it.

The Political and Geopolitical Context

When Abe began his historic second term at the helm of the Japanese government in 2012, his country was in the midst of a challenging period. Less than a year had passed since the Fukushima nuclear disaster, the Japanese economy faced numerous challenges and the country had cycled through six prime ministers (including Abe himself) in the six preceding years. The West was still recovering from the global financial crisis of 2008 and China had begun asserting itself not only in its own neighbourhood but also more broadly in Asia.

Abe undertook an ambitious and multi-pronged reform effort to address the challenges he saw in Japan's domestic and international environment. He sought to revive the Japanese economy through a mix of monetary expansion and fiscal policy while also putting an emphasis on concluding the Trans-Pacific Partnership (TPP), a regional mega trade agreement. He chipped away at Japan's ingrained reluctance to act boldly in the realm of national and international security, sometimes with remarkable success. Not only did Abe spearhead the creation of a defence ministry, a National Security Council, and an official National Security Strategy, he also expanded the role of the Japanese Self-Defence Forces abroad. The latter was achieved through a crucial reinterpretation of Article 9 of the Japanese constitution, which has historically banned Japan from resorting to war in order to achieve its external objectives.

In Japanese politics and society, Abe was a nationalist and a revisionist. He preferred a stronger role for Japan in international politics and supported a revisionist view of Japan's history, particularly in connection with blame and responsibility for World War II. He sought for Japan to become a 'normal nation' unashamed of its history and ready and able to take on the security challenges of the twenty-first century. 'Japan is back,' Abe had declared in a speech in Washington, D.C. in early 2013, less than two months after starting his second term.

Yet, Japan's re-emergence as a major power under Abe did not always bode well for Japan itself. His official and unofficial ties to ultraconservative groups such as Nippon Kaigi, his government's efforts to revise school textbooks to include a more nationalistic approach to Japanese history, his controversial visits to the Yasukuni Shrine and his prevarication on the issue of 'comfort women' with South Korea all significantly complicated not only his legacy within Japan but also Japan's relations with its neighbours during his political career.

Outside its neighbourhood, a more assertive Japan was welcomed by traditional allies such as the United States and Australia as well as new strategic partners such as India and member countries of the Association of Southeast Asian Nations (ASEAN). Abe doubled down on the US–Japan alliance while also seeking a greater regional security role for Japan. From 2016 onwards, he astutely cultivated a friendship with President Donald Trump to ensure that the latter remained a partner in these efforts. His personal relationship with Prime Minister Narendra Modi is also widely known. Abe saw India–Japan ties as the defining relationship of this century and invested a great deal of effort in raising India's profile in the Japanese political establishment as well as in Japan's global outlook.

Abe's strategy for Southeast Asia involved taking the longstanding Fukuda Doctrine of peaceful engagement with Asian countries and changing its orientation towards competing with China's growing influence among these nations. To this end, Japan began to see itself as a cornerstone of regional order against the potential excesses of Chinese power, a position that was buttressed by an expanding portfolio of foreign aid and infrastructure investments across Southeast Asia.

Perhaps what Abe will be most remembered for is the concept of the Indo-Pacific and the loose coalition of countries known as the Quad—which comprises the United States, Japan, India and Australia. Abe was not only an ardent champion of the new strategic space created by greater geopolitical links across the Indian and Pacific Oceans but also sought to formalize a grouping of major democratic powers and like-minded countries that could contain the rise of China.

The Indo-Pacific

To understand Abe's vision for the Indo-Pacific, it is important to consider the core ideas underpinning his foreign policy and vision for Japan. These can be categorized under four concepts: value-based diplomacy, the 'arc of freedom and prosperity', rules-based order and Japan as a 'normal' nation. These ideas are mutually reinforcing and together unveil Abe's vision of the Indo-Pacific as an integrated geopolitical entity in which Japan can play a central role for decades to come.

The idea of value-based diplomacy was articulated by Abe and his foreign minister Taro Aso when they first took office in 2006. In addition to the existing pillars of Japanese foreign policy at the time—reinforcing the US–Japan alliance, multilateral cooperation and improved relations with neighbouring countries—they added a new pillar, which involved 'placing emphasis on universal values such as freedom, democracy, fundamental human rights, the rule of law and the market economy'. These universal values working within countries would create a transnational space—or 'arc'—of freedom and prosperity, which would extend from Northern Europe at one end to Northeast Asia at the other, encompassing Europe, the Middle East, the Indian subcontinent and Southeast Asia.

Pointedly, China was not a part of this vision. However, in its earliest articulations of the concept, the Japanese government had argued that the universal values underpinning the arc of freedom and prosperity could be shared with China, Latin America and Africa as well. More relevant for China was Japan's emphasis on a rules-based order in Asia and in the world. An outgrowth of the American concept of a so-called liberal international order of free markets, democracy and multilateralism, the rules-based order became shorthand for foundational international principles such as sovereignty, territorial integrity and freedom of navigation.

These principles were all vital to Japan, especially after the flaring up of the Senkaku Islands dispute with China in 2002 and the intensification of the dispute after 2005. Equally, the rules-based order was essential for securing the sea lanes used for importing the bulk of Japan's energy following the Fukushima crisis—and through which Japan conducted most of its trade with the world.

China's own growing power and assertiveness also evoked a turn to rules and the shoring up of the existing regional order in Japan's foreign policy. The rapid growth of Beijing's military budget, the increasing grey-zone tactics of Chinese maritime vessels in the South and East China seas, the construction of artificial islands, the declaration of an air defence identification zone and other provocative manoeuvres made it clear that China's rulebook was rather different from Japan's.

In this context, some Japanese analysts argued that lofty principles and rules were little more than a cover for Abe's realpolitik approach to China and regional security issues. Nonetheless, the language of universal values and rules became a cornerstone—authentic or otherwise—in Japan's ideas of the Indo-Pacific. If nothing else, it was a way of Japan contesting and normatively competing with any Chinese efforts at laying the ground for a Sino-centric regional order.

Abe's realpolitik was more visible in his efforts at remaking Japan as a 'normal' nation. This involved not only loosening the fetters on Japanese defence and foreign policy that had been in place since the end of World War II, but also reinforcing the existing alliance with the United States and building new strategic partnerships with countries such as India. In fact, it was in India that Abe introduced the idea of the Indo-Pacific into global political discourse (though the concept had already been circulating in Indian and Japanese thinktank circles for a few months at the time) during his historic speech to the Indian Parliament in August 2007.

In the speech, titled 'Confluence of the Two Seas', Abe emphasized the pivotal role that India and Japan could play in bringing about freedom and prosperity in a 'Broader Asia'. In doing so, Abe at once broadened Japan's strategic horizon and ambition as a provider of order in this newly constituted region. He also presaged the formation of the Quad by suggesting that India and Japan cold join together with 'like-minded countries'—specifically the United States and Australia—to take responsibility for security and economic growth in the Indo-Pacific.

In cultivating ties with India, Abe built on the legacy of his predecessors Yoshiro Mori and Junichiro Koizumi, who had overseen Japan's warming relations with India since the turn of the century. He went much further than Mori or Koizumi could, in part due to his political affinity for—and personal friendship with—Narendra Modi, who became Prime Minister of India in 2014. Abe aggressively promoted economic ties between Japan and India. Under his leadership, Japan invested billions of dollars for the development of industrial corridors, high-speed railways and regional connectivity projects in India. These efforts had the double advantage of providing lucrative contracts and incentives for Japanese firms—who brought their technology and expertise to the task of infrastructure development in India—while also contributing to the economic and industrial base that would serve as the foundation for India's own rise.

India was an attractive partner to Abe not just for strategic but also for ideological reasons. It was a major Asian power with whom Japan had no historical baggage. In fact, Indian freedom fighter Subhas Chandra Bose and his Indian National Army had sought to work with Japan to liberate India from British rule. Indian judge Radha Binod Pal was the sole dissenter on the Far East Tribunal that tried Japanese officials for war crimes at the end of World War II. Prime Minister Jawaharlal Nehru sought very early to rehabilitate Japan into the international community and invited Abe's grandfather, Nobusuke Kishi, to India in 1957.

Abe, who had a keen understanding of the importance of history, mentioned Kishi's visit in his speech to the Indian Parliament in 2007, stating that it was of great importance to his grandfather, who at the time was 'the leader of a defeated nation'. He also made it a point during that trip to visit the former home of Subhas Chandra Bose and to meet with the son of Radha Binod Pal. India, which was one of the first countries to call for Japan to be reintegrated into the international order after World War II, would be a key player in Japan's re-emergence as a normal nation under Abe.[1]

Even though Abe did not last more than a year in office during his first term as Prime Minister of Japan, during that short period his speech to the Indian Parliament and further diplomatic efforts ensured that the concept of the Indo-Pacific took root in key capitals in the region and beyond. After returning to office in 2012, Abe continued working to give substance to the idea. In 2016, Japan officially announced its strategy of working towards a Free and Open Indo-Pacific (FOIP). Underlying this concept were exactly the ideas that Abe and Aso had articulated in 2006: freedom of markets and navigation; the pursuit of economic prosperity; and a commitment to regional peace and stability.

Equally important was an emphasis on including East Africa—which was not included in Abe's original arc of freedom and prosperity—in the Indo-Pacific region. This conceptual evolution would enable Japanese firms to access new markets within a framework of state-endorsed economic diplomacy. It would also help Japan, India and other countries to compete with China's growing Belt and Road Initiative in Africa. Abe subsequently used his good offices with Trump to bring the United States on board, with the US President himself endorsing the FOIP concept in November 2017 during a speech at the Asia Pacific Economic Cooperation (APEC) CEO summit in Vietnam.

Although the United States and Japan seemed keen at the time to exclude China from the arc of freedom and prosperity envisioned by the FOIP, India disagreed with this approach. In June 2018, during a speech at the Shangri-La Dialogue in Singapore, Modi declared, 'India does not see the Indo-Pacific Region as a strategy or as a club of limited members. Nor as a grouping that seeks to dominate. And by no means do we consider it as directed against any country.'

At the time, having resolved the 2017 Doklam military crisis with China by standing firm, Indian decision-makers were open to negotiating the architecture of a future regional order with China (a position that has been abandoned since the People's Liberation Army's occupation of territory along the disputed India–China border in mid-2020). Equally, this position would allow ASEAN countries to have a greater say in the reshaping of their regional order. Abe was attuned to these considerations and flexible enough to adapt his preferred strategy to ground realities. In December 2018, both Japan and the United States endorsed India's formulation of the FOIP.

The United States under Donald Trump did not make it easy for Abe's vision of the Indo-Pacific to flourish. Although Abe's foreign policy relied on reinforcing the US–Japan alliance, Trump's vision of the region was premised on US allies bearing more of the economic and military burden of containing China's growing power and ambition. Washington dealt a further blow to Abe's hopes of fostering prosperity through free trade by abandoning the TPP negotiations. Japan then had no option but to do what Trump had wanted them to do: salvage what was left of the TPP and refashion it into the Comprehensive and Progressive Agreement for Trans-Pacific Partnership (CPTPP)—without the United States.

Ultimately, Abe's Japan was the progenitor, promoter and guardian of the Indo-Pacific as a strategic concept and a normative rallying point against an alternative—perhaps Sino-centric—regional order. So much so that in a span of just fifteen years, the erstwhile United States Pacific Command has been renamed to the Indo-Pacific Command, India's Ministry of External Affairs has seen the creation of an Indo-Pacific Division, and the Quad has become a firm reality.

These surface-level realities are indicative of a fundamental reimagining of Asian security and economics. More than ever, and largely due to Shinzo Abe's efforts, capitals around the world are thinking transnationally and in terms of regional order when formulating their foreign policies. And by 'regional order', more often than not, diplomats, analysts, journalists and the informed public mean the Indo-Pacific regional order.

The Quad

The idea of the Quad originated in the early 2000s in the aftermath of the 2004 Indian Ocean tsunami, when the navies of India, the United States, Australia and Japan (among others) had successfully coordinated their disaster management and relief efforts. The United States, Japan and Australia had already initiated a Trilateral Security Dialogue in 2002, and the George W. Bush administration looked favourably upon the idea of creating a security-based coalition of countries in Asia.

Abe was one of the earliest and most enthusiastic champions of a strategic dialogue of democratic major powers in the Indo-Pacific, and momentum behind the Quad peaked following his election as Japan's Prime Minister in late 2006. During Prime Minister Manmohan Singh's visit to Tokyo in December that year, Abe and he officially agreed on 'the usefulness of having dialogue among Japan, India and other like-minded countries in the Asia-Pacific region on themes of mutual interest'.

In April 2007, India and the US conducted their annual Malabar naval exercises off the coast of Okinawa and included Japan for the first time. In May, the United States, Japan, India and Australia met informally in Manila, and another round of the Malabar exercises took place in September, this time including Japan, Australia and Singapore. The exercises were conspicuously held 350 kilometres southwest of the Andaman Islands in proximity to the sea lanes China relies on for international trade. These events led to strenuous protests by Beijing through diplomatic channels and through the Chinese media.

Although Japan remained enthusiastic about the Quad in spite of these Chinese protests, India and Australia responded by publicly distancing themselves from the initiative. For several subsequent years, India did not invite Japan to the Malabar exercises when it was the host (though Japan did host trilateral exercises with the United States and India in 2009 and 2014). The momentum behind the Quad dissipated as Abe resigned as Prime Minister in late 2007 and Bush left the White House a little over a year later.

Despite this initial setback, the four countries steadily deepened their bilateral and trilateral relationships after 2007. A four-way strategic partnership continued to evolve—in essence a 'Quad without the Quad', in the words of David Brewster. While the form of this arrangement was not official, the substance increasingly resembled it. Abe returned to office in 2012 and immediately authored a high-profile article titled 'Asia's Democratic Security Diamond' that advocated a resumption of the Quad. It would still take five more years and a deterioration in India–China relations before India would come around to the idea.

Less than three months after the Doklam crisis of 2017 came to an end, senior officials of the four governments met once again when they were all in Manila for an ASEAN summit. By then, China was much more powerful than ten years prior. Therefore, perhaps less concerned by the security implications of the Quad, it was restrained in its criticism. So began a new phase of cooperation that led to the re-emergence of the Quad as a significant grouping in the Indo-Pacific region.

Although Abe would undoubtedly have liked the Quad to have a harder edge, the grouping downplayed its military aspects and focused instead on becoming a regional provider of public goods. However, military exercises and strategic dialogues continued between Quad members in bilateral and multilateral settings. Notably, India invited Japan back to the Malabar exercises in 2015 and Japan has remained a participant ever since.

Over time, the Quad has developed its institutional architecture and objectives. In 2019, Quad members upgraded their interaction to the ministerial level. In October 2020, the Quad held its first standalone ministerial meeting, focusing primarily on the COVID-19 pandemic. The following month, after years of speculation over Australia's exclusion from the Malabar naval exercises, the Royal Australian Navy was invited to participate for the first time since 2007. Australia remained a participant in the 2021 and 2022 iterations as well.

In March 2021, Quad leaders held a virtual summit in which they announced a vaccine initiative for the Indo-Pacific as well as working groups on climate change and emerging technologies. The statement issued from this meeting announced that the four countries would collaborate 'to meet challenges to the rules-based maritime order' in the East and South China seas. In terms of diplomatic signalling at least, the Quad was inching closer to Abe's vision of a democratic security diamond.

In September 2021, Quad leaders held their first in-person summit and reiterated their commitment to tackling the effects of the pandemic in the Indo-Pacific. They also agreed to cooperate in the fields of high-standards infrastructure (an area in which Japan is a leader), climate change mitigation, critical and emerging technologies, cybersecurity and space. As Russia's invasion of Ukraine unfolded in early 2022, the Quad leaders met virtually on 4 March to reaffirm their commitment to sovereignty and territorial integrity and agree that large-scale aggression of this nature should not be allowed to occur in the Indo-Pacific—which many took to be a reference to any potential designs China may have on Taiwan.

The Quad has thus evolved gradually over time, initially hesitatingly, but subsequently with greater vigour and purpose. Abe's ideas and diplomatic efforts have led the way and he is widely regarded as the chief architect and greatest supporter of the Quad. Although the Quad is still far away from Abe's ideal of security cooperation, it is built on ideas and practices that might in the future enable it to take on overt coordinated security missions—particularly in partnership with like-minded countries such as South Korea, Vietnam, the United Kingdom and France.

Abe's Legacy

This essay began with the observation that in the complex arena of international affairs—where multiple domestic and international variables are operating simultaneously with all kinds of feedback loops and unintended consequences in play—it is difficult to isolate the role of any single leader, except in extreme circumstances. This remains true of Shinzo Abe's overall legacy in Japanese politics and international affairs. If we ask ourselves whether Japan would have acted differently under any other leader, the answer may well be 'not by a big margin' given the foreign and domestic compulsions faced by the Japanese state. Other leaders who shared his ideological commitments—such as Taro Aso—may well have steered the ship of state into similar waters as Abe did.

Yet, in a concrete sense, it *was* Abe that led Japan through a tumultuous period, bringing some semblance of stability to domestic politics and greatly enhancing Japan's stature on the world stage. His legacy is by no means unblemished, especially when viewed in the context of Japan's domestic politics. Nonetheless, his reputation as an astute thinker and politician, his steadfast support for a specific vision of regional order and his unrelenting strategic pursuit of that vision are likely to endure in most corners of the global collective memory.

Abe sought to create an arc of freedom and prosperity that stretched from Europe to Japan. He believed that a regional order based on universal values such as free markets, rule of law, freedom of navigation, democracy and human rights would not only attract other countries but also create a bulwark against Chinese authoritarian expansionism. He sought to shore up the rule-based nature of order in the Indo-Pacific region and to remake Japan as a normal nation that could take up its responsibility as an underwriter of regional rules. To achieve these goals, he sought the institutionalized cooperation of like-minded democratic major powers such as the United States, India and Australia.

The story, of course, is far from over, and may well take twists and turns entirely unexpected by Abe or anyone else involved in the high politics of this era. For now, it is safe to say that Abe has already found his place in the historical record as a leader who deeply understood—as Max Weber did a hundred years ago—that 'politics is a strong and slow boring of hard boards'. In a very Weberian sense, Shinzo Abe was a politician who consistently reached out for the impossible, and occasionally achieved something approximating it.

ACKNOWLEDGEMENTS

L IKE MANY AROUND THE world, we in India, too, received the shocking news of the assassination of Shinzo Abe in July 2022 with disbelief, dismay and deep sadness. Weeks before this tragic event, I was at a conference on Japan–India relations in Chennai, recollecting his contribution to the bilateral relationship in the company of the distinguished Japanese scholar Takenori Horimoto, and a young Indian scholar, Swasti Rao, who was a research scholar in Japan during the Abe years. It was Rao who suggested to me that I put together a volume recording Abe's contribution to not just the bilateral relationship but also to the conceptualization of the Indo-Pacific as a geopolitical construct.

I then drew up a list of potential contributors and was delighted to find that each one of them readily accepted my invitation to write, and delivered the essays within a short period of time. I am grateful to each of the authors, all distinguished individuals, for their contribution to this volume. I am grateful in particular to Horimoto San and my friend Masayuki Taga for encouraging me to take this initiative forward.

It was then only natural for me to reach out to India's external affairs minister, S. Jaishankar, and request him to write a foreword. Jaishankar knew Abe well and he readily agreed to do the honour of writing a fine tribute to Abe in this volume. I am grateful to him for this.

I am grateful to Swati Chopra and her colleagues at HarperCollins Publishers India for their professional support and for making it possible for this book to be published in time for commemorating Abe on his first death anniversary.

NOTES

3. Shinzo Abe: Prime Minister of a New Japan

1. Statement by Prime Minister Shinzo Abe, 15 August 2015. https://japan.kantei.go.jp/97_abe/statement/201508/0814statement.html
2. Ibid.
3. Address by Prime Minister Shinzo Abe at the opening session of the Sixth Tokyo International Conference on African Development (TICAD VI) on 27 August 2016 at Kenyatta International Convention Centre, Nairobi, Kenya. https://www.mofa.go.jp/afr/af2/page4e_000496.html
4. 'Confluence of the Two Seas', speech by Prime Minister Shinzo Abe at the Parliament of the Republic of India on 22 August 2007. https://www.mofa.go.jp/region/asia-paci/pmv0708/speech-2.html
5. Jack Detsch, 'Stop worring about the Pacific and love the Indo-Pacific: The United States has a new lens for its rivalry with China', *Foreign Policy*, 30 July 2021. https://foreignpolicy.com/2021/07/30/biden-pacific-china/

4. The Political Significance of Shinzo Abe

1. The LDP entered coalition with the Japan Socialist Party (JSP) and the smaller New Party Sakigake from 1994 to 1996 under Prime Minister

Tomiichi Murayama of the JSP. Since 1999—except from 2009 to 2012 when it was out of power—the LDP has ruled in coalition with Komeito.

2. 'Sōsenkyo ga Yurasu Habatsu Seiji Tōwareru Seisaku no Kyūshinryoku', *Nihon Keizai Shimbun*, 9 September 2021. https://www.nikkei.com/article/DGXZQODE07CTU0X00C21A9000000/

3. See Central Government Reform of Japan, 'Establishing a System with More Effective Political Leadership', January 2001. https://japan.kantei.go.jp/central_government/frame.html

4. 'The vote that changed Japan', *The Economist*, 3 September 2009. https://www.economist.com/leaders/2009/09/03/the-vote-that-changed-japan

5. The CDP was formed after the DPJ split before the 2017 lower-house election.

6. In addition to the Four-Minister Meeting, the NSC also convenes Nine-Minister Meetings (*Kyū Daijin Kaigō*)—which includes the Four-Minister members and the ministers of finance, economy, trade and industry, public management, home affairs, posts and telecommunications and the national security advisor—and a meeting to address national-security emergencies (*Kinkyū Jitai Daijin Kaigō*), which includes the Prime Minister, the chief Cabinet secretary and others as circumstances dictate.

7. Shinzo Abe, *Utsukushii Kuni E (Towards a Beautiful Country),* Tokyo: Bunshun Shinsho, 2006. Article 9 of Japan's constitution states: 'Aspiring sincerely to an international peace based on justice and order, the Japanese people forever renounce war as a sovereign right of the nation and the threat or use of force as means of settling international disputes.In order to accomplish the aim of the preceding paragraph, land, sea, and air forces, as well as other war potential, will never be maintained. The right of belligerency of the state will not be recognized.' See 'Prime Minister of Japan and his Cabinet' and 'The Constitution of Japan' at: https://japan.kantei.go.jp/constitution_and_government_of_japan/constitution_e.html

8. Article 96 of Japan's constitution states: 'Amendments to this Constitution shall be initiated by the Diet, through a concurring vote of two-thirds or more of all the members of each House and shall thereupon be submitted to the people for ratification, which shall require the affirmative vote of a majority of all votes cast thereon, at a special referendum or at such election as the Diet shall specify.'

9. Turnout in the six national elections that Abe fought remained below 60 per cent, a post-war low and well below the nearly 70 per cent turnout that brought the DPJ to victory in 2009. See https://www.soumu.go.jp/main_content/000824111.png for data on turnout at Japanese elections since 1947.

10. See *'Yasukuni Hihan wa Itsu Kara Hajimatta ka* (When did Yasukuni criticism start?)' in *Utsukushii Kuni E* by Shinzo Abe.

11. Rob Fahey, 'Abe's "nightmare" is a warning over LDP disunity', *Tokyo Review*, 14 February 2019. https://www.tokyoreview.net/2019/02/abes-nightmare-is-a-warning-over-ldp-disunity/

12. The timing of upper-house elections is fixed at broadly three-year intervals.

13. *'Fueru Habatsu Shozoku, Onkei ni Kitai? Posuto Eru Chansu / Tō, Kokkai no Jōhō mo Jimin Giin, 8 Wari Made Jōshō* (MPs belonging to factions increase. Are they looking for benefits? MPs in factions increase to 80 per cent as they look for chances to secure posts and party/parliamentary information)', *Asahi Shimbun*, 23 April 2022. https://www.asahi.com/sp/articles/DA3S15274638.html

14. 'Abe and Suga big with Japan's youth', https://asia.nikkei.com/Politics/Abe-and-Suga-big-with-Japan-s-youth-polls-show, *Nikkei*, August 10, 2021.

15. 'The 13th IISS Asian Security Summit: The Shangri-La Dialogue keynote address by Shinzo Abe, Prime Minister, Japan', Ministry of Foreign Affairs of Japan, 30 May 2014. https://www.mofa.go.jp/fp/nsp/page4e_000086.html

5. Remaking Japan: The Abe Way

1. The Anpo protests of the summer of 1960 were staged against revisions to the US-Japan security treaty. See https://visualizingcultures.mit.edu/tokyo_1960/anp2_essay01.html

2. Nobukatsu Kanehara, 'Japan's grand strategy— state, national interests and values', JIIA, Japan Diplomacy Series, Japan Digital Library, page no.14 https://www2.jiia.or.jp/en/pdf/digital_library/japan_s_diplomacy/160325_Nobukatsu_Kanehara.pdf

3. Yuri Kase, 'The costs and benefits of Japan's nuclearization: An insight into the 1968/70 internal report', *The Nonproliferation Review*, Summer 2001. https://www.nonproliferation.org/wp-content/uploads/npr/82kase.pdf

4. Yukinori Komine, 'Okinawa confidential, 1969: Exploring the linkage between the nuclear issue and the base issue', Diplomatic History, Vol. 37, No. 4 pp. 807–840, September 2013. https://www.jstor.org/stable/44254329

   The declassification of documents from the Nixon-Kissinger years, the Record Collections of the Ministry of Foreign Affairs of Japan, diaries and memoirs, as well as newspaper 'front channel' between the state department and the Ministry of Foreign Affairs(MOFA) principally examined the issue of continued free-use of US bases in Okinawa for conventional combat operations to address regional contingencies in the Korean Peninsula, the Taiwan Strait, and Indochina (for the continuation of the Vietnam War in particular). State officials insisted on drafting confidential written agreements; MOFA officials attempted to focus on public documents (the joint communique and the unilateral statement).

   The 'backchannel' between the National Security Advisor Henry Kissinger and Sato's secret emissary Kei Wakaizumi produced the confidential 'Agreed Minute' between Nixon and Sato regarding the reintroduction of nuclear weapons into Okinawa in case of emergencies. Newly declassified documents disclose that state and MOFA diplomats had also made their respective contributions to the nuclear issue. Senior state officials, especially Undersecretary U.

Alexis Johnson maintained private contact with Kissinger and provided expert input to prepare a draft 'Agreed Minute'. Without knowing the existence of the background, MOFA officials prepared separate confidential arrangements regarding re-entry of nuclear weapons. Together, the two governments assessed the nuclear issue and the base issue, known as the 'Okinawa Package', in order to ensure continued US deterrence in East Asia.

5. Yuichi Hosoya, 'On Prime Minister Abe Shinzo—Creating a new foreign policy to replace the Yoshida Doctrine', Japan Foreign Policy Forum No. 73, 16 November 2022. https://www.japanpolicyforum.jp/politics/pt20221116103501112684.html

6. Policy speech by Prime Minister Shinzo Abe to the 165th Session of the Diet, 29 September 2006. https://japan.kantei.go.jp/abespeech/2006/09/29speech_e.html

7. Shinzo Abe, 'Japan is Back', CSIS, 22 February 2013. https://www.mofa.go.jp/announce/pm/abe/us_20130222en.html

8. Richard L. Armitage and Joseph S. Nye, 'The U.S.-Japan alliance: Anchoring stability in Asia', CSIS, August 2012.

9. 'The 13th IISS Asian Security Summit: The Shangri-La Dialogue—keynote address by Shinzo Abe, Prime Minister, Japan', Ministry of Foreign Affairs, 30 May 2014. https://www.mofa.go.jp/fp/nsp/page4e_000086.html

10. H.Amdt.261 to H.R.1777100th Congress (1987–1988) https://www.congress.gov/amendment/100th-congress/house-amendment/261?q=%7B%22search%22%3A%5B%22hr+2%22%5D%7D&s=a&r=5

11. Shinzo Abe, 'US strategic ambiguity over Taiwan must end', *Project Syndicate*, 12 April 2022. https://www.project-syndicate.org/commentary/us-taiwan-strategic-ambiguity-must-end-by-abe-shinzo-2022-04

6. Shinzo Abe and Japan's Nuclear Dilemmas

1. Constitution of Japan. https://japan.kantei.go.jp/constitution_and_government_of_japan/constitution_e.html Accessed on 12 September 2022.

2. For details of the amendment see Jonah Bhide, 'Rearming a forbidden military: Japan's SDF and constitutional revisions', *The Baines Report*, 15 February, 2019. https://sites.utexas.edu/bainesreport/2019/02/15/rearming-a-forbidden-military-japans-self-defense-force-constitutional-revisions/#:~:text=Since%20the%20end%20of%20the%20Second%20World%20War%2C,created%20for%20defensive%20purposes%2C%20rather%20than%20prohibited%20belligerency, accessed on 3 September 2022.

3. Anthony DiFilippo, *Japan's Nuclear Disarmament Policy and the US Security Umbrella* (New York: Palgrave Macmillan, 2006), p. 194.

4. Sayuri Romei, 'The legacy of Shinzo Abe: A Japan divided about nuclear weapons', *Bulletin of Atomic Scientists*, August 2022.

5. Prime Minister of Japan and his cabinet, *National Security Strategy*, Tokyo, 17 December 2013, http://japan.kantei.go.jp/96_abe/documents/2013/__http://japan.kantei.go.jp/96_abe/documents/2013/__icsFiles/afieldfile/2013/12/17/NSS.pdf; and Prime Minister of Japan and his Cabinet, *National Defence Program Guidelines for FY2014 and Beyond* (Tokyo, 17 December 2013).

6. Ayako Mie, 'Abe drops SDF combat mission proposal', *Japan Times*, 6 June 2014.

7. Masakatsu Ota, 'Japanese nuclear policy after Hiroshima, after Abe, and after Nov. 3', *War on the Rocks*, 14 September 2020.

8. Ibid.

9. Ibid.

10. The arrangements consist of nuclear capabilities, aircraft and infrastructure provided by a number of NATO countries for the collective defence of all. To guarantee the security of its allies, the United States has deployed a limited number of B-61 nuclear weapons to certain locations in Europe, which remain under US custody. For more, see 'NATO's nuclear sharing arrangements', *NATO Factsheet*, February 2022. https://www.nato.int/nato_static_fl2014/assets/pdf/2022/2/pdf/220204-factsheet-nuclear-sharing-arrange.pdf#:~:text=NATO%E2%80%99s%20nuclear%20sharing%20arrangements%20ensure%20that%20the%20benefits%2C,the%20

weapons%20stationed%20in%20Europe%20at%20all%20times Accessed on 2 October 2022.

11. 'Shinzo Abe: No country will fight alongside a defence Japan', Interview of Shinzo Abe, *Japan Forward*, April 1, 2022. Available at https://japan-forward.com/interview-shinzo-abe-no-country-will-fight-alongside-a-defenseless-japan/

12. According to estimates, Japan has '45 tons of separated plutonium, enough for several Nagasaki-type bombs'. Its overall plutonium stockpile of more than 150 tons is one of the world's largest, although much smaller than those of the US, Russia or Great Britain. See Jeff Kingston, 'Abe's nuclear energy policy and Japan's future', *The Asia Pacific Journal*, vol. 11, issue 34, no. 1, 18 August 2013. https://apjjf. org/-Jeff-Kingston/3986/article.pdf, Accessed on 21 September 2022.

13. Tokyo Governor Shintaro Ishihara, an outspoken conservative, repeatedly said this.

14. Anthony DiFilippo, p. 201–02.

15. Jeff Kingston, p. 8.

16. Thomas Feldhoff, 'Post-Fukushima energy paths: Japan and Germany compared', *Bulletin of Atomic Scientists*, October 2014.

17. Jeff Kingston, p. 8.

18. 'Japan is the Second-Largest Net Importer of Fossil Fuels in the World', US Energy Information Administration, 7 November 2013.

19. Naoto Kan, *My Nuclear Nightmare: Leading Japan through the Fukushima Disaster to a Nuclear-Free Future,* translated by Jeffrey S. Irish, Ithaca and London: Cornell University Press, 2017, p. 27.

20. Ibid., p. 126.

21. Jeff Kingston, p. 8.

22. Naoto Kan, p. 127.

23. Ibid., p. 165.

24. NaotoKan, p. 165.

25. Jeff Kingston, p. 8.

26. Susan Carpenter, *Japan's Nuclear Crisis: The Routes to Responsibility,* New York: Palgrave Macmillan, 2012, p. 206.

27. 'Three years after Fukushima, Japan forges ahead with nuclear energy', *DW.com,* 11 April 2014. https://www.dw.com/en/three-years-after-fukushima-japan-forges-ahead-with-nuclear-energy/a-17560046, accessed on 27 January 2020.

28. 'Shinzo Abe says Japan cannot do without nuclear power', Agence France-Presse, 10 March 2016.

29. Jeff Kingston, p. 8.

30. *Tokyo Shimbun,* 22 September 2012.

31. Jeff Kingston, p. 8.

32. Maxime Polleri, 'The Legacy of Shinzo Abe in Fukushima', *Japan Today,* 23 July 2022.

33. Thomas Feldhoff, p. 12.

34. Susan Carpenter, p. 120.

35. Anthony DiFilippo, p. 2.

36. Kimiaki Kawai, 'Mission unaccounted: Japan's shift of role in US extended nuclear deterrence', *Journal for Peace and Nuclear Disarmament,* vol.5, no. 2, 15 August 2022, p. 423.

7. Abe and the Evolution of India-Japan Relations

1. Most recent international relations literature on India–Japan relations tends to view the bilateral relationship through the prism of 'Big Power' relations, especially against the backdrop of China's rise. See for example: Brahma Challaney, *Asian Juggernaut: The Rise of China, India and Japan.* New Delhi: HarperCollins, 2010; Bill Emmott,. *Rivals: How the Power Struggle Between China, India and Japan Will Shape Our Next Decade,* Mariner Books, 2009; H. Hirabayashi, *India: The Last Superpower,* Aleph Books, 2021; Takenori Horimoto and Lalima Varma, *India-Japan Relations in Emerging Asia.* Delhi: Manohar, 2013; Rohan Mukherjee and Anthony Yazaki, *Poised for Partnership: Deepening India–Japan Relations in the Asian Century,* Delhi: Oxford University Press, 2016; Jagannath Panda and Titli Basu, *China–India–Japan in the Indo-Pacific: Ideas, Interests and Infrastructure,* Delhi: IDSA Pentagon Press, 2018; N.S. Sisodia and G.V.C. Naidu *India–Japan*

Relations: Partnership for Peace and Security in Asia, Delhi: IDSA Pentagon Press, 2006.

2. P.A.N. Murthy, *India and Japan: Dimensions of their Relations,* Delhi: ABC Publishing House, 1986, p. 321.

3. Kato, in U.S. Bajpai, *India and Japan: A New Relationship*, Delhi: South Asia Books, 1988, p. 24.

4. Naveena C.K., 'Swami Vivekananda's admiration for the Japanese', https://www.swamivivekananda.guru/2018/09/22/swami-vivekanandas-admiration-for-the-japanese/

5. Sanchari Pal, 'What connects Swami Vivekananda to Jamsetji Tata?', https://parsikhabar.net/history/what-connects-vivekananda-and-jamsetji-tata-a-sea-voyage-that-changed-india/19131/; Also, 'Meeting aboard the Empress India', https://www.tata.com/newsroom/jamsetji-tata-letter-to-swami-vivekananda

6. Rabindranath Tagore, Nationalism in Japan. https://tagoreweb.in/Essays/nationalism-216/nationalism-in-japan-2625

7. Anirudh Deshpande, 'Revisiting Nehruvian idealism in the context of contemporary imperialism', *Economic and Political Weekly*, vol.41, no.52,30 December 2006–5 January 2007, pp.. 5408–13

8. Quoted by Shinzo Abe in his address to the Indian Parliament, 'Confluence of the Two Seas', 22 August 2007. https://www.mofa.go.jp/region/asia-paci/pmv0708/speech-2.html

9. Toshio Yamanouchi, *India Through Japanese Eyes,* Delhi: Sterling Publishers, 2000, p. 57.

10. P.A.N. Murthy (1986), p. 131.

11. Email correspondence with Jagdish Bhagwati,June 2022.

12. Takenori Horimoto and Lalima Varma, *India–Japan Relations in Emerging Asia,* Delhi: Manohar, 2013. Also see K.V. Kesavan, *Building a Global Partnership: Fifty Years of Indo-Japanese Relations,* Delhi: Lancer's Books, 2002.

13. Ibid.

14. First India–Japan Consultative Committee Meeting, Tokyo, 1 November 1966. Quoted in Murthy (1986), p. 330-31.

15. Ibid, p. 334.

16. T.N. Ninan, 'After 23 years, Japanese Prime Minister to visit India', *India Today*, 15 May 1984, www.indiatoday.in/magazine/economy/story/19840515-after-23-years-japanese-prime-minister-to-visit-india-803609-1984-05-15

17. The conference proceedings are compiled in U.S. Bajpai, *India and Japan: A New Relationship?*, New Delhi: India International Centre/Lancer Group, 1988.

18. Saburo Okita quoted in U.S. Bajpai (1988), p. 2.

19. Ibid, pp. 2–3.

20. Ibid, pp. 7–8.

21. Ibid, p. 7.

22. K.J. Joseph, 'India's technology transfer from Japan and the US under economic liberalisation', in K.V. Kesavan, (2002), p. 184.

23. T,N, Ninan, (1984).

24. U.S. Bajpai (1988), p. 60.

25. Ibid, p. 23.

26. OECD, 'Main Determinants and impacts of foreign direct investment on China's economy', OECD Working Paper No. 2000/4, 2000, Table 2, p. 7. www.oecd.org/daf/inv/investment-policy/WP-2000_4.pdf

27. Katherine G. Burns, *China and Japan: Economic Partnership to Political Ends,* Washington, D.C.: Stimson Centre, 2011. https://www.stimson.org/wp-content/files/file-attachments/china-japan-economic-partnership-political-ends.pdf

28. See Nagesh Kumar, 'Liberalisation and Japanese foreign direct investments in India', in Kesavan (2002), pp. 165–177.

29. 'Japan-India summit meeting', Ministry of Foreign Affairs, Japan, 23 August 2000. https://www.mofa.go.jp/region/asia-paci/pmv0008/india_s.html

30. India, 'Joint statement, India–Japan artnership in a new asian era: strategic orientation of India–Japan global partnership', Ministry of External Affairs, 29 April 2005. https://www.mea.gov.in/bilateral-documents.htm?dtl/6627/joint

31. 'Joint statement towards India–Japan Strategic and global partnership', Ministry of External Affairs, India, 15 December 2006. https://mea.gov.in/bilateral-documents. htm?dtl/6368/Joint+Statement+Towards+IndiaJapan+Strategic+and+Global+Partnership

32. Shinzo Abe, 'Confluence of the Two Seas', Address to Indian Parliament, 22 August 2007. https://www.mofa.go.jp/region/asia-paci/pmv0708/speech-2.html

33. Makoto Kojima, 'Japan–India economic ties: Current trends and future prospects', 20 May 2020. https://www.nippon.com/en/in-depth/a06702/

34. 'Tokyo declaration for India— Japan special strategic and global partnership', 1 September 2014. https://www.mea.gov.in/bilateral-documents.htm?dtl/23965/Tokyo+Declaration+for+India++Japan+Special+Strategic+and+Global+Partnership

35. Shotaro Kumagai and Ratul Rana, 'Current structure of and outlook for Japan–India human exchange' in *Pacific Business and Industries*, vol. xvii, no. 66, Japan Research Institute, 2017. www.jri.co.jp/MediaLibrary/file/english/periodical/rim/2017/66.pdf

8. Japan–India Relations: Mapping Abe's Diplomacy

1. Detailed discussions are presented in Takenori Horimoto and Lalima Varma (eds.) *India–Japan Relations in Emerging Asia,* Manohar, 2013, and Takenori Horimoto (ed.), *Introduction to Contemporary Japan–India Relations,* University of Tokyo Press, 2019 (in Japanese). Excellent examinations of the bilateral relations are presented by Srabani Roy Choudhury et al., (ed.), *India–Japan Relations at 70: Building Beyond the Bilateral,* K.W. Publishers, 2022.

2. *India Today,* 15 June 1990.

3. United States Senate Intelligence Committee Hearings,19 May 2018. Can be accessed at: Hearings | Intelligence Committee (senate.gov)

4. Horimoto Takenori, 'Japan, Asia and India— The many legacies of Shinzo Abe', *The Wire,* 10 July 2022. See https://thewire.in/world/japan-asia-and-india-the-many-legacies-of-shinzo-abe

5. Abduction of Japanese citizens by North Korea, Ministry of Foreign Affairs, Japan, 1 June2022. https://www.mofa.go.jp/region/asia-paci/n_korea/abduction/index.html

6. Joshua Walker and Hidetoshi Azuma, 'Shinzo Abe's unfinished deal with Russians' in *War on the Rocks*, 11 September 2020. https://warontherocks.com/2020/09/shinzo-abes-unfinished-deal-with-russia/

7. 'Japan–India Rapprochement and Its Future Issues', Japan's Diplomacy Series, Japan Digital Library of Japan Institute of International Affairs, April 2016. http://www2.jiia.or.jp/en/pdf/digital_library/japan_s_diplomacy/160411_Takenori_Horimoto.pdf

8. Shinzo Abe, *Utsukushii Kuni E (Towards a Beautiful Country)*, Bungeishunju, 2006, p. 159.

9. Sanjaya Baru, *The Accidental Prime Minister: The Making and Unmaking of Manmohan Singh*, Viking, 2014, p. 170.

10. Shinzo Abe, 'Confluence of the Two Seas', Address to Indian Parliament, 22 August2007. https://www.mofa.go.jp/region/asia-paci/pmv0708/speech-2.html

11. Takenori Horimoto, 'Japan–India relations beyond coping with China in the Indo-Pacific region' in the Journal of Indian and Asian Studies, Vol. 2, Issue 2 (July 2021) and 'Japan–India Relations: coexisting closeness and discrepancy' in *Contemporary India Forum*, Spring 2022 (in Japanese).

12. S. Jaishankar, *The Indian Way: Strategies for an Uncertain World*, Harper Collins, 2020, p. 163. Also see Takenori Horimoto, 'Modi diplomacy and the future of Japan–India relations', *Nippon Com*, 18 May 2020. https://www.nippon.com/en/in-depth/a06701/?cx_recs_click=true

13. Takenori Horimoto, 'Indo-Pacific order and Japan–India relations in the midst of Covid-19', *Journal of Asian Economic Integration*, July 2020. https://www.researchgate.net/publication/343128948_Indo-Pacific_Order_and_Japan-India_Relations_in_the_Midst_of_COVID-19

14. Ian Johnson, 'Xi Jinping exposed', *Asia Unbound*, 23 October 2022. https://www.cfr.org/blog/xi-jinping-exposed

15. Masuda Tsuyoshi, 'Japan's security strategy at a crossroad', *NHK World* 27 July 2020. https://www3.nhk.or.jp/nhkworld/en/news/backstories/1216/

16. J.J. Mearsheimer, *The Tragedy of Great Power Politics*, W.W. Norton & Co., 2014, p. 385. He has maintained that opinion to the present day.

9. India and Abe—A Special Connect

1. Blog by Prime Minister Narendra Modi, 8 July 2022.

2. Ibid.

3. *The Economic Times*, 31 Aug 2014.

4. Shinzo Abe, 'Confluence of the Two Seas', Speech in Indian Parliament, 22 August 2007.

5. Address by Shinzo Abe at TICAD VI, 27 August 2016.

6. Keynote speech by Narendra Modi at IISS Shangri-La Dialogue, 1 June 2018.

7. www.jica.go.jp

8. National Security Strategy 2014, www.mofa.go.jp

10. Abe and India: A Bond Bred in the Bone

1. Author's interview with Aftab Seth, who is also a professor at Keio University and recipient of the Grand Cordon of the Order of the Rising Sun from Japan's Emperor. 20 December 2022.

2. Carl Marziali, 'Prime Minister Shinzo Abe visits USC', USCNews,https://news.usc.edu/80768/japans-prime-minister-shinzo-abe-visits-usc/

3. Shinzo Abe, Address to Indian Parliament, New Delhi, 22 August 2007. https://www.mofa.go.jp/region/asia-paci/pmv0708/speech-2.html

4. 'Mr. Kishi in Delhi', *The Hindu*, 23 May 1957.

5. 'Joint Appeal by Prime Ministers: Suspension of nuclear tests', *The Hindu*, 24 May 1957.

6. Suhasini Haider, 'Shinzo Abe considered Manmohan Singh a mentor, Narendra Modi a friend: Japan leader's advisor', *The Hindu*, September 5, 2022. https://www.thehindu.com/news/national/shinzo-abe-considered-pm-manmohan-singh-a-mentor-top-adviser/article65850327.ece

7. Interview with Aftab Seth, 20 December 2022.

8. 'India–Japan relations, Ministry of External Affairs, Government of India, September 2019'. https://mea.gov.in/Portal/ForeignRelation/India_japanBilateral_Brief_September_2019.pdf

9. Author interview with Sujan Chinoy, director general of the Manohar Parrikar Institute for Defence and Strategic Analysis. 23 December 2022.

10. Janis Mimura, *Planning for Empire: Reform Bureaucrats and the Japanese Wartime State*, Ithaca: Cornell University Press, 2011.

11. Dan Kurzman, *Kishi and Japan: The Search for the Sun*, US: Ivan Obelensky Inc.1960.

12. Yuka Hayashi, 'For Japan's Shinzo Abe, unfinished family business', *The Wall Street Journal*, 11 December 2014. https://www.wsj.com/articles/for-japans-shinzo-abe-unfinished-family-business-1418354470

13. Isaac Chotiner, 'How Shinzo Abe sought to rewrite Japanese history', *The New Yorker*, 9 July 2022. https://www.newyorker.com/news/q-and-a/how-shinzo-abe-sought-to-rewrite-japanese-history

14. Kallol Bhattacherjee, 'India–Japan Guwahati summit cancelled in view of protests', *The Hindu*, 13 December 2019. https://www.thehindu.com/news/international/india-japan-guwahati-summit-cancelled/article61607607.ece

15. Suhasini Haider, 'Shinzo Abe considered Manmohan Singh a mentor, Narendra Modi a friend: Japan leader's advisor', *The Hindu*, September 5, 2022. https://www.thehindu.com/news/national/shinzo-abe-considered-pm-manmohan-singh-a-mentor-top-adviser/article65850327.ece

16. Robert Eldridge, 'The assassination attempt of Nobusuke Kishi' *The Japan Times*, 13 July 2020. https://www.japantimes.co.jp/

opinion/2020/07/13/commentary/japan-commentary/assassination-attempt-nobusuke-kishi/

11. Abe's Japan in India: Acting through the Northeast

1. Fumio Kishida, 'Special Partnership for the era of the Indo-Pacific', Ministry of Foreign Affairs, Japan. 18 January 2015. https://www.mofa.go.jp/s_sa/sw/in/page3e_000291.html

2. Ibid.

3. Ibid.

4. Samriddhi Roy, 'India–Japan cooperation in Northeast India' under Kishida, *Strategic Perspectives,* October–December 2021. United Service Institution of India, Delhi. https://usiofindia.org/publication/cs3-strategic-perspectives/the-india-japan-cooperation-in-northeast-india-under-kishida/

5. Ibid.

6. Ibid.

7. Rahul Karmarkar, 'Centre keen on lifting AFSPA from northeast: PM Modi', *The Hindu*, 28 April 2022. https://www.thehindu.com/news/national/pm-modi-promises-to-remove-afspa-completely-from-northeast/article65362781.ece

8. Dr Madhab said that with expansion of trade between India and China and the ASEAN countries in recent years, the ports in the country will not be able to handle the increasing volume and ultimately the land route will have to be opened up via the Northeast. https://assamtribune.com/dr-madhab-calls-for-building-infrastructure

9. Act East Forum, 'India–Japan sustainable development initiative for the North Eastern region of India', Embassy of India in Japan. Tokyo, https://www.in.emb-japan.go.jp/files/100319132.pdf

10. Ibid.

11. Mayumi Murayama, Sanjoy Hazarika and Preeti Gill (eds.), *Northeast India and Japan: Engagement through Connectivity* (Francis and Taylor, 2022).

12. Act East Forum, op.cit.

13. Mayumi Murayama, 'Mutual perspectives of people of Japan and Northeast India during World War II' in *Northeast India and Japan: Engagement through Connectivity* (2022).

14. Ibid.

15. Takenori Horimoto, 'Connectivity of India and Japan's cooperation' in *Northeast India and Japan: Engagement through Connectivity* (2022).

16. Ibid.

17. Yaiphaba Meetei Kangjam and Hemant Singh Katoch,'Northeast India, World War II and Japan: Past, Present and Future' in *Northeast India and Japan: Engagement through Connectivity* (2022).

18. Ibid.

12. The Mastermind behind Indo-Pacific and Quad Initiatives

1. Tobias Harris, *The Iconoclast: Shinzo Abe and the New Japan,* London: Hurst & Co, 2020; Also see Michael Green, *Line of Advantage: Japan's Grand Strategy in the era of Abe Shinzo,* New York: Columbia University Press, 2022; Also see George Mulgan, *The Abe Administration and the Rise of the Prime Ministerial Executive,* Routledge, 2019 and Christopher Hughes, *Japan's Foreign and Security Policy under the 'Abe Doctrine',* New York: Palgrave Pivot, 2015.

2. https://apnews.com/article/shinzo-abe-shooting-world-leaders-react-e163d6212ab8a76ff88ac66a7287172c

3. https://www.whitehouse.gov/briefing-room/statements-releases/2022/07/08/statement-by-president-joe-biden-prime-minister-anthony-albanese-and-prime-minister-narendra-modi-mourning-former-prime-minister-abe/

4. Suhasini Haidar, 'Shinzo Abe considered Manmohan Singh a mentor, Narendra Modi a friend', *The Hindu,* 4 September 2022.

5. Yoichi Funabashi, *Asia-Pacific Fusion: Japan's Role in APEC,* Columbia University Press, 1995.

6. Shinzo Abe, 'Confluence of the Two Seas', 2007. https://www.mofa.go.jp/region/asia-paci/pmv0708/speech-2.html

7. https://www.mofa.go.jp/regio, n/asia-paci/pmv0708/speech-2.html

8. Purnendra Jain, 'Japan–India relations: From weak links to stronger ties' in *The Oxford Handbook of Japanese Politics*, eds. Robert Pekkanen and Saadia Pekkanen, New York, 2021.

9. For most of the post-war period, the LDP—to which Abe belonged—remained in power. The LDP was briefly defeated in 1993 and again in 2009. But it returned to power in 2012 and continues to rule.

10. Shinzo Abe, 'Two democracies meet at sea: For a better and safer Asia', 2011. https://en.jinf.jp/wp-content/uploads/2011/09/HP-E%E3%8 2%A4%E3%83%B3%E3%83%89%E6%BC%94%E8%AA%AC%E4%B C%9A%E5%A0%B4%E9%85%8D%E5%B8%83%E7%94%A8916.pdf

11. At the time, the Japanese Democratic Party was ruling Japan and Abe's LDP was not in power.

12. Shinzo Abe, 'The bounty of the open seas', 2013. https://www.mofa.go.jp/announce/pm/abe/abe_0118e.html

13. Address by Prime Minister Shinzo Abe at the opening session of the sixth Tokyo International Conference on African Development (TICAD VI), 2016. https://www.mofa.go.jp/afr/af2/page4e_000496.html#:~:text=I%20say%20hello%20to%20you,witnessing%20a%20%E2%80%9Cquantum%20leap.%E2%80%9D

14. Shinzo Abe, 'Asia's democratic security diamond', *Project Syndicate*, 27 December 2012. https://www.project-syndicate.org/magazine/a-strategic-alliance-for-japan-and-india-by-shinzo-abe

15. Purnendra Jain and Takenori Horimoto, 'Japan and the Indo-Pacific' in *New Regional Geo-Politics in the Indo-Pacific: Drivers, Dynamics and Consequences*, ed. Priya Chacko, Routledge, 2016.

16. https://www.mea.gov.in/bilateral-documents.htm?dtl/26176/Joint_Statement_on_India_and_Japan_Vision_2025_Special_Strategic_and_Global_Partnership_Working_Together_for_Peace_and_Prosperity_of_the_IndoPacific_R

17. https://mea.gov.in/Speeches-Statements.htm?dtl/29943/Prime_
Ministers_Keynote_Address_at_Shangri_La_Dialogue_June_01_2018

18. Rory Medcalf, *Contest for the Indo-Pacific: Why China Won't Map the
Future,* Melbourne: La Trobe University Press, 2022. and Priya Chacko
(ed.), *New Regional Geo-Politics in the Indo-Pacific: Drivers, Dynamics and
Consequences,* Routledge, 2016.

19. Commonwealth of Australia, Defence White Paper, 2013. www.
defence.gov.au (pdf download)

20. https://www.whitehouse.gov/wp-content/uploads/2022/02/U.S.-
Indo-Pacific-Strategy.pdf

21. Louisa Brooke-Holland, *Integrated Review 2021: The Defence Tilt to the
Indo-Pacific* , 11 October 2021. House of Commons Library, https://
commonslibrary.parliament.uk/research-briefings/cbp-9217/

22. https://asialink.unimelb.edu.au/insights/quad-momentum-continues

23. Shinzo Abe, 'Realizing the Free and Open Indo-Pacific', *Project
Syndicate,* 2022. https://www.japantimes.co.jp/opinion/2022/10/03/
commentary/japan-commentary/abes-indo-pacific-vision/

24. Tobias Harris, 2020.

13. Shinzo Abe and the Indo-Pacific: Beyond a Quasi-Alliance

1. For a philosophical and historical argument on the nature of Japan's
grand strategy by an highly influential Japanese official under Abe,
see Nobukatsu Kanehara, 'Japan's grand strategy—State, national
interests and values . https://www.google.com/url?sa=t&rct=j
&q=&esrc=s&source=web&cd=&ved=2ahUKEwjPzZu91Y_7
AhVV33MBHbU0AFkQFnoECA0QAQ&url=https%3A%2F%
2Fwww2.jiia.or.jp%2Fen%2Fpdf%2Fdigital_library%2Fjapan_s_
diplomacy%2F160325_Nobukatsu_Kanehara.pdf&usg=AOvVaw1
4NDQ4qCjJLvcKnosuDvWw. Kanehara was assistant chief cabinet
secretary to Prime Minister Shinzo Abe from 2012 to 2019. In the
paper, which was first published in 2011 in Japanese, Kanehara
suggests that cosmopolitanism, rule of law, democracy and commerce

are key elements of Japanese grand strategy and have their roots in Japan's distant and modern past. While the paper barely mentions the term 'Indo-Pacific', Kanehara cannot have been far from Abe's and Aso's conceptualization of the Indo-Pacific and arc of democracy. These key elements of Japanese grand strategy surely influenced the conceptualization of the Indo-Pacific initiative.

2. Taro Aso, 'Arc of freedom and prosperity: Japan's expanding diplomatic horizon', speech at the Japan Institute of International Affairs seminar, 30 November 2006. https://www.mofa.go.jp/announce/fm/aso/speech0611.html

3. Professor Purnendra Jain, who has an essay in this volume, has had access to a speech Abe made at the Indian Council of World Affairs, New Delhi, which may have a longer statement on the Indo-Pacific.

4. Shinzo Abe, 'Confluence of the Two Seas', speech at the Parliament of the Republic of India, 22 August 2007. https://www.mofa.go.jp/region/asia-paci/pmv0708/speech-2.html

5. Gurpreet Khurana, 'The "Indo-Pacific" concept: Retrospect and prospect', National Maritime Foundation, New Delhi, 2 February 2017. https://cimsec.org/indo-pacific-concept-retrospect-prospect/. Khurana was an Indian naval officer. In the PDF version of the paper, see p. 4 where Khurana notes that Secretary of State Hillary Clinton used the term as early as 2010. Khurana recounts that the first time the term 'Indo-Pacific' was used in an academic paper was in 2007 in a paper he authored. It was mentioned earlier, in a 'brainstorming' session with Japanese counterparts in October 2006 at the Institute of Defence Studies and Analyses, New Delhi. He notes too that the Australians had been using the term even before then (see p. 1 of his paper).

6. Shinzo Abe, 'Asia's democratic security diamond', *Project Syndicate*, 27 December 2012. https://www.project-syndicate.org/magazine/a-strategic-alliance-for-japan-and-india-by-shinzo-abe

7. Abe was also due to deliver a major lecture titled 'The bounty of the open seas: Five new principles for Japanese diplomacy' in Jakarta, Indonesia, on 18 January 2013, in which he argues for Japan–ASEAN

cooperation in the Indo-Pacific (though he did not use the term). https://www.mofa.go.jp/announce/pm/abe/abe_0118e.html

8. Shinzo Abe, speech at the opening session of the Sixth Tokyo International Conference on African Development (TICAD VI) on 27 August 2016 at the Kenyatta International Convention Centre in Nairobi, Kenya, https://www.mofa.go.jp/afr/af2/page4e_000496.html. This address is often cited by the Japanese as his announcement of a free and open Indo-Pacific. In fact, he never used the phrase during the speech. As far as I can tell, he first used the term officially in a speech to the Japanese parliament on 22 January 2018. See https://japan.kantei.go.jp/98_abe/statement/201801/_00002.html.

9. Rex Tillerson, 'Defining our relationship with India for the next century', 18 October 2017, https://www.csis.org/analysis/defining-our-relationship-india-next-century-address-us-secretary-state-rex-tillerson

10. See 'The Department of Defense Indo-Pacific strategy report: Preparedness, Partnerships, and Promoting a networked region', 1 June 2019. https://media.defense.gov/2019/Jul/01/2002152311/-1/-1/1/DEPARTMENT-OF-DEFENSE-INDO-PACIFIC-STRATEGY-REPORT-2019.PDF

11. Ibid.

12. 'Towards a Free and Open Indo-Pacific', Ministry of Foreign Affairs, Government of Japan, November 2019, https://www.google.com/url?sa=t&rct=j&q=&esrc=s&source=web&cd=&ved=2ahUKEwiHgKnH0I_7AhXkXnwKHfk5DV0QFnoECAsQAQ&url=https%3A%2F%2Fwww.mofa.go.jp%2Ffiles%2F000407643.pdf&usg=AOvVaw24cXsGUF3ycFfe2VLHvzxB. A later documentation of the Free and Open Indo-Pacific is 'Japan's effort for a "Free and Open Indo-Pacific"'. https://www.mofa.go.jp/policy/page25e_000278.html

13. T.V. Paul, *Restraining Great Powers: Soft Balancing from Empires to the Global Era,* New Haven: Yale University Press, 2018.

14. Richard J. Samuels, *Securing Japan: Tokyo's Grand Strategy and the Future of East Asia,* Ithaca: Cornell University Press, 2007, pp. 109–132.

15. Hiroshi Nakanishi, 'Redefining Comprehensive Security in Japan' in Ryosei Kokubu, (ed.), *Challenges to China–Japan–US Cooperation*, Tokyo: Japan Centre for International Exchange, 1998, pp. 45–48.

16. Ibid, pp. 48–50.

17. Ibid, pp. 54–56.

18. Nobumasa Akiyama, 'Human security at the crossroad: Human security in the Japanese foreign policy context', IPSHU English Research Report Series No. 19 in *Conflict and Human Security: A Search for New Approaches of Peace Building* (2004), p. 262.

19. Ibid, pp. 263–267.

20. Narendra Modi, 'Keynote address at Shangri-La Dialogue', 1 June 2018. https://www.pmindia.gov.in/en/news_updates/pms-keynote-address-at-shangri-la-dialogue/

14. The Roots of Abe's Indo-Pacific Vision

1. Liu Xiaoming, 'China and Britain won the war together', *The Telegraph* (UK), 1 January 2014. https://www.telegraph.co.uk/comment/10546442/Liu-Xiaoming-China-and-Britain-won-the-war-together.html

15. Shinzo Abe's Grand Strategy: Drivers and Legacy

1. Shinzo Abe, 'Japan is Back', Policy Speech by the Prime Minister at the Centre for Strategic and International Studies (CSIS), 22 February 2013. https://japan.kantei.go.jp/96_abe/statement/201302/22speech_e.html

2. Shinzo Abe, policy speech by the Prime Minister to the 198th Session of the Diet, 29 January 2019. https://japan.kantei.go.jp/98_abe/statement/201801/_00003.html

3. Prime Minister of Japan's Office. https://www.kantei.go.jp/jp/feature/gaikou/index.html

4. Shinzo Abe, *Utsukushii Kuni E (Towards a Beautiful Country)*, Tokyo: Bunshun Shinsho, 2006.

5. Joint Statement between the Government of Japan and the Government of the People's Republic of China on Comprehensive Promotion of a Mutually Beneficial Relationship Based on Common Strategic Interest, Japan Ministry of Foreign Affairs, 7 May 2008. https://www.mofa.go.jp/region/asia-paci/china/joint0805.html

6. See for example his comment that 'Japan's relations with China stand out as among the most important' in his speech 'Japan is back' at CSIS on 22 February 2023. https://www.mofa.go.jp/announce/pm/abe/us_20130222en.html

7. 'Interview with Shinzo Abe', Japan Ministry of Foreign Affairs, *Gaikō*, Vol. 64, Nov–Dec 2020. https://www.mofa.go.jp/mofaj/files/100121866.pdf

8. 'The Guidelines for Japan-US Defence Cooperation', Japan Ministry of Foreign Affairs, 27 April 2015. https://www.mofa.go.jp/files/000078188.pdf

9. Steve Holland and Kiyoshi Takenaka, 'Trump says US committed to Japan security, in change from campaign rhetoric', *Reuters*, 10 February 2007,\. https://www.reuters.com/article/us-usa-trump-japan-idUSKBN15P17E; Japan Ministry of Foreign Affairs, Japan–US Security Treaty, 19 January 1960. https://www.mofa.go.jp/region/n-america/us/q&a/ref/1.html

10. 'Interview with Shinzo Abe', Japan Ministry of Foreign Affairs, *Gaikō*, (2020). https://www.mofa.go.jp/mofaj/files/100121866.pdf

11. Shinzo Abe, 'Confluence of the Two Seas', speech by the Prime Minister of Japan at the Parliament of the Republic of India, 22 August 2007. https://www.mofa.go.jp/region/asia-paci/pmv0708/speech-2.html

12. Shinzo Abe, 'Asia's democratic security diamond', *Project Syndicate*, 27 December 2012. https://www.project-syndicate.org/magazine/a-strategic-alliance-for-japan-and-india-by-shinzo-abe?barrier=accesspaylog

13. 'Japan's effort for a "Free and Open Indo-Pacific"' Japan Ministry of Foreign Affairs,. https://www.mofa.go.jp/files/100056243.pdf

14. 'US–Japan joint statement on advancing a Free and Open Indo-Pacific through energy, infrastructure and digital connectivity cooperation', The White House,13 November 2018. https://trumpwhitehouse. archives.gov/briefings-statements/u-s-japan-joint-statement-advancing-free-open-indo-pacific-energy-infrastructure-digital-connectivity-cooperation/

15. President Trump's first mention of the term 'free and open Indo-Pacific' was at his speech at the APEC CEO Summit in Vietnam in November 2017. https://vn.usembassy.gov/20171110-remarks-president-trump-apec-ceo-summit/; former Secretary of State Mike Pompeo laid out the 'Indo-Pacific Economic Vision' on 30 July 2018. https://vn.usembassy.gov/20171110-remarks-president-trump-apec-ceo-summit/

16. For Australia's Indo-Pacific policy, see '2017 Foreign Policy White Paper'. https://www.dfat.gov.au/sites/default/files/2017-foreign-policy-white-paper.pdf; for ASEAN's vision, see 'ASEAN outlook on the Indo-Pacific'. https://asean.org/asean2020/wp-content/uploads/2021/01/ASEAN-Outlook-on-the-Indo-Pacific_FINAL_22062019.pdf; for India's vision, see Prime Minister Narendra Modi's keynote address at the Shangri-La Dialogue on 1 June 2018. https://mea.gov.in/Speeches-Statements.htm?dtl/29943/Prime_Ministers_Keynote_Address_at_Shangri_La_Dialogue_June_01_2018

17. On Japan's open posture to work with China under FOIP, see for example Shinzo Abe's policy speech to the 196th Session of the Diet on 22 January 2018. https://japan.kantei.go.jp/98_abe/statement/201801/_00002.html,

18. 'US–Japan Joint Leaders' Statement: "US–Japan global partnership for a new era"',The White House 16 April 2021. https://www. whitehouse.gov/briefing-room/statements-releases/2021/04/16/u-s-japan-joint-leaders-statement-u-s-japan-global-partnership-for-a-new-era/

19. Fumio Kishida, Keynote address at the IISS Shangri-La Dialogue, 10 June 2022. https://www.mofa.go.jp/files/100356160.pdf

20. 'Australia–Japan joint declaration on security cooperation', Australian Government, Department of Foreign Affairs and Trade,22 October

2022. https://www.dfat.gov.au/countries/japan/australia-japan-joint-declaration-security-cooperation

21. ISEAS-Yusof Ishak Institute, 'The state of Southeast Asia: 2022 survey report', 16 February 2022. https://www.iseas.edu.sg/articles-commentaries/state-of-southeast-asia-survey/the-state-of-southeast-asia-2022-survey-report/

16. Abe's Foreign Policy: The Strategic and the Normative

1. 'India-Japan Relations', Ministry of External Affairs, Government of India. See https://www.mea.gov.in/Portal/ForeignRelation/Japan_December_2014.pdf

INDEX

NOTES ON THE CONTRIBUTORS

Tomohiko Taniguchi is a specially appointed professor at the University of Tsukuba in Japan. He worked as Shinzo Abe's foreign-policy speech-writer for fifteen years. Some of the speeches he drafted include 'Confluence of the Two Seas', which Abe delivered to the Indian Parliament and which served as an original inspiration for the Indo–Pacific concept.

Heizo Takenaka is a professor emeritus at Keio University in Japan. He was formerly the minister for economic and fiscal policy (2001–06), and played a key role in the design and articulation of Abenomics. In his capacity as an economist and as part of his social activities, he serves on several advisory boards and committees, including the World Economic Forum.

Nobukatsu Kanehara served as the assistant chief cabinet secretary to Prime Minister Shinzo Abe from 2012 to 2019. In 2013, he also became the inaugural deputy secretary-general of the newly constituted National Security Secretariat. He served in a number of notable positions at the Ministry of Foreign Affairs, including that of the director-general of the Bureau of International Law.

Robert Ward is the Japan chair at the International Institute for Strategic Studies, London, and director of its geo-economics programme. Before joining the IISS, Ward was editorial director of The Economist Intelligence Unit, a sister company of *The Economist*. He worked in Japan in 1989–96. Ward has a bachelor's and a master's degree from Cambridge University, England.

Titli Basu is an associate professor at Jawaharlal Nehru University, New Delhi. Her research interests include strategic affairs in East Asia, with special focus on Japanese domestic politics and foreign policy. Earlier she was a fellow at the Manohar Parrikar Institute for Defence Studies and Analyses, New Delhi. Basu was a visiting fellow at the National Institute for Defense Studies, Ministry of Defence, Tokyo, in 2017; and a Japan Foundation fellow at the Institute of Social Science, University of Tokyo, in 2010–11.

Manpreet Sethi is a distinguished fellow at the Centre for Air Power Studies, New Delhi, where she has led the nuclear policy vertical for twenty years. She has nine books and more than 120 articles to her credit. She is also senior research adviser at the Asia–Pacific Leadership Network and a member of the International Group of Eminent Persons for a World without Nuclear Weapons, constituted by Prime Minister Fumio Kishida of Japan.

Takenori Horimoto is a visiting professor at Gifu Women's University in Japan and a highly regarded scholar on Japan–India relations. He served as director-general of the Research and Legislative Reference Bureau, National Diet Library, in Japan. He was a professor at Shobi University Graduate School and the project professor at Kyoto University's Graduate School of Asian and African Area Studies. He has published fifteen books, including *Indo daisan no taikoku e: 'Senryakuteki jiritsu' gaikō no tsuikyū* (*India, Tomorrow's Third Great Power: Pursuing a Foreign Policy of 'Strategic Autonomy'*).

Deepa Gopalan Wadhwa joined the Indian Foreign Service in 1979. She served as the ambassador of India to Sweden, Qatar and Japan. In the course of her career, she has handled issues related to India's relations with Pakistan, China and Japan, and participated in international negotiations on climate change, disarmament and human rights. She is currently chairperson of the India–Japan Friendship Forum and a member of the governing councils of the Institute of Chinese Studies in New Delhi and the Asian Confluence in Meghalaya, which works on development and connectivity of the Northeast.

Suhasini Haidar is the diplomatic and national editor of *The Hindu*. Over the course of her twenty-five-year reporting career, Haidar has covered some of the most challenging stories and conflicts from the most diverse regions of the world, including Pakistan, Sri Lanka, Libya, Lebanon and Syria. She has interviewed a number of global leaders on the biggest stories of the time and published extensively on foreign affairs. Haidar was the foreign affairs editor and the prime-time anchor of the English news channel CNN-IBN (2005–14), and correspondent for CNN International's New Delhi bureau (1995–2005).

Sanjoy Hazarika is an author, a researcher and practitioner, journalist, filmmaker, policy analyst and human rights advocate. A former award-winning reporter for *The New York Times*, Hazarika founded the Centre for North East Studies and Policy Research in Guwahati, which pioneered the boat clinics on the Brahmaputra in Assam. Between 2016 and 2022, he was the international director of the Commonwealth Human Rights Initiative (CHRI). He is also the founder of the Centre for North East Studies at Jamia Millia Islamia, New Delhi. He has published several books, including a co-edited volume, *Northeast India and Japan: Engagement through Connectivity* (2022).

Purnendra Jain is an emeritus professor at the University of Adelaide. He is also a senior visiting research fellow at the Institute of South Asian Studies, National University of Singapore, and a visiting research fellow at the JICA Ogata Research Institute, Tokyo. He received the Order of the Rising Sun, Gold Rays with Neck Ribbon, in 2021.

Kanti Bajpai is Wilmar Professor of Asian Studies, Lee Kuan Yew School of Public Policy, National University of Singapore. His latest book is the edited volume *How Realist Is India's National Security Policy?* (Routledge, 2023). He has also authored *India versus China: Why They Are Not Friends* (Juggernaut, 2021).

Ravi Velloor is associate editor and senior Asia columnist, *The Straits Times*, Singapore. Widely travelled in Japan, China and South Korea, he was formerly the foreign editor and South Asia bureau chief of *The Straits Times*. Velloor has spent more than four decades in journalism. He is a regular podcaster on Asian issues, and a speaker and moderator at global conferences. His book, *India Rising: Fresh Hopes, New Fears*, was published in 2016.

Yuka Koshino is a research fellow for security and technology policy at the International Institute for Strategic Studies, and co-author of *Japan's Effectiveness as a Geo-Economic Actor: Navigating Great-Power Competition* (2022). She holds a master's degree in Asian Studies from the Edmund A. Walsh School of Foreign Service at Georgetown University.

Rohan Mukherjee is an assistant professor of international relations at the London School of Economics and Political Science. He is the author of *Ascending Order: Rising Powers and the Politics of Status in International Institutions* (Cambridge University Press, 2022).

ABOUT THE EDITOR

Sanjaya Baru is a public policy analyst and a former newspaper editor. He was the media adviser to Prime Minister Manmohan Singh. He has taught at the Lee Kuan Yew School of Public Policy in Singapore, the Indian School of Public Policy in New Delhi and the Kautilya School of Public Policy in Hyderabad. He was the director of geo-economics and strategy at the International Institute of Strategic Studies, London. His most recent book is *India's Power Elite: Class, Caste and a Cultural Revolution* (2021). He has also co-edited a collection of essays published by HarperCollins India, *A New Cold War: Henry Kissinger and the Rise of China* (2021).

30 Years *of*

 HarperCollins *Publishers* India

At HarperCollins, we believe in telling the best stories and finding the widest possible readership for our books in every format possible. We started publishing 30 years ago; a great deal has changed since then, but what has remained constant is the passion with which our authors write their books, the love with which readers receive them, and the sheer joy and excitement that we as publishers feel in being a part of the publishing process.

Over the years, we've had the pleasure of publishing some of the finest writing from the subcontinent and around the world, and some of the biggest bestsellers in India's publishing history. Our books and authors have won a phenomenal range of awards, and we ourselves have been named Publisher of the Year the greatest number of times. But nothing has meant more to us than the fact that millions of people have read the books we published, and somewhere, a book of ours might have made a difference.

As we step into our fourth decade, we go back to that one word – a word which has been a driving force for us all these years.

Read.

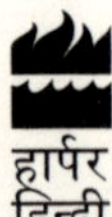